HARDY'S INFLUENCE ON THE MODERN NOVEL

Hardy's Influence on the Modern Novel

Peter J. Casagrande
Professor of English
University of Kansas

BARNES & NOBLE BOOKS
TOTOWA, NEW JERSEY

© Peter J. Casagrande 1987

All rights reserved.

First published in the USA 1987 by
BARNES & NOBLE BOOKS
81 ADAMS DRIVE
TOTOWA, NEW JERSEY, 07512

ISBN 0–389-20683–0

Printed in Hong Kong

Library of Congress Cataloging-in-Publication Data
Casagrande, Peter J.
Hardy's influence on the modern novel.
Bibliography: p.
Includes index.
1. Hardy, Thomas, 1840–1928—Influence. 2. English fiction—20th century—History and criticism.
3. French fiction—20th century—History and criticism.
I. Title.
PR4757.I52C37 1987 823'.8   86–22159
ISBN 0–389-20683–0

To Mattie

Biographers of great men are as a rule satisfied to recount the life of their subjects while on earth, but usually another life should be added. . . . This is their life after death, their influence on the world, the varied fortunes of their writings, the turn given by these writings to other minds, . . . the impetus they have added at different times to the thoughts of men.

(Ernest Renan, *Cahiers de Jeunesse*, quoted in Carl J. Weber, *Hardy in America*)

The [Wessex N]ovels . . . are full of inequalities; they are lumpish and dull and inexpressive; but they are never arid; there is always about them a little blur of unconsciousness, that halo of freshness and margin of the unexpressed which often produce the most profound sense of satisfaction. It is as if Hardy himself were not quite aware of what he did, as if his consciousness held more than he could produce, and he left it for his readers to make out his full meaning and to supplement it from their own experience.

(Virginia Woolf, 'The Novels of Thomas Hardy')

Contents

Preface		ix
Acknowledgements		xv
Note on the Texts		xvii
Selective Chronology		xix
1	Introductory: Hardy, George Moore and Others	1
2	'Now it Remains': Hardy and D. H. Lawrence	32
3	'An Undying Underground Stream': Hardy and John Cowper Powys	62
4	Three 'Nostalgicians': Hardy, Marcel Proust and Alain-Fournier	110
5	'The Immortal Puzzle': Hardy and John Fowles	150
6	'The Pathetic Side of the World': Hardy and Theodore Dreiser	173
7	'Canst thou be Virgil': A Hardy Legacy in the Novel	204
Notes		217
Select Bibliography		234
Index		240

Preface

This study originated in an observation, made while surveying the extensive scholarship on Hardy's novels, that Hardy the novelist has been valued and praised by fellow novelists in a way he has not been by reviewers and critics. I do not mean simply that his fellow novelists turned to him for reasons of their own and therefore said things about his fiction that his critics were not called upon to say. This was undoubtedly true. D. H. Lawrence, for example, contemplated the people of the Wessex Novels as an enormous achievement to be at once imitated and surpassed. F. R. Leavis contemplated the same people as an approximation of life, in essential ways inadequate. Even if one allows for this inevitable difference, however, Hardy's fellow novelists have generally been more enthusiastic about his accomplishments and his stature than their critical brethren. And his failures seem to have bothered them less. Perhaps because they are creative artists rather than commentators on creative art, they know in a way they cannot conceal that the best that is in a novelist cannot manifest itself but in company with error. Perhaps, on the other hand, as successors to Hardy, they welcomed as an opportunity to be exploited the imperfections they found in their precursor. Whatever the case, what they recognized and most prized in Hardy's fiction was the emergence there of a 'new' beauty. I shall have more to say of this later. Suffice it to note here that Hardy as the creator of a new beauty has not been a strong concern of Hardy's critics.

Since so much that critics have complained of in Hardy can be traced to that greatest of novelist-critics, Henry James, the suggestion that Hardy stands high in the esteem of fellow novelists may sound odd, or even inaccurate. As I hope to show in the pages that follow, however, the aesthetic reservations of James, Robert Louis Stevenson and George Moore, as well as the objections (less aesthetic than social) of G. K. Chesterton, T. S. Eliot and F. R. Leavis, form only a part, and by no means the determining part, of the story of Hardy's reputation and influence among novelists of the twentieth century. For example, Hardy's novels (this has long been known) played a critical part in D. H. Lawrence's development as a novelist, as revealed in Lawrence's *Study of Thomas Hardy* (1914) and the proximity of Lawrence's writing of that essay to his writing of both *The Rainbow* (1915) and *Women in Love* (1920). Similarly, looking to France for a moment, it seems clear that Hardy influenced Marcel Proust in important ways in *Remembrance of Things Past* (1907–22). Proust had high praise for Hardy's novels, especially *A Pair of Blue Eyes*, *Jude the Obscure* and *The Well-Beloved*. He considered the last – a work much maligned by Hardy's critics – as worthy of comparison with *Remembrance*. George Painter, Proust's great biographer, has stated that the three novels were in Proust's mind throughout the writing of his masterpiece. And again, looking to America, there can be no doubt, especially since the publication in 1981 of the Pennsylvania Edition of Theodore Dreiser's *Sister Carrie*, that Hardy's *Tess of the d'Urbervilles* and *Mayor of Casterbridge* were of importance to Dreiser in the conception and writing of that major American novel. One would think that the nineteenth-century novelist whose work influenced *The Rainbow*, *Remembrance of Things Past* and *Sister Carrie* would have been recognized long ago as a potent force behind twentieth-century fiction. But such has not been the case, even though the list of twentieth-century novelists influenced by the Wessex Novels by no means ends with Proust, Lawrence and Dreiser.

The subject of this study is, then, Thomas Hardy's influence on some important modern novels, most of which appeared before 1945. Its purpose is to order, extend and clarify what is at present a scattered account of Hardy's influence on prose fiction of the twentieth century. So great has been critical concern with the influence of the early twentieth-century experimenters in fiction – Joyce, Conrad, Woolf, Proust and Faulkner, for example – that Hardy, a traditionalist in method though not in vision, whose last novel appeared in 1897, has been neglected as an influence on the

Preface   xi

novel after 1900. But certain insistent facts suggest that he was an important influence – on George Moore, D. H. Lawrence, John Cowper Powys and John Fowles in England; on Marcel Proust and Alain-Fournier in France; and on Theodore Dreiser and others in America. It is to these more or less neglected facts of literary history that each of the chapters that follows calls attention, at least initially. In each chapter, documentary evidence for Hardy's influence on the writing of an author is given first; that account is followed by a close examination of the novel or novels influenced by one or more of the Wessex Novels. In short, each chapter consists of an historical segment and a critical one, the latter a careful and I hope judicious look into kinships between novels. My purpose is not to prove the seven later novelists mere borrowers from Hardy, but rather to describe some of their debts to him, their often-intriguing departures from him, and in this way to attempt to throw light on how a number of important novels came into being. In connection with this, I have not hesitated to quote at length from remarks on Hardy by his fellow novelists in their letters, essays or novels. Since much of this commentary has been lost to view, it seems worthwhile to bring the best of it back into perspective.

No claim is made for anything so grand as a 'Hardy tradition' or a 'Hardy school' in twentieth-century fiction. The evidence suggests, however, that something important – best described I think as a 'Hardy legacy' – has come down to us through novels so distinguished, and yet so different and dispersed, as *Esther Waters* (1894), *Sister Carrie* (1900) and *Jennie Gerhardt* (1911), *Remembrance of Things Past* (1907–22), *Le Grand Meaulnes* (1913), *The Rainbow* (1915) and *Women in Love* (1920), *Wolf Solent* (1929) and *Maiden Castle* (1936), and *Daniel Martin* (1977). More than many of us have been led to believe by F. R. Leavis's exclusion of Hardy (on Jamesian testimony) from the 'great tradition' of English fiction, Hardy has been a potent force in the novel of the twentieth century.

The question of literary influence, long a sub-category of literary history viewed as mere source-hunting, was elevated to the realm of poetic theory a decade ago with the appearance of Harold Bloom's *The Anxiety of Influence* (1973). In this provocative book, and in several subsequent ones, Bloom attempts to give the reader interested in the working of influence a 'rhetoric' of influence; for Bloom, in an at once highly systematic and highly intuitive way, moves beyond source study and the tracing of similarities of thought and manner into the murky depths of the creative mind in its struggle simultaneously to learn from and to break with its precursors. Though Bloom's language is often daunting, and his intuitive leaps sometimes difficult to imitate, his achievement is real: he has restored to prominence, and in new perspective, the reading of a writer and his use of his reading in what he writes. I have tried to preserve this emphasis on the attitudes of the writer toward his precursor, though less by emphasis on art as anxiety neurosis than on personal history – that is, on what a particular author read of Hardy's, what he said of Hardy and his work, and how he incorporated Hardy into his own writing. In spite of this difference, I am indebted to Bloom's analysis of the complex of feelings at work when one writer reads and adapts another writer, as well as to his insistence on the value of intertextual criticism.

What follows begins with George Moore's *Esther Waters* because, though not a twentieth-century novel, it is one of the first, and in several ways still the most remarkable, of Hardy's fictional offspring; and because discussion of Moore's vehement dislike of Hardy's work naturally occasions discussion of the still-influential case against Hardy made by James, Stevenson, Eliot, Chesterton and Leavis between the 1890s and the 1940s. Chapter 2, on Hardy and Lawrence, must of necessity negotiate some well-travelled roads; for Hardy's influence on Lawrence has been more carefully studied to date than his influence on any other novelist. What has been neglected, however, is Lawrence's explicit concern, particularly in his *Study of Thomas Hardy*, with the working of this influence. My focus is on Lawrence's *Study* as a 'meditation on influence', and on Lawrence's discussion there of the relations between men and women in Hardy's *Tess* and *Jude* as Lawrence's 'rehearsal' for the use of sexual reversals and androgynous characters, especially in *The Rainbow* and *Women in Love*. Chapter 3 is devoted to the discipleship of John Cowper Powys to Thomas Hardy, both in life and his own 'Wessex Novels' – particularly *Wolf Solent* (1929), *Weymouth Sands* (1934) and *Maiden Castle* (1936). Chapter 5, on Hardy and John Fowles, a novelist who is an avowed admirer of Hardy and who at present lives and writes in Dorset, is an account of Fowles's *Daniel Martin* as an instance of Hardy's hold on a strong post-war novel. Fowles has openly acknowledged the influence of Hardy, and Fowles is unusual in being as interested in Hardy's psychology as in his novels, especially the connections between Hardy's sexual temperament and his art brought to light by the work of Robert Gittings and other Hardy biographers since 1960.

Chapters 4 and 6 are attempts on topics that might in themselves be treated in monographs – Hardy's influence on, respectively, French and American novelists. Chapter 4 describes Hardy's status among French novelists and critics to about 1928, with particular attention to Marcel Proust and his younger contemporary Alain-Fournier, author of *Le Grand Meaulnes*. Chapter 6 demanded a tight focus if it was not to become a short book in its own right, perhaps titled 'Thomas Hardy and the Regional Novel in America, 1900–45'. Hardy's influence on William Faulkner has been much discussed; less well-known is his importance to Sherwood Anderson, Hamlin Garland, Willa Cather, Ellen Glasgow and others. For two reasons – the opportunity to examine the career of *Tess* in America, and Theodore Dreiser's refusal to turn away from the severity of Hardy's tragic view of things – I have chosen to describe Dreiser's debt to Hardy in *Sister Carrie* and *Jennie Gerhardt*.

As these remarks may suggest, one assumption here is that study of some of the great progeny of the Wessex Novels may improve our critical estimate of those novels. It is my view throughout that the way a novelist uses a precursor is a critical as well as a creative gesture, and a critical gesture worthy of note. It has also been my assumption that, in treating so varied a group of writers in their relation to one predecessor, I was obliged to accept what I was offered by way of opportunities for discussion. To superimpose a method or set of categories – Harold Bloom's six revisionary ratios, for example – would have been to risk reducing to near-uniformity a rich variety of responses. George Moore mocked the vision and style of *Tess* and yet in *Esther Waters* succumbed to both the subject and the poetry of *Tess*. Lawrence lamented Hardy's diffidence before the reality of human passion and at the same time praised Hardy's awareness of that reality and the larger order of which he made it a part. Powys, taking Hardy as both his living hero-as-man-of-letters and poetic sire, repeatedly sought to explore his own identity in novels that explore the wayward passions of characters much like certain of Hardy's heroes and heroines. Proust wove into the mighty geometry of *Remembrance of Things Past* his high regard for the 'stone-mason's geometry' of three of the Wessex Novels. Fowles found in *The Well-Beloved* an instructive anticipation of his own intention in *Daniel Martin*. He explored this Hardyan precedent and intention not just through his novel, but in a highly personal critical essay on *The Well-Beloved*, 'Hardy and the Hag'. Fowles's essay, reminiscent of Lawrence's 'Study of Thomas Hardy' in being a companion to creative effort, sheds light on how a practising novelist can come to terms with a precursor through the terms provided by critical theory and literary biography. Fowles's recent novel, *Mantissa* (1982), continues this critical-creative probing, though without explicit reference to Hardy. Theodore Dreiser, drawn to Hardy's tragic vision and to the depth of Hardy's pity for his people, re-enacted in *Sister Carrie* and *Jennie Gerhardt* the situation of the ruined woman, but in terms affected as much by his personal and cultural as by his literary experience.

Needless to say, perhaps, the challenge of writing a book that describes the connections between major writers of different cultures and eras is an enormous one. Though I have never lost faith in my governing idea, I confess to never having been without a certain sense of inadequacy before the emerging spectacle, for it is after all a spectacle not just of greatness, but of greatness manoeuvring before greatness.

P.J.C.

Acknowledgements

As always, thanks must go first to those students of Hardy whose work has been a guide and inspiration. Particularly in a study of this kind, in which an attempt is made to trace Hardy's influence on the French and American as well as on the English novel, one goes deeply into debt. Though it is impossible to mention all, the work of several scholars has been critical to my own effort: that of Harold Bloom, L. A. Bisson, the editors of the Pennsylvania Edition of Theodore Dreiser's *Sister Carrie*, Robert Giannoni, John Fowles in his capacity as critic in 'Hardy and the Hag', Mark Kinkead-Weekes and George Painter. I am grateful also to colleagues at the University of Kansas who shared with me their knowledge of English, American and French literature: Professor James Carothers, Professor Thomas O'Donnell and Professor Theodore Johnson. Since a portion of my fifth chapter, on Hardy and Fowles, first saw light as a talk at the 1980 Thomas Hardy Summer School at Weymouth, I am grateful to the directors of the School for inviting me to lecture. Because investigation for this study began more than a decade ago in response to an invitation from Helmut E. Gerber (now deceased) to contribute to his and W. E. Davis's *Thomas Hardy: An Annotated Bibliography*, I take this opportunity to remember Professor Gerber's very important contribution over the years to the progress of Hardy studies. Financial support from the University of Kansas General Research Fund, as well as a sabbatical leave, granted me by the Regents of the University, freed me from other duties and enabled me to complete much of the work for this study in 1981–2.

The author and publishers wish to thank the following who have kindly given permission for the use of copyright-material:

John Fowles, for the extract from his essay originally published in Lance St John Butler's *Thomas Hardy after 50 Years* (Macmillan Press, 1977);

Anthony Sheil Associates Ltd and Little, Brown and Company, for the extract from *The French Lieutenant's Woman* by John Fowles, first published by Jonathan Cape; © 1969 by John Fowles;

The New York Times (Book Review) for the extracts from John Fowles's essay, which was published on 21 June, 1970; copyright © 1970 by The New York Times Company;

Laurence Pollinger Ltd and the Estate of John Cowper Powys, for the extracts from *Weymouth Sands, Wolf Solent, Maiden Castle* and *Autobiography* and for the poem 'To Thomas Hardy' by John Cowper Powys.

Every effort has been made to trace all copyright-holders but if any have been inadvertently overlooked the publishers will be pleased to make the necessary arrangement at the first opportunity.

Note on the Texts

Hardy's fiction is quoted from the paperback version of the New Wessex Edition (London: Macmillan, 1974–6). Chapter references, with, where necessary, an abbreviation identifying the work in question, appear in parentheses following quotations and allusions in the text. The following list includes all the Wessex novels of special importance to this study, their dates of first publication in book form, and, for the most frequently cited, the abbreviations used to identify them.

A Pair of Blue Eyes (1873)
Far from the Madding Crowd (1874)
The Return of the Native (1878)
The Mayor of Casterbridge (1886)
The Woodlanders (1887)
Tess of the d'Urbervilles (1891) (abbreviated as *TD*)
Jude the Obscure (1895) (abbreviated as *JO*)
The Well-Beloved (1897)

Quotations from and references to Hardy's autobiography relate to the following edition, cited as *Life:* Florence Emily Hardy, *The Life of Thomas Hardy 1840–1928* (London: Macmillan, 1962). This work was first published in two volumes, *The Early Life of Thomas Hardy* (1928) and *The Later Years of Thomas Hardy* (1930). Though the name of the second Mrs Hardy appears on the title-page, the *Life* is Hardy's own work. Page references appear in parentheses following quotations.

Page or chapter references to frequently cited works by the other

xvii

novelists discussed also appear in the text. For each such work, the first reference appears in the Notes, specifying the edition cited and the abbreviation (if any) used in subsequent references, following quotations and allusions in the text.

Title abbreviations are not used for repeated references to the same work.

Selective Chronology

1840	Thomas Hardy born (d. 1928)
1852	George Moore born (d. 1933)
1871	Theodore Dreiser born (d. 1945)
	Marcel Proust born (d. 1922)
1872	John Cowper Powys born (d. 1963)
1873	Thomas Hardy, *A Pair of Blue Eyes*
1874	Thomas Hardy, *Far from the Madding Crowd*
1878	Thomas Hardy, *The Return of the Native*
1882	Thomas Hardy, *Le Trompette-Major* [*The Trumpet-Major*, 1880], tr. Yorick Bernard-Derosne
1885	D. H. Lawrence born (d. 1930)
1886	Thomas Hardy, *The Mayor of Casterbridge*
	Henri-Alban Fournier (Alain-Fournier) born (d. 1914)
1887	Thomas Hardy, *The Woodlanders*
1888	George Moore, *Confessions of a Young Man*
1891	Thomas Hardy, *Tess of the d'Urbervilles*
1894	George Moore, *Esther Waters*
1895	Thomas Hardy, *Jude the Obscure*
1897	Thomas Hardy, *The Well-Beloved* (published in serial in 1892)
	Lorimer Stoddard's *Tess* opens in New York City (2 March)
1900	Theodore Dreiser, *Sister Carrie*
1901	Thomas Hardy, *Tess d'Urberville*, tr. Madeleine Rolland; *Barbara* [*Far from the Madding Crowd*], tr. Mathilde Zeys; *Jude l'Obscur*, tr. Firmin Roz

1907–12	Marcel Proust, *Remembrance of Things Past* (revised and expanded until 1922)
1909	Thomas Hardy, *La Bien-aimée* [*The Well-Beloved*], tr. Eve Paul-Marguerite
1911	Theodore Dreiser, *Jennie Gerhardt*
1913	Alain-Fournier, *Le Grand Meaulnes*
	Thomas Hardy, *Deux yeux bleus* [*A Pair of Blue Eyes*], tr. Eve Paul-Marguerite
1912–23	Wessex Edition of the Novels of Thomas Hardy (Macmillan)
1914	D. H. Lawrence, *Study of Thomas Hardy*
1915	D. H. Lawrence, *The Rainbow*
	John Cowper Powys, *Wood and Stone* (dedicated to Thomas Hardy)
1916	John Cowper Powys, *Rodmoor*
1919	Sherwood Anderson, *Winesburg, Ohio*
1920	D. H. Lawrence, *Women in Love*
1922	Thomas Hardy, *Le Maire de Casterbridge* [*The Mayor of Casterbridge*], tr. Philippe Neel
1925	John Cowper Powys, *Ducdame*
	Ellen Glasgow, *Barren Ground*
1926	John Fowles born
1929	John Cowper Powys, *Wolf Solent*
1932	John Cowper Powys, *A Glastonbury Romance*
1934	John Cowper Powys, *Weymouth Sands; Autobiography*
1936	John Cowper Powys, *Maiden Castle*
1969	John Fowles, *The French Lieutenant's Woman*
1977	John Fowles, *Daniel Martin*

1
Introductory: Hardy, George Moore and Others

In the long career of Thomas Hardy, George Moore occupied a special place, for Moore was undoubtedly one of the two literary contemporaries Hardy most despised. The other was G. K. Chesterton. On 11 January 1928, when Hardy lay dying, one of his last gestures was to dictate two epitaphs, one to Chesterton, the other to Moore. The epitaph to Chesterton, as the opening and closing couplets show, distilled Hardy's lingering bitterness toward a critic who had attacked him fifteen years before as 'a sort of village atheist brooding and blaspheming over the village idiot': 'Here lies nipped in this narrow cyst / The literary contortionist. . . . If one with him could not see / He'd shout his choice word "Blasphemy".' Chesterton had been perhaps the harshest critic of Hardy's heterodoxy. Moore, on the other hand, had been the most savage critic of Hardy's style, and to Moore Hardy bequeathed an 'Epitaph for George Moore: On One Who Thought No Other Could Write Such English as Himself':

> 'No mortal man beneath the sky
> Can write such English as can I.
> They say it holds no thought my own
> What then, such beauty (perfection) is not known.'
>
> Heap dustbins on him:
> They'll not meet
> The apex of his self-conceit.[1]

If this bitter last volley reveals an unflattering capacity for brooding resentment, it also reflects Hardy's stubborn belief in the integrity of his work. And, to be sure, the epitaphs were not without provocation, especially from Moore. At least Chesterton, by 1930, would find it possible to recant somewhat.[2] But Moore, from 1888 to 1924, had kept up a viciously personal, one-sided attack on Hardy. So far as can be determined, Hardy did nothing to provoke Moore except write the Wessex Novels, *Tess of the d'Urbervilles* in particular, and thereby establish himself as the leading English novelist of the last two decades of the nineteenth century.

Moore's first blast was sounded in *Confessions of a Young Man* (1888), where, as J. O. Bailey has noted, he labelled Hardy 'inferior to George Eliot', and described *Far from the Madding Crowd* as 'one of George Eliot's miscarriages'.[3] Thirty-five years later, in an article in the *Dial* (New York), Moore would denounce Hardy as a popularizer of pessimism who 'coaxed his readers into drinking from an old tin pot a beverage that had hitherto only been offered to them in golden and jewelled goblets [i.e. in Shakespeare and Ecclesiastes]'. Hardy's prose style Moore called the worst of the nineteenth century, and he mocked its diction, grammar and imagery. Hardy's plots, he charged, 'shrank from the essential' out of a 'lack of invention, brain paralysis, something of the sort'. Moore could not understand 'why the public should have selected for their special adoration ill-constructed melodramas, feebly written in bad grammar'.[4]

John Middleton Murry replied to Moore's assault in the following year, and Hardy wrote Murry a letter of thanks:

> I doubt if he was worth such good powder and shot as you gave him! . . . Somebody once called him a putrid literary hermaphrodite, which I thought funny, but it may have been an exaggeration. The reviewers . . . have timidly waited till you came along to show at any rate that (to change the image) this lion, so great at roaring, is only Snug the Joiner.[5]

An entry for early April 1924 in one of Hardy's notebooks continues in this same vein: 'George Moore. *The Times* in its notices of the monthly reviews agrees with Mr. Middleton Murry, . . . in the latter's smashing criticism of that ludicrous blackguard George Moore's book called *Conversations in Ebury Street*, in which I believe I am libelled wholesale, though I have not seen the book.'[6]

Murry's 'smashing criticism' is a minor masterpiece of critical invective whose brutal point is that Moore is a mere writer of talent attacking Hardy out of malicious envy for Hardy's genius:

To know so much – to be so little able; . . . to watch that 'absurd' Hardy – that . . . is Mr. Moore's word, not mine – clothing his melodramatic skeletons with flesh and blood which lives and moves and has its being, and with a touch of his fingers filling his stories with the fragrance of the great earth itself, while Mr. Moore's smell chiefly of the midnight oil; to have talent enough to know what genius is and to have no genius – that is bitter indeed.[7]

There is injustice in Murry's scathing denunciation, injustice in the denunciation and irony in the entire situation. Murry might have noted that Moore did not limit his attacks to Thomas Hardy. He lashed out at many of his contemporaries – at James and Conrad, as well as Hardy, among the novelists. Moore was irritable, quick-tempered, sharp-tongued, and apparently humourless.[8] Hardy was not his only target, though Hardy was undoubtedly one of his favourite ones, possibly because Hardy, as novelist and then as poet, dominated the English literary scene for so long, and in spite of certain recognized shortcomings as a stylist. Furthermore, the years have proved somewhat inaccurate Murry's dismissal of Moore as a mere writer of talent. Moore's autobiographical writings enjoy a growing reputation, and *Esther Waters*, the best of Moore's novels, is something more than mere fiction of talent.[9] And in the endurance of *Esther Waters* lies the irony Murry might have perceived, and exploited, had he been able to curb his indignation – that in his finest novel Moore is most deeply indebted to the novelist he apparently most despised, as a thinker, as a stylist, and as a maker of plots. For *Esther* is Moore's *Tess*, Moore's attempt to rewrite Hardy's masterpiece along certain of the lines set down by Balzac, Flaubert and Zola, whom Moore admired and sought to imitate. If Moore despised Hardy's melodramatic treatment of the story of a ruined maid, he was clearly fascinated by the possibilities in the story itself. If he disliked Hardy's poetic use of language, he was not immune, even within the constraints of his realism, to the influence of Hardy's language.

Esther Waters (1894) is in one sense a parody of the highest order, and, if in all parody there is imitation, and in all imitation a degree of admiration, then Moore – in spite of his attacks on Hardy – was an admirer of Hardy in *Tess*. Moore's criticism of Hardy exists in inverse proportion to his depth of attachment to him. Moore is driven not to reject but to revise Hardy, and in this impulse to revise lies a measure of approbation, if not affection.[10] Moore had views in common with Hardy that his ripping criticisms do not betray. Like Hardy, Moore was an enemy of organized religion, and hostility toward the churches figures in both *Tess* and *Esther*. Like Hardy, Moore championed the individual, especially the superior individual of the lower classes who struggles against the imperatives of nature and society. Like Hardy, Moore loved the poetry of Swinburne and Shelley, and, again like Hardy, Moore followed them in their effort to exhibit candidly the sexual behaviour of human beings. Finally, both Moore and Hardy were humanitarian idealists whose *Esther* and *Tess* express a struggle to come to terms with certain grim realities – social, psychological and cosmic. So Moore's antipathy is born of strong affinity as well as of powerful alienation.

Moore was reading *Tess of the d'Urbervilles* (1891) while he was writing *Esther Waters* in 1893–4.[11] His objections to it are the objections of a literary realist and devoted stylist confronted with the language and narrative method of a writer of tragic romance intended for serial publication. His complaints are worth examining in some detail, for his sense of Hardy's weaknesses in *Tess* is shrewder than the intemperance of his (or Murry's) remarks imply. Moore read *Tess* as a fellow craftsman who found its workmanship at variance with, at points inferior to, his own. That Hardy is at times a clumsy writer cannot be denied. And that by 1893–4, when Moore was writing *Esther*, Hardy had become England's leading novelist in spite of his occasional lapses must only have increased Moore's irritation and anxiety; for Moore was devoted to a meticulous use of English, even though he himself was less than a master of it. Moore saw Hardy's success as an outrage, but out of this mixture of envy and indignation was to come *Esther Waters*. Moore published his objections to *Tess* some twenty years later, in *Conversations in Ebury Street*:

> I have read *Tess of the d'Urbervilles* and my doubts began when Alec came riding by and called her to jump up behind him. We are told that he rode into a wood. Now, a wood may be large or small; it may wander hither and thither, or grow in patches. A wood may be dense, dark, solemn, forbidding, or it may be blithe, enticing, with delightful interspaces; it may be overgrown with scrub, littered with uncouth rocks, or it may be

smooth.... A wood may be described in two words. When Scott wrote: *Land of brown heath and scraggy wood*, we are in Scotland. But the woods and fields that Mr. Hardy speaks of are never before our eyes. I think he tells us that Alec rode some distance into the wood and made a couch for Tess in the dead leaves. He buttons his overcoat round her shoulders and goes away for a little while, and returns to find her asleep. The situation is one which seems to Mr. Hardy opportune for a meditation, wherefore he begins: 'But some might say, where was Tess's guardian angel? Where was the providence of her simple faith?'... The French have a good word for this kind of story: *coco*, and *coco* may be translated into English as *Mother Goose*. After the accident in the wood Tess returns to her home, and about a year afterwards we read of her in a cornfield with a baby, who is taken ill and whom she baptizes herself in the middle of the night. When the baby dies, Tess continues to work in her parents' house, and then becomes a dairymaid; and in the dairy she meets Angel Clare, whom she marries, without, however, telling him that she has had a baby. But on the night of the wedding she makes up her mind to confess everything to him, and is glad when Angel Clare confides to her the fact that he had once *plunged into eight and forty hours' dissipation with a stranger*, and that he has *never repeated the offence*. You will see ... that the interest of the story concentrates not so much on Tess's confession but on the character the author gives to the confession, for, like a wood, a confession can take every kind of shape.[12]

Moore objects to *Tess* because it reflects too sharply the imprint of Hardy's temperament. As a result, for Moore *Tess* does not imitate with sufficient fidelity what he perceives as human reality. According to Moore, *Tess* fails for its insufficient detachment from what it exhibits. In particular, he objects to the intrusiveness of Hardy's narrator. One notes also, however, how closely and retentively Moore has read this novel he so detests. More than twenty years after its publication, he is still familiar with the details of its plot.

Moore's objections to the famous 'gargoyle episode' in *Far from the Madding Crowd* (ch. 46) illustrate the reason he deplored Hardy's style:

The persistent torrent from the gargoyle's jaws directed all its vengeance into the grave. . . . Had there not been purple in his eye, he would have written: The pour of water from the gargoyle washed away the grave-mound. A simple statement was all that was needed, and perhaps the very first among our literary instincts is the one that tells us the theme that may be developed and the theme that offers no opportunities for development.[13]

Moore's revision of Hardy's sentence indeed simplifies it. But it does so at the cost of destroying Hardy's sense of nature as a force active, sometimes spitefully active, in human affairs. With an eye on Hardy's grammar, which he never tired of ridiculing, Moore argues, 'The gargoyle may direct its vengeance, but not the torrent.' Aside from the amusing fact that Moore's sentence is itself ambiguous, his reading is a misreading, but surely a creative one. Moore is unable to see, or chooses not to see, that, given Hardy's view of things, the antecedent for the possessive pronoun 'its' could very well be 'torrent', for in the world of the Wessex Novels torrents, as well as other things of nature, are frequently made to seem hostile toward the people of Wessex. One thinks, for example, of the storm in *Far from the Madding Crowd*, the heath in *The Return of the Native*, the cliff and rock formations in *A Pair of Blue Eyes*, the Hintock woodlands in *The Woodlanders*, and of course the soil and weather at Flintcomb-Ash in *Tess*. Hardy's grammar is not so bad here as Moore insists, but then Hardy's grammar is not really at issue. Rather, as some of Moore's other remarks on *Tess* suggest, what is at issue (in 1893–4) is how to 'rewrite' *Tess*; for Moore is as caught up in reconceiving the whole of *Tess* as he is in reconceiving a single sentence from *Far from the Madding Crowd*:

> Let us take *Tess of the d'Urbervilles*. Now, George Eliot, not a great genius, would have seen that the key-stone of that book – no, not the key-stone, the whole theme – was where the girl confesses her previous relations to her husband. Not only George Eliot, but any writer who touched the story, would be unable to avoid the knowledge that the whole thing depended on the handling of the incident. Now, mark what Hardy does. The husband is sitting in a chair, his wife at his knee; and then in a few pages, and in the third person, Hardy disposes of it all. This incident, to which everything should lead up, which

we should never be allowed to overlook, is over almost as soon as we realize that it has begun.[14]

It is not enough to respond to Moore with phrases such as 'malicious envy', 'ludicrous blackguard', 'yelping terrier' or 'putrid literary hermaphrodite'. It is more useful to see that Moore, devoted to the principles and practices of a realism he was in the 1880s and 1890s learning from French masters, was demanding of Hardy's fiction a degree of verisimilitude that Hardy himself, devoted to what he called his 'idiosyncratic mode of regard', did not wish to effect. Hardy's sense of the working of a malign or indifferent nature and the intermittent pessimism that derived from that sense seemed absurd to Moore. And yet much of this distaste for Hardy can be seen as Moore's need to defend his own idea of the novel and of human destiny in order to make room for the kind of fiction he was moved to write. Out of this hostility toward the tragic romance of Tess Durbeyfield came the realism of the story of Esther Waters.

Esther and *Tess* are strongly like and yet unlike one another. Central to both is the dilemma of the 'ruined' maid and the poignancy of her effort to come to terms, practically and spiritually, with her ruin. This effort is exhibited in both novels through the heroine's movement between a sensual male companion and a repressed, puritanical one, through her troubled connections with her family, and through her relationships with her community and its values. Though the setting of Tess's 'campaign' is wholly rural, and the setting of Esther's mainly urban, there are striking similarities: between Tess and Esther in their initial simplicity and innocence; between the sensuality of William Latchett (Esther's seducer) and that of Alec d'Urberville; between the puritan morality of Angel Clare and that of Fred Parsons; between the poverty of Tess's family and that of Esther's; between the religiosity of Fred's family and that of Angel's; between Tess's harried movements between her home at rural Marlott and other places and Esther's wandering between her London home and rural Woodview, where her story begins and ends. Tess is violated by Alec, bears his child, cares for it, then loses it and goes off to start anew at Talbothays dairy. There, where her renewal of spirit is closely associated with the regenerative power of a lush and fertile nature, she falls in love with Angel Clare. They marry, but, when on their wedding-night she confesses her past, Angel abandons her; and she, in complete despair, takes up a wandering life that leads her back to Alec when she sees that relief for her impoverished family can be had only with Alec's help. When Angel (too late) returns to her, Tess kills Alec and rejoins Angel for a few precious weeks of happiness before being taken by the police at Stonehenge. She is hanged for murder, as the notorious 'President of the Immortals' looks on. This is the tragedy of sexual ruin, of lost and outraged innocence, and Moore's handling of a similar set of events in *Esther* differs fundamentally from Hardy's because Moore rejects tragedy. Moore seeks instead to exhibit the tawdry and yet in certain ways heroic reality of sexual ruin and its aftermath.

Esther is seduced by William, bears his child (Jackie), keeps it with her, and then, at enormous personal sacrifice, struggles to rear the child. After miserable and degrading situations as a wet-nurse and a servant, Esther finds a temporary haven with a Miss Rice, a novelist who admires Esther's courage and has sufficient scorn for conventional morality to ignore Esther's past. While recovering at Miss Rice's home (this haven approximates Esther's 'Talbothays'), Esther meets Fred Parsons, who might be described as an Angel Clare with a heart. They plan to marry, for Fred is as forgiving of Esther's ruin as Angel is outraged by Tess's. But their growing affection is thwarted when Esther, meeting William by chance in London, agrees to return to him even though he is married; for she is attracted by both his physical charm and his wealth. He has become a prosperous publican and, more often than not, a lucky better on the horses. Though Fred makes several appeals to Esther's religious principles (like Tess, she has a religious morality), Esther sets aside morality and appearances to return to William because he was her first love and is the father of her son. She even agrees to aid him secure a divorce by living with him out of wedlock. Like Tess, Esther returns to her seducer; but Esther does so willingly and even happily, not out of desperation, not with murder in her heart. The result for Esther is mixed, not tragic. William loses his health and his public house when his bookmaking attracts the attention of the authorities, and at the novel's end Esther is left in reduced circumstances. She returns to the spot of her ruin, Woodview, where her old mistress and friend, Mrs Barfield, still resides. And all is not lost, for Jackie, her son by William, is now a staunch soldier and a loyal, loving son. For Esther – and this has been the case from the beginning – the love and well-being of her son is enough. This is the mixed reality of sexual ruin, Moore seems to be saying, with Tess and her irreparable losses in mind. There is loss, but also gain, sweetness amidst bitterness and pain:

> All was forgotten in the happiness of the moment – the long fight for his [Jackie's] life, and the possibility that any moment might declare him to be mere food for powder and shot. She was only conscious that she had accomplished her woman's work – she had brought him up to man's estate; and that was her sufficient reward.[15]

How unlike, and yet like, the closing moment of *Tess*:

> 'Justice' was done, and the President of the Immortals, in Aeschylean phrase, had ended his sport with Tess. And the d'Urberville knights and dames slept on in their tombs unknowing. The two speechless gazers [Angel and Liza-Lu] bent themselves down to the earth, as if in prayer, and remained thus a long time, absolutely motionless: the flag continued to wave silently. As soon as they had strength they arose, joined hands again, and went on. (Ch. 59)

Tess was not, of course, entirely responsible for *Esther*. Before he published *Esther* in 1894, and even before the appearance of *Tess* three years earlier, Moore had shown interest in treating the life of a girl of the working class in fiction. Prototypes of Esther appear in several of his earlier novels: Gwynnie Lloyd in *A Modern Lover* (1883), his first novel; 'Awful Emma' in *Confessions of a Young Man*; and Alice Barton in *A Drama in Muslin* (1886). Moore's novel *Vain Fortune* (1892) has been called a parody of Tess's confession to Angel Clare, a scene Moore would single out for particular censure, as has been noted.[16] Undoubtedly the publication of *Tess* amidst great acclaim struck Moore as an unwarranted intrusion into his particular fictional 'territory'. His remarks on Hardy's novels between 1888 and 1923 indeed suggest that he set out in effect to 'rewrite' *Tess* and that he did so for several reasons, all of which centre on his distaste for Hardy's interpretation of life and for Hardy's style. First, Moore disliked Hardy's melodramatic treatment of things, particularly Tess's confession, again because the 'reality' of such a confession had been compromised. Moore's teeth are set on edge by Hardy's use of language, not just his grammar but his impassioned and poetic use of words. Finally, though he does not say so, it seems certain that Moore disliked Hardy's idealized conception of Tess, his notion of her as 'a pure woman', one somehow untouched in her essence by all that assails her. In all this, Moore is demanding a greater faithfulness to objective reality than Hardy offers.

Moore's demand could not have been made of a less willing source, for the demands of physical and social reality are precisely what Hardy, in remarks of 1886–7, said he chose to set aside in his fiction:

> My art is to intensify the expression of things . . . so that the heart and inner meaning is made vividly visible. . . .
>
> Novel-writing as an art cannot go backward. Having reached the analytic stage it must transcend it by going still further in the same direction. Why not by rendering as visible essences, spectres, etc., the abstract thoughts of the analytic school? . . .
>
> The Realities to be the true realities of life, hitherto called abstractions. The old material realities to be placed behind the former, the shadowy accessories. (*Life*, p. 177)

Here is Hardy again, speaking now not of novel-writing, but of the landscapes of R. P. Bonington and J. M. W. Turner:

> The exact truth as to material fact ceases to be of importance in art – it is a student's style – the style of a period when the mind is serene and unawakened to the tragical mysteries of life; when it does not bring anything to the object that coalesces with and translates the qualities that are already there, – half-hidden, it may be – and the two united are depicted as the All. (p. 185)

No two approaches to the writing of fiction could be more strikingly opposed than Moore's realistic and Hardy's symbolic, or abstract, approach. With this in mind, it is interesting to compare the seduction and confession scenes in *Tess* and *Esther* – especially their language and the illusion of reality created through that language. We shall begin with *Tess*, with Alec's discovery and violation of Tess in her sleep, amidst the shadows of The Chase:

'Tess!' said d'Urberville.

There was no answer. The obscurity was now so great that he could see absolutely nothing but a pale nebulousness at his feet, which represented the white muslin figure he had left upon the dead leaves. Everything else was blackness alike. D'Urverville stooped, and heard a gentle regular breathing. He knelt and bent lower, till her breath warmed his face, and in a moment his cheek was in contact with hers. She was sleeping soundly, and upon her eyelashes there lingered tears.

Darkness and silence ruled everywhere around. Above them rose the primeval yews and oaks of The Chase, in which were poised gentle roosting birds in their last nap; and about them stole the hopping rabbits and hares. But, might some say, where was Tess's guardian angel? where was the providence of her simple faith? Perhaps, like that other god of whom the ironical Tishbite spoke, he was talking, or he was pursuing, or he was in a journey, or he was sleeping and not to be awaked.

Why it was that upon this beautiful feminine tissue, sensitive as gossamer, and practically blank as snow as yet, there should have been traced such a coarse pattern as it was doomed to receive; why so often the coarse appropriates the finer thus, the wrong man the woman, the wrong woman the man, many thousand years of analytical philosophy have failed to explain to our sense of order. One may, indeed, admit the possibility of a retribution lurking in the present catastrophe. Doubtless some of Tess d'Urberville's mailed ancestors rollicking home from a fray had dealt the same measure even more ruthlessly towards peasant girls of their time. But though to visit the sins of the fathers upon the children may be a morality good enough for divinities, it is scorned by average human nature; and it therefore does not mend the matter.

As Tess's own people down in those retreats are never tired of saying among each other in their fatalistic way: 'It was to be.' There lay the pity of it. An immeasurable social chasm was to divide our heroine's personality thereafter from that previous self of hers who stepped from her mother's door to try her fortune at Trantridge poultry-farm. (Ch. 11)

The following is Moore's account of Esther's seduction. It too occurs in the eleventh chapter and it too is preceded by a dance:

The ball had brought amusement to all, to Esther it brought happiness. Her happiness was now visible in her face and audible in her voice, and Sarah's ironical allusions to her inability to learn to read no longer annoyed her, no longer stirred her temper – her love seemed to induce forgiveness for all and love for everything.

In the evenings when their work was done Esther and her lover lingered about the farm buildings, listening to the rooks, seeing the lights die in the west; and in the summer darkness about nine she tripped by his side when he took the letters to post. The wheat stacks were thatching, and in the rickyard, in the carpenter's shop, and in the whist of the woods they talked of love and marriage. They lay together in the warm valleys, listening to the tinkling of the sheep-bell, and one evening, putting his pipe aside, William threw his arms around her, whispering that she was his wife. The words were delicious to her fainting ears, and her will died in what seemed like irresistible destiny. She could not struggle with him, though she knew that her fate depended upon her resistance, and swooning away she awakened in pain, powerless to free herself. . . . Soon after, thoughts betook themselves on their painful way, and the stars were shining when he followed her across the down, beseeching her to listen. But she fled along the grey road and up the stairs to her room. Margaret was in bed, and awakening a little asked her what had kept her out so late. She did not answer . . . and hearing Margaret fall asleep she remembered the supper-table. Sarah, who had come in late, had sat down beside her; William sat on the opposite side; Mrs. Latch was in her place, the jockeys were all together; Mr. Swindles, his snuff-box on the table; Margaret and Grover. Everyone had drunk a great deal; and Mr. Leopold had gone to the beer cellar many times. She thought that she remembered feeling a little dizzy when William asked her to come for a stroll up the hill. They had passed through the hunting gate; they had wandered into the loneliness of the hills. Over the folded sheep the rooks came home noisily through a deepening sky. So far she remembered, and she could not remember further; and all night lay staring into the darkness, and when Margaret called her in the morning she was pale and deathlike.

The location of each episode in its respective chapter is

important. Hardy's account of Tess's ruin ends not just his eleventh chapter, but also the first 'Phase' (titled 'The Maiden') of her tragic career. The reader moves directly from Tess's violation and the end of her maidenhood to the beginning of 'Phase the Second' of her life, the Phase titled 'Maiden No More', where we find her trudging homeward, bitter and disheartened, wanting nothing more to do with Alec. Hardy's placement of Tess's violation lends it an emphasis appropriate to its decisive place in her story. By contrast, Moore places Esther's ruin at the beginning of his eleventh chapter, thereby freeing himself to use what remains of that long chapter to exhibit Esther's angry sulking, William's half-hearted attempt to make amends, and then his impulsive elopement with another woman, an act that leaves Esther to face the consequences entirely alone. This Esther does by holding her position as servant at Woodview as long as she can conceal her pregnancy, saving her wages, then returning to the squalor of her parents' home in London to have the child. Though deeply distressed by the event, Esther is without Tess's spiritual desolation, her sense of irretrivable loss. Tess's 'views of life had been totally changed for her by the lesson' (*TD*, ch. 12); she is paralysed with shame and wants nothing further to do with Alec. On the other hand, Esther wants William if he will only repent; and so she can respond to Mrs Barfield's kindly 'Tell me, it was not your fault' in a matter-of-fact way:

> It is always a woman's fault, ma'am. But he should not have deserted me as he did, that's the only thing I reproach him with, the rest was my fault – I shouldn't have touched the second glass of ale. Besides, I was in love with him, and you know what that is. I thought no harm, and I let him kiss me. He used to take me out for walks on the hill and round the farm. He told me he loved me, and would make me his wife – and that's how it was. (*EW*, ch. 12)

This contrast between Tess's trauma and Esther's relative composure suggests the high value Hardy placed on Tess's purity. Her ruin has a dimension that Esther's lacks because Esther is conceived by Moore as a woman without powerful and controlling moral ideals. For Esther, sexual ruin is a matter for resignation: 'She had sinned, and the Lord had punished her for her sin, and she must bear her punishment uncomplainingly, giving Him thanks that He had imposed no heavier one upon her' (ibid.). For Tess, sexual ruin is a matter for the bitterest anger and deepest fear, emotions rooted in her belief in the eternal consequences of her slip. At the same time, she believes unjust the punishment her beliefs teach her awaits the impure. This is why she rejects in strong language the theology of the inscriber of religious texts she meets soon after fleeing Alec:

> 'Do you believe what you paint?' she asked in low tones.
> 'Believe that tex? Do I believe in my own existence!'
> 'But,' said she tremulously, 'suppose your sin was not of your own seeking?' . . .
> 'I cannot split hairs on that burning query', he said. 'I have walked hundreds of miles this past summer, painting these texes. . . . I leave their application to the hearts of the people who read 'em.'
> 'I think they are horrible', said Tess. 'Crushing! killing!'
> (*TD*, ch. 12)

Tess's anger has depths and shadows that Esther's lacks, something revealed most dramatically when Esther lunges at William with a sharp kitchen knife, an act that recalls Tess's murder of Alec with a similar instrument. Tess's lunge is climactic and decisive, Esther's inconsequential: 'William retreated from her, and Mrs. Latch, coming suddenly in, caught her arm. Esther threw the knife; it struck the wall, falling with a rattle on the meat screen. Escaping from Mrs. Latch, she rushed to secure it, but her strength gave way, and she fell back in a dead faint' (*EW*, ch. 11). This is a far cry from the melodrama of the murder at the hotel at Sandbourne in *Tess*, with the dripping of Alec's heart's blood, Tess's mad flight to Angel, their short-lived happiness and her subsequent death by hanging. Moore had complained particularly of the melodrama in Alec's death ('murder with a carving knife and the blood to soak through the ceiling, and . . . Tess hanged later on, after spending a splendid honeymoon among the monoliths at Stonehenge'). There is some justice in his remark that this melodrama, unlike that of *Macbeth*, is 'melodrama unredeemed by poetry'.[17] On the other hand, when set beside Esther's actions, Tess's almost always have a resonance, an absurdity, a mythic quality that is the legitimate effect of romance written, in Hardy's words, in an attempt to project 'the tragical mysteries of life'.

Moore may be said to seek in *Esther* what Hardy termed 'the exact truth as to material fact', though even this truth, as shall be seen, is coloured by the poetry of Moore's language. Hardy seeks the 'exact truth' combined with and transformed by a temperament, and he seeks this because he believes there are at work in human affairs mysterious powers – internal and external – that art and language can merely intimate, never capture.

This contrast is nowhere so clear as on the occasion of Tess's confession to Angel Clare (*TD*, ch. 34) and Esther's to Fred Parsons (*EW*, ch. 23):

> 'I've been thinking of you a good deal, Esther, in the last few days. I want to ask you to marry me.'
> Esther did not answer.
> 'Will you?' he said.
> 'I can't; I'm very sorry; don't ask me.'
> 'Why can't you?'
> 'If I told you I don't think you'd want to marry me. I suppose I'd better tell you. I'm not the good woman you think me. I've got a child. There, you have it now, and you can take your hook when you like.'

Satisfied that she has repented and that she has been 'a good woman' since her slip eight years before, Fred responds, 'I did not mean to reproach you; I know that a woman's path is more difficult to walk in than ours. It may not be a woman's fault if she falls, but it is always a man's. He can always fly from temptation.' Unlike Angel Clare, Fred has no sexual lapse in his own past to confess, and Esther 'did not like him any better for his purity, and was irritated by the clear tones of his icy voice'. But Fred manages to convince her that he can forgive her, and she tells him the story of her betrayal, with this result: ' "I love you, Esther; it is easy to forgive those we love." "You're very good; I never thought to find a man so good." '

What Moore revises in *Tess* in this way of depicting Esther's confession and Fred's forgiveness is Hardy's insistence that hidden motives and unanticipated consequences define human experience. Tess's confession, like her seduction, ends one Phase of her life ('The Consequence') and begins another ('The Woman Pays'). Both the seduction and the confession completely transform her, suggesting what is indeed the case for Hardy's people – that against their wills they must contend with forces, within themselves and without, beyond their comprehension. Tess, as we know, had been thwarted in an earlier attempt to confess – her letter had slipped under the rug at Talbothays. Esther and William see into themselves and their surroundings in a way that Tess and Angel cannot, for Tess and Angel are made conversant with multiple, shifting realities, and with chance: for instance, their first meeting at Marlott, the collision at the Durbeyfield cart and the mail cart. A new and terrible knowledge, whether Tess's after her encounter with Alec in The Chase, or Angel's after his conversation with Tess at Wellbridge, alters their way of seeing, alters the appearance of ordinary things, and therefore alters them.

Angel has seemingly paved the way for Tess's confession, for he himself confesses to a similar error in his past – 'eight-and-forty hours' dissipation with a stranger' in London. 'O, Angel,' Tess replies, 'I am almost glad – because now *you* can forgive *me*! I have not made my confession. I have a confession, too – remember, I said so.'

> Their hands were still joined. The ashes under the grate were lit by the fire vertically, like a torrid waste. Imagination might have beheld a Last Day luridness in this red-coaled glow, which fell on his face and hand, and on hers, peering into the loose hair about her brow, and firing the delicate skin underneath. A large shadow of her shape rose upon the wall and ceiling. She bent forward, at which each diamond on her neck gave a sinister wink like a toad's; and pressing her forehead against his temple she entered on her story of her acquaintance with Alec d'Urberville and its results, murmuring the words without flinching, and with her eyelids drooping down.

With this gesture of intimacy, Hardy ends chapter 34 of *Tess* and 'Phase the Fourth' of his heroine's life. The next phase, the beginning of Tess's decline unto death, begins with this:

> Her narrative ended; even its re-assertions and secondary explanations were done. Tess's voice throughout had hardly risen higher than its opening tone; there had been no exculpatory phrase of any kind, and she had not wept.
>
> But the complexion even of external things seemed to suffer transmutation as her announcement progressed. The fire in the

grate looked impish – demoniacally funny, as if it did not care in the least about her strait. The fender grinned idly, as if it too did not care. The light from the water-bottle was merely engaged in a chromatic problem. All material objects around announced their irresponsibility with terrible iteration. And yet nothing had changed since the moments when he had been kissing her; or rather, nothing in the substance of things. But the essence of things had changed. (*TD*, ch. 35)

If Angel Clare's response to Tess differs from that of Fred Parsons to Esther, it is because Angel no longer *sees* the woman he once had seen and had married only hours before: 'The woman I have been loving is not you', he remarks bitterly. Tess, like Esther, wants forgiveness. Fred can forgive Esther because, as he says, 'it is easy to forgive those we love'. But for Angel, the lover whose beloved has been transformed in his mind from the embodiment of Purity into the tarnished reality of a fallen woman, 'forgiveness does not apply. . . . You were one person; now you are another. My God – how can forgiveness meet such a grotesque – prestidigitation as that!'

He looked upon her as a species of impostor; a guilty woman in the guise of an innocent one. Terror was upon her white face as she saw it; her cheek was flaccid, and her mouth had almost the aspect of a round little hole. The horrible sense of his view of her so deadened her that she staggered; and he stepped forward, thinking she was going to fall. (Ibid.)

To pair the seductions and confessions from *Esther* and *Tess* is to see not the superiority of one novel to the other, of Moore's realism to Hardy's romance, or of a tragic vision of life to a realistic one. Rather it is to see the legitimacy of both. A reader contemplates the reaction of Esther and Fred to their growing affection with the feeling that love can indeed emerge in this way, not without emotion, but with subdued emotion, without heightened passion, without tragic consequences or cosmic overtones. It is plausible, one reflects, that some persons will live their lives, even in times of crisis, in this rather matter-of-fact way. And it is a very attractive plausibility, for it encompasses courage as well as compromise; and its superb result is that life goes on. The will to live that moves Esther toward Fred and then back to William is the will to let live that makes her refuse to sacrifice the life of her son to her own comfort. On the other hand, the passion in Tess and Angel's response is equally plausible and equally human. It is consistent with Tess's morality and Angel's nostalgia. If the main issue is Hardy's truth-to-life, as it seems to be for Moore in his remarks on Tess, then one can reply that uncompromising idealism is as much a human reality as moral compromise, that sexual assault is not infrequently followed by retaliation, and retaliation by punishment under the law. Finally, then, the validity of Moore's realistic and Hardy's symbolic treatment of the plight of a ruined maid is not a question of verisimilitude. It is a question of style and of vision.

The reality of Esther's seduction and subsequent recovery is created by Moore's use of words. Moore's realistic treatment of the affairs of Esther is an interpretation of reality, every bit as subject to the influence of temperament, and even to a poetic tendency in that temperament, as Hardy's treatment in *Tess*. For example, one of Moore's favourite devices in his avowedly realistic treatment of things is repetition, through which he produces the attractive double effect of poetic rhythm on the one hand and prosaic monotony on the other, as in the following five sentences from the seduction scene cited above (p. 12):

> In the evenings when their work was done Esther and her lover lingered about the farm buildings, listening to the rooks, seeing the lights die in the west; and in the summer darkness about nine she tripped by his side when he took the letters to post. The wheat stacks were thatching, and in the rickyard, in the carpenter's shop, and in the whist of the woods they talked of love and marriage. They lay together in the warm valleys, listening to the tinkling of the sheep-bell, and one evening, putting his pipe aside, William threw his arm around her, whispering that she was his wife. The words were delicious to her fainting ears, and her will died in what seemed like irresistible destiny. She could not struggle with him, though she knew that her fate depended upon her resistance, and swooning away she awakened in pain, powerless to free herself. (*EW*, ch. 11)

One is drawn here to the assonance and the repetition of consonants: in 'lovers', 'lingered', 'listening', 'lights', 'lay', 'tinkling', 'delicious', 'will', 'irresistible', 'struggle', 'powerless' – even in the name 'William'; also to the alliteration of 'when their work was done', 'whist of the woods', 'warm', 'whispering', 'wife', 'will', 'swooning away', 'awakened' and, again, 'William'. Adding to this poetry in the passage is the repetition of present participles – 'thatching', 'listening', 'tinkling', 'whispering', 'fainting', 'swooning' – and of prepositional phrases: 'in the rickyard, in the carpenter's shop, and in the whist of the woods', 'in the warm valleys', 'in what seemed like irresistible destiny', and, finally, 'in pain'. The consonants 'l' and 'w' join in the name 'William' with striking appropriateness. One infers from this that Moore's avowed realism, in this most important scene, is more than mere reportage. It is an expressive and interpretative technique both in its use of repetition and parallel structure and in its lyrical treatment of romantic love. Moore would have his reader experience a subdued poetry of sexual surrender. Moore's complaint that Hardy allowed his feeling about a similar situation in *Tess* to intrude upon depiction of the reality of the situation might be levelled against Moore himself in this scene. On the other hand, the pace of Moore's sentences, his withholding of narrative comment, and his refusal to linger too long over the scene suggest his wish to convey its relative uneventfulness, even its routineness, and this is in keeping with his aversion for the heightened manner.

Let us look now at nine sentences from the parallel passage in *Tess* (also cited above), a passage Moore almost certainly read before he wrote his own:

> The obscurity was now so great that he [Alec] could see absolutely nothing but a pale nebulousness at his feet, which represented the white muslin figure he had left upon the dead leaves. Everything else was blackness alike. D'Urberville stooped; and heard a gentle regular breathing. He knelt and bent lower, till her breath warmed his face, and in a moment his cheek was in contact with hers. She was sleeping soundly, and upon her eyelashes there lingered tears.
>
> Darkness and silence ruled everywhere around. Above them rose the primeval yews and oaks of The Chase, in which were poised gentle roosting birds in their last nap; and about them stole the hopping rabbits and hares. But, might some say, where was Tess's guardian angel? where was the providence of her simple faith? Perhaps, like that other god of whom the ironical

Tishbite spoke, he was talking, or he was pursuing, or he was in a journey, or he was sleeping and not to be awaked.

Moore was offended by Hardy's commentary in this passage (see pp. 4–5 above), by his digression on the whereabouts of her 'guardian angel'. A violation of reality, Moore seems to be saying, lies in Hardy's too-sudden move from an exhibiting of events to an interpretation of them. For Hardy, to ask why Tess should be a victim is to occasion a fairytale – that is, a theological or philosophical 'explanation' that destroys the illusion of reality the novel ought to create.

But Hardy's 'reality' is not Moore's. The irony of Hardy's 'meditation', founded on his sense of a tragic futility in things, occasions the beauty of the sentences that precede the meditation. Central to this is Hardy's sense that the sleeping Tess is somehow like the 'gentle roosting birds', a quite prosaic notion deriving, in part, from Hardy's reflections on nineteenth-century biological thought. Hardy possessed an unusual ability to make poetry of matters usually treated in prose. Certain ideas charged him poetically; his way of responding to ideas could be deeply emotional, for he saw instinctively their implications for individual human lives. Interestingly enough, the 'poetry' of the first seven sentences of this passage is produced through the intermingling of 'l' and other sounds, especially 's' sounds, as in the passage in Moore; and the name 'd'Urberville', like the name 'William', becomes a focus both of sounds and of action. The 'pale' and 'nebulous' figure in 'muslin' at d'Urberville's feet in the forest reaches back phonetically in the passage to atmospheric words such as 'obscurity' and 'absolutely nothing'. At the same time, 'pale' and 'nebulous' anticipate other atmospheric terms, such as 'blackness', 'darkness and silence', 'primeval yews' and 'gentle roosting birds', as well as Tess's 'gentle regular breathing', her 'sleeping soundly', and her 'eyelashes' on which tears linger. Both her 'gentle' breathing and the birds' 'gentle' roosting are literally disturbed by, at the same time that they mingle phonetically with, 'd'Urberville'. If Moore's 'l' – laden account of Esther's seduction captures something of the bright pleasure as well as the banality of sexual encounter, then Hardy's 'l'-laden account depicts its dark and painful mystery, its inexplicable need-to-be.

In part, the mystery and romance of Hardy's vision derives from his sense, clearly illustrated in this passage, of human and nonhuman lives as coeval aspects of a single process called nature. This is another point on which Hardy and Moore part ways. Moore's neglect of or contempt for this in Hardy accounts for his misreading of the gargoyle episode in *Far from the Madding Crowd* (see p. 6 above). Moore's realism, though 'scientific' in its insistence on observing and recording human behaviour, can be seen as naïve in its dualism. That is, it is founded on an assumption that human behaviour, though possessing some resemblances to animal behaviour, is distinct from and superior to animal behaviour. Men and women may on occasion behave like animals, but they are not for Moore animals in any essential sense. At least, they are not so near to sharing the situation of animals and plants as they are in Hardy's novels, especially the novels Hardy wrote after he wrote *The Woodlanders* (1887). Hardy, for all his departures from ordinary reality in *Tess*, can lay claim to a scientific realism largely absent from *Esther Waters*. For example, in *Tess* the death of the gamebirds under the guns of the hunters, and the slaughter of the rodents by the harvesters, are connected by the imagery of blood with the violation and death of Tess. The ruin of Tess by Alec is brutally and vividly prefigured when Prince, the Durbeyfield horse, is gored by the shaft of a mail cart and Tess is splashed with his blood. Similarly, Tess's recuperation at Talbothays after the death of her child is not merely *like* the coming of spring to the pastures of the Valley of the Great Dairies. Her recuperation is made one with the return of spring, apart from it and yet one with it. Shame, death and despair behind her, she feels 'the pulse of hopeful life still warm within her'; 'the recuperative power which pervaded organic nature was surely not denied to maidenhood alone' (*TD*, ch. 15). And so, when 'a particularly fine spring came round, and [when] the stir of germination was almost audible in the buds [,] it moved her, as it moved the wild animals, and made her passionate to go'; 'Some spirit within her rose automatically as the sap in the twigs' (ibid.). Once at Talbothays, Tess is happy because 'physically and mentally suited among these new surroundings. The sapling which had rooted down to a poisonous stratum on the spot of its sowing had been transplanted to a deeper soil' (ch. 20). At Talbothays, Tess and Angel find themselves 'converging, under an irresistible law, as surely as two streams in one vale' (ibid.).

Moore occasionally uses similar images, as when Esther, confined to a hospital bed and fearful for the life of her newborn son, 'experienced the sensation of the captured animal' (*EW*, ch. 18); or when, just having given birth to the child, she is likened to 'a convalescent plant trying to lift its leaves to the strengthening light' (ch. 16). On another occasion, Esther's time at rural Woodview, the place of her seduction, is described as the time when 'the sap of life was flowing fastest in her' (ch. 26). When she first arrived at Woodview and was shown around by William (much as Tess was shown around The Slopes by Alec), 'inanimate nature – the most significant objects – seemed inspired, seemed like symbols of her emotion' (ch. 6). On an earlier occasion at Woodview, Esther finds it 'a pleasure to touch anything, especially anything alive':

> She even noticed that the elm trees were strangely tall and still against the calm sky, and the rich odour of some carnations which came through the bushes from the pleasure-ground excited her; the scent of earth and leaves tingled in her, and the cawing of the rooks coming home took her soul away skyward in an exquisite longing; she was, at the same time, full of romantic love for the earth, and of a desire to mix herself with the innermost essence of things. The beauty of the evening and the sea breeze instilled a sensation of immortal health. . . .
>
> (ch. 6)

The echoes of *Tess* in Moore's language here (aside from marking a degree of sympathy with a style he later disparaged) show Moore's inability to exhibit his heroine in the transformative way Hardy exhibits Tess. For Hardy the recuperative power working in nature is working in Tess. Tess is not merely like a transplanted tree: she is a sapling taken out of its poisonous place of germination and rerooted in a better soil. In the same way, she is the stricken birds, the trapped rodents, the gored horse; the redness of her blood is the redness of theirs. Nonhuman nature is not for her, as it is for Esther, 'inanimate' or even 'symbolic'. Nor is her love of the earth 'romantic'. In a sense, the difference between Esther and Tess in their relation to nature is the difference between a real and a merely symbolic presence. Nature is present in Tess; Esther is a natural woman. Esther is Tess-not-mysterious; she is humanity denuded of its mysterious origins and destiny.

There is, obviously, more to be said about the kinships between

Tess and *Esther*. What has been said here should suggest, however, the decisive importance of *Tess* to the making of *Esther*. It may also suggest a basis for Hardy's appeal to later novelists, to American realists such as Theodore Dreiser and Ellen Glasgow, for example, both of whom also 'rewrote' *Tess* – Dreiser in *Sister Carrie* (1900) and *Jennie Gerhardt* (1911), and Glasgow in *Barren Ground* (1925). On the other hand, Moore's reservations about Hardy were echoed by at least two of his contemporaries among novelists, Henry James and Robert Louis Stevenson. It is useful, by way of introduction to the chapters that follow, to note Hardy's standing among some of his fellow writers of fiction.

Henry James had greeted *Far from the Madding Crowd* in the New York *Nation* (December 1874) with scorn for the artificiality of its plot and ridicule for what he called its 'ingeniously verbose and redundant style'. Like Moore later, James found it a clever imitation of George Eliot. Though he praised Hardy's depiction of the rural scene and his gift for dialogue, he excoriated Hardy's characters: 'he rarely gets beyond ambitious artifice – the mechanical stimulation of heat and depth and wisdom that are absent. . . . Everything human in the book strikes us as factitious and insubstantial; the only things we believe in are the sheep and the dogs.[18] Some twenty years later, when writing to Robert Louis Stevenson about 'the faults and falsity' of *Tess*, James was writing to a long-time admirer of Hardy's fiction who had suddenly come to dislike it. Stevenson had praised *A Pair of Blue Eyes* as 'one of the best dramatic novels of the day', and so admired *The Mayor of Casterbridge* that he had made a pilgrimage to Dorchester to meet its author and seek permission to dramatize the novel. In 1887, on the eve of sailing for America, Stevenson had sent Edmund Gosse searching about London for a copy of *The Woodlanders* to read on the voyage. But, upon reading *Tess*, Stevenson underwent the violent change he described in a letter to James in 1892. James had opened the exchange in a letter of March of the same year with this: 'The good little Thomas Hardy has scored a great success with *Tess of the d'Urbervilles*, which is chock-full of faults and falsities and yet has a singular beauty and charm.[19] Stevenson responded with a tirade worthy of George Moore:

> Hurry up with another book of stories. I am now reduced to two of my contemporaries, you and Barrie – O and Kipling! . . . As for Hardy – you remember the old gag? – Are you wownded,

my lord? – Wownded, Ardy – Mortually, my lord? – Mortually, Ardy. – Well, I was mortually wownded by Tess of the Durberfields. . . . Tess is one of the worst, weakest, least sane, most *voulu* books I have yet read. Bar the style, it seems to me about as bad as Reynolds . . . or to be more plain, to have no earthly connection with human life or human nature; and to be merely the ungracious portrait of a weakish man under a vow to appear clever, as a ricketty schoolchild setting up to be naughty and not knowing how. I should tell you in fairness I could never finish it; there may be treasures of the Indies further on; but so far as I read, James, it was, in one word, damnable. *Not alive, not true*, was my continual comments as I read; and at last – *Not even honest!* was the verdict with which I spewed it from my mouth. I write in anger? I almost think I do; I was betrayed in a friend's house – and I was pained to hear that other friends delighted in that barmicide [sic] feast. I cannot read a page of Hardy for many a long day, my confidence [in him] is gone.[20]

James replied with these now-notorious words:

I grant you Hardy with all my heart and even with a certain quantity of my boot-toe. I am meek and ashamed where the public clatter is deafening – so I bowed my head and let 'Tess of the D's' pass. But oh yes, Dear Louis, she is vile. The pretence of 'sexuality' is only equalled by the absence of it, and the abomination of the language by the author's reputation for style. There are indeed some pretty smells and sights and sounds. But you have better ones in Polynesia.[21]

This exchange would rate as little more than a particularly nasty bit of literary gossip if James's words had not been taken up and virtually institutionalized by F. R. Leavis some fifty years later, in *The Great Tradition* (1948), where Leavis excludes Hardy from the ranks of the greatest English novelists because he lacked 'profound sureness of . . . essential purpose':

On Hardy (who owes enormously to George Eliot) the appropriately sympathetic note is struck by Henry James: 'The good little Thomas Hardy has scored a great success with *Tess of the d'Urbervilles*, which is chock-full of faults and falsity, and yet has a singular charm.' This concedes by implication all that properly can be conceded – unless we claim more for *Jude the Obscure*, which, of all Hardy's works of a major philosophic – tragic ambition, comes nearer to sustaining it, and, in its clumsy way – which hasn't the rightness with which the great novelists show their profound sureness of their essential purposes – is impressive. It is all the same a little comic that Hardy should have been taken in the early 1920s . . . as pre-eminently the representative of the 'modern consciousness' or the modern 'sense of the human situation'.[22]

Leavis's decree is itself a 'little comic' in retrospect. First, it seems odd to include D. H. Lawrence in the 'tradition' with no mention whatsoever of Lawrence's *Study of Thomas Hardy* and the evidence there of Lawrence's profound debt to Hardy.[23] Though Leavis notes Joseph Conrad's debt to Dickens, he wholly ignores Lawrence's reliance on Hardy. What is more, Leavis's inability to understand Hardy's appeal in the 1920s appears peculiar when one looks not just to Lawrence, but to James Joyce and Virginia Woolf. If Lawrence found in the Wessex Novels a surpassing exhibition of the struggle between human passion and various forms of repression, Virginia Woolf found in Hardy one of the great writers of poetic prose, and Joyce found him one of the first champions in the fight for candour in fiction.

The case of Joyce is particularly instructive because, unlike Lawrence and Woolf, he had to overcome an early distaste for Hardy as strong as Moore's, James's and Stevenson's. In 1900, in an essay entitled 'Ibsen's New Drama', Joyce praised Ibsen's portraits of women at the expense of Meredith's, Turgenev's and Hardy's: 'He [Ibsen] appears to have sounded them to almost unfathomable depths. Beside his portraits, the psychological studies of Hardy and Turgénieff, or the exhaustive elaborations of Meredith, seem no more than sciolism. With a deft stroke, in a phrase, in a word, he does what costs them chapters.'[24] Joyce condemned Hardy's story 'The Tragedy of Two Ambitions', and placed Hardy among those nineteenth-century novelists who failed to advance the methods of prose fiction. By 1906, however, when he was faced with the refusal of Grant Richards to honour an agreement to publish *The Dubliners*, Joyce had learned to value, in the words of one critic, 'Hardy's role in the expansion of the subject matter of the novel and at the same time to base his right to trespass on so-called forbidden ground on the practice of his predecessor.'[25] Joyce quizzed Richards as follows: 'Do you think that *The Second Mrs. Tanqueray* would not have been denounced by a manager of the middle Victorian period, or that a publisher of that period would not have rejected a book by George Moore or Thomas Hardy?'[26] If Hardy's method in fiction seemed crude to Joyce, Hardy's struggle against Mrs Grundy seemed heroic, and this is apparent again in a letter Joyce wrote in 1928 to the editor of *La Revue nouvelle*. Joyce's letter formed part of a 'Homage to Thomas Hardy' occasioned by Hardy's death in January 1928. Responding in French, Joyce confessed to being touched at being asked to honour a venerable writer whose novels he had read years before. Though he declined to pass judgement on Hardy's writings, he firmly praised Hardy's integrity and courage as an artist.

> Mais quelque diversité de jugement qui pourrait exister sur cette oeuvre (s'il en existe), il paraît par contre évident à tous que Hardy offrait dans son attitude de poète vis-à-vis du public, un honorable exemple de probité et d'amour-propre dont nous autres clercs avons toujours un peu besoin, spécialement à une époque où le lecteur semble se contenter de moins en moins de la pauvre parole écrite et où, par consequent, l'écrivain tend à s'occuper de plus en plus des grandes questions qui, du reste, se règlent très bien sans son aide.[27]

What Joyce admired in Hardy was his 'integrity, the probity and pride of authorship by dint of which Hardy remains an honourable example for other writers to follow'.[28] The spirit of Hardy's 'Candour in English Fiction' (1890) and his lament there on 'the fearful price [a writer] has to pay for the privilege of writing in the English language' is echoed in a letter of Joyce's of 1918, in which he remarked that 'writing in English is the most ingenious torture ever devised for sins committed in previous lives'.[29]

Virginia Woolf found in Hardy's novels not just the integrity of great art, but something she cultivated in her own fiction: a powerfully suggestive lyricism. Acknowledging that Hardy's fiction suffers from a degree of incoherence, the result of his inability to depict character through his 'sense of poetry', she yet urged that poetry is the supreme virtue of Hardy's prose fiction:

Thomas Hardy is . . . akin to Charlotte Brontë in the power of his personality and the narrowness of his vision. . . . As we read *Jude the Obscure* we are not rushed to a finish; we brood and ponder and drift away from the text in plethoric trains of thought which build up around the characters an atmosphere of question and suggestion of which they are themselves, as often as not, unconscious. Simple peasants as they are, we are forced to confront them with destinies and questionings of the hugest import, so that often it seems as if the most important characters in a Hardy novel are those which have no names. Of this power, of this speculative curiosity, Charlotte Brontë has no trace. She does not attempt to solve the problems of human life; she is even unaware that such problems exist. . . .[30]

Woolf's regard for Hardy's 'speculative curiosity' deserves to be set alongside Leavis's complaint that Hardy lacked philosophic depth, just as the following sentences on Hardy's style offset Moore's, Stevenson's and James's complaints about Hardy's use of language:

Self-centred and self-limited writers have a power denied the more catholic and broad-minded. Their impressions are close packed and strongly stamped between their narrow walls. Nothing issues from their minds which has not been marked with their own impress. They learn little from other writers, and what they adopt they cannot assimilate. Both Hardy and Charlotte Brontë appear to have founded their styles upon a stiff and decorous journalism. The staple of their prose is awkward and unyielding. But both with labour and the most obstinate integrity by thinking every thought until it has subdued words to itself, have forged for themselves a prose which takes the mould of their minds entire; which has, into the bargain, a beauty, a power, a swiftness of its own.[31]

Woolf admires Hardy's prose for the strange beauty of its poetry, which she sees as an expression of Hardy's 'overpowering personality', of

some untamed ferocity perpetually at war with the accepted order of things which makes [him] desire to create instantly rather than to observe patiently. . . . It makes [him a poet], or, if [he chooses] to write in prose, intolerant of its restrictions. Hence it is that . . . [Hardy is] always invoking the help of nature. [He feels] the need of some more powerful symbol of the vast and slumbering passions in human nature than words or actions can convey.[32]

Because Woolf was fully aware of the imperfections of Hardy's narratives as novels – that is, as representations of social reality – she could enumerate his great virtues as a writer of romance:

(1) 'He is driven by some sense that human beings are the sport of forces outside themselves, to make use of an extreme and even melodramatic use of coincidence.'
(2) 'He is . . . possessed of the conviction that a novel is not a toy, nor an argument; it is a means of giving truthful if harsh and violent impressions of the lives of men and women.'
(3) 'He [is] . . . a minute and skilled observer of nature. . . .'
(4) He is a philosophic novelist in whose best fiction, such as *The Mayor of Casterbridge*, 'conscious ordering' does not impair his 'impression of life as it came to him'.
(5) His style, though more difficult to analyse than any novelist's except Scott's, achieves its aim 'unmistakably' even though 'on the face of it it [is] so bad'.
(6) His plots, filled with 'violence and convolution', win our acceptance because

> as we read . . . it becomes obvious that his violence and his melodrama, when they are not due to a curious peasant-like love of the monstrous for its own sake, are part of that wild spirit of poetry which saw with an intense irony and grimness that no reading of life can possibly outdo the strangeness of life itself, no symbol of caprice and unreason be too extreme to represent the astonishing circumstances of our existence.[33]

Woolf's sympathy in the face of Hardy's imperfections is, quite simply, her response to a strange and new beauty she found in Hardy's characters, settings and plots. Her sympathy is also stimulated by the opportunity she finds to complete an incompleteness she detects in Hardy:

> The novels . . . are full of inequalities; they are lumpish and dull and inexpressive; but they are never arid. there is always about them a little blur of unconsciousness, that halo of freshness and margin of the unexpressed which often produce the most profound sense of satisfaction. It is as if Hardy himself were not quite aware of what he did, as if his consciousness held more than he could produce, and he left it for his readers to make out his full meaning and to supplement it from their own experience.[34]

Like Moore, like Lawrence, Powys, Dreiser and Fowles, Woolf was attached to Hardy not just for what he had written, but also for what he left to be written.

Taken in the context of Moore's, James's and Stevenson's, and Leavis's complaints, not to mention T. S. Eliot's at about this same time,[35] Woolf's praise may seem somewhat eccentric, the product of an obituary occasion or of the nostalgia of a daughter looking back fondly to Hardy's connections with her father, for Hardy's *Far from the Madding Crowd* and *Hand of Ethelberta* had first appeared under the flag of Leslie Stephen and the *Cornhill*. But Woolf's admiration had loud echoes. From the 1880s on, in England, France and America, other novelists found much to praise and imitate in the Wessex Novels. It is worth quoting just a few of these remarks, if only to balance the more-publicized statements of James, Moore, Chesterton and others. James's 'poor little Thomas Hardy', Chesterton's 'village atheist brooding and blaspheming over the village idiot', Eliot's 'powerful personality uncurbed . . . by submission to any objective beliefs' – all these famous phrases seem incomplete, even off the mark, when set beside the opinions of some of Hardy's fellow novelists.

In 1886, George Gissing called on Hardy for some advice on novel-writing and later in the same year wrote to Hardy as follows:'I have not been the least careful of your readers, and in your books I have constantly found refreshment and onward help.' William Dean Howells, a respected novelist and the leading American critic of his day, wrote in 1895,

> I love even the faults of Hardy; I will let him play me any trick he chooses . . . if only he will go on making his peasants talk, and his rather uncertain ladies get in and out of love. . . . His people live very close to the heart of nature, and no one, unless

it is Tourguenief, gives you a richer and sweeter sense of her unity with human nature.

One year later, Willa Cather, a journalist in Pittsburgh and not yet a novelist, proclaimed her deep admiration for 'Thomas Hardy, ... [for] the lofty conception of *Tess*, ... [for] the finished execution of *A Pair of Blue Eyes*, [for] the beautiful simplicity of *Far from the Madding Crowd*.' The future author of *O Pioneers* and *My Ántonia* found Hardy's depiction of rural life 'the one thing in which Hardy excels all the novelists of his time and country'. In 1902, Theodore Dreiser described Hardy as 'the greatest figure in all English literature'. Because Hardy had written both great novels and 'rousingly beautiful' poetry, Dreiser knew of 'no one to set beside him'. In 1904, Arnold Bennett declared that Hardy had created a new fiction, distinct from the realism of Richardson and the romance of Scott: 'it contains a new beauty, a new thrill for the amateurs of beauty; it does not derive'. And it is worth noting again that in 1910 Marcel Proust sang the praises of *The Well-Beloved*, ranked Hardy among the greatest writers of fiction and singled out *The Well-Beloved* as 'very beautiful' and 'a thousand times better' than what he saw as his similar effort in *Remembrance of Things Past*.[36]

D. H. Lawrence, in 1914, found in six of the Wessex Novels heroes and heroines who fascinated him with their struggle to 'come into being' and for their disdain for money or 'immediate self-preservation'. Lawrence cherished in Hardy what he cherished in Shakespeare, Sophocles and Tolstoy: 'that there exists a great background, vital and vivid, which matters more than the people who move upon it. . . . The vast, unexplored morality of nature, surrounds us in its eternal incomprehensibility, and in its midst goes on the little human morality play.' Sinclair Lewis, the American realist, was 'joining a majority of intelligent readers' when he wrote in 1925,

> Hardy is probably the greatest living novelist. . . . There is in Hardy such a combination of nobility with closeness to earth, of dignity with quick humanity, as can be equaled only in one or two of the Russians. *Jude* and *Tess* and *The Return of the Native* are revelations of somber splendor which yet is never ponderous, which even to the most timorous romantic is forever 'interesting'.

Hardy's work, concluded Lewis, is the expression of a 'great and original vision charged with warm humaneness'.[37]

A generation later, in 1958, one finds Joyce Cary praising the magnitude of Hardy's achievement in fiction. Hardy, writes Cary, is one of 'the masters' of the modern novel because he opens to the reader the 'fearful truth' of 'the injustice of life, the cruelty [in *Tess*] of blind fate destroying innocent and guilty alike'. Citing the scene at Stonehenge in *Tess* and the episode in *The Mayor of Casterbridge* in which Henchard discovers his effigy floating in the river, Cary remarks,

> Hardy is among the greatest. The more we recede from him in time, the greater he seems, like Wordsworth's mountain. He is master, like Shakespeare, of the great dramatic scene. . . . It is Hardy who, more than anyone, has devised . . . scenes of which we can barely put the meaning into words, and, like Shakespeare, he goes to great lengths to contrive them.

Yet another generation later, in the late 1960s, one finds John Fowles, amidst work on *The French Lieutenant's Woman*, speaking of the 'shadow' of Hardy he cannot and will not avoid.[38]

Praise does not, of course, constitute influence. But, as the following chapters show, in a significant number of cases praise was accompanied by imitation. Not just *Esther Waters*, but Dreiser's *Sister Carrie* and *Jennie Gerhardt*, Proust's *Remembrance of Things Past*, Alain-Fournier's *Le Grand Meaulnes*, Lawrence's *The Rainbow* and *Women in Love*, J. C. Powys's *Wolf Solent* and *Maiden Castle*, and John Fowles's *Daniel Martin* are indebted to the Wessex Novels. If one adds to these the available evidence for Hardy's influence on some of the English and American regionalists of the early twentieth century, on novelists such as Romain Rolland and V. S. Naipaul, we have the stuff of a Hardy legacy in the twentieth-century novel.[39]

2
'Now it Remains': Hardy and D. H. Lawrence

> *Hardy [demolished] our faith in our own endeavour. . . .*
> (Lawrence, 1913)
>
> *My book on Thomas Hardy has turned out to be a sort of story of my own heart, or a* Confessio Fidei. *. . .*
> (Lawrence 1914)
>
> *Where* Jude *ends* The Rainbow *begins.*
> (Ian Gregor, 1973)

If the first two remarks above suggest ambivalence in Lawrence's attitude toward Hardy, the third asserts that ambivalence's creative result. Lawrence had disdain as well as respect for Hardy's accomplishment in the Wessex Novels, which he read and reread throughout his life. Though I have found no reference to Hardy in Lawrence's history before 1910, he had almost surely read Hardy before this, his twenty-fifth, year, probably with Jessie Chambers and her family. Jessie recalled her father's reading of *Tess* in the kitchen of the Haggs, the farm to which the Chambers moved in about 1897. Lawrence visited them there frequently from about 1900 on and of course transformed Haggs Farm into the Willey Farm of *Sons and Lovers* (1913).[1] Equally important, four volumes of the Wessex Novels were in the Eastwood Mechanics' Library, and Lawrence in all likelihood read them.[2] In December 1910, Lawrence mentioned *Jude the Obscure* in a letter to his fiancée, Louie Burroughs. And at about this same time Lawrence wrote a poem titled 'And Jude the Obscure and his Beloved', a poem that indicates, as one critic has said, that Lawrence 'had given the character relationships of *Jude* some analysis while the first version of *Sons and Lovers* was in progress'.[3] This poem, a dialogue between 'Jude' and 'Sue', exhibits a relationship similar to Paul and

Miriam's in *Sons and Lovers*, as well as to George and Lettie's in Lawrence's first novel, *The White Peacock* (1911). Not just in the distressed heroine of this first novel, but also in the use there of symbolic scenes as structural devices, Lawrence was reaching back to Hardy.[4] Lawrence was 'consciously or unconsciously . . . attempting to correct his mentor [Hardy]' by correcting Hardy's pessimism – that is, by demonstrating that in 'passionate, willful individuality lies the only hope for survival'.[5] The style, tone and atmosphere of the Wessex Novels mark *The White Peacock* and it is apparent already that *Jude the Obscure* was a touchstone for Lawrence.

In Lawrence's search for his own voice and manner, as well as for his own distinctive philosophy, Hardy was, among the novelists, the chief precursor to reckon with; and this was true because Lawrence, though repelled by Hardy's frequent expressions of sexual pessimism, was powerfully attracted to Hardy's subject – men and women passionately in love against a natural background at once beautiful and sinister. In March 1913, in his review of *Georgian Poetry, 1911–1912* (in which his own 'Snap Dragons' was included), Lawrence placed Hardy, almost scornfully, among 'the nihilists, the intellectual, hopeless people' who represent 'a dream of demolition', a dream, moreover, that Lawrence believes his generation is obliged to awaken from. This passage in which Lawrence mentions Hardy is worth quoting *in extenso*, for it at several points anticipates the better-known *Study of Thomas Hardy*, which Lawrence would begin just one year later:

> This collection is like a big breath taken when we are waking up after a night of oppressive dreams. The nihilists, the intellectual, hopeless people – Ibsen, Flaubert, Thomas Hardy – represent the dream we are waking from. It was a dream of demolition. Nothing was, but was nothing. Everything was taken from us. And now our lungs are full of new air, and our eyes see it is morning, but we have not forgotten the terror of the night. We dreamed we were falling through space into nothingness, and the anguish of it leaves us rather eager. . . .
>
> The last years have been years of demolition. Because faith and belief were getting pot-bound, and the Temple was made a place to barter sacrifices, therefore faith and belief and the Temple must be broken. This time art fought the battle, rather than science or any new religious faction. And art has been

demolishing for us: Nietzsche, the Christian religion as it stood; Hardy, our faith in our own endeavour; Flaubert, our belief in love. Now, for us, it is all smashed, we can see the whole again. We were in prison, peeping at the sky though loop-holes. The great prisoners smashed at the loop-holes, for lying to us. And behold, out of the ruins leaps the whole sky.

It is we who see it and breathe in it for joy. God is there, faith, belief, love, everything. We are drunk with the joy of it, having got away from the fear. . . .

It is all the same – hope, and religious joy. Nothing is really wrong. Every new religion is a waste-product from the last, and every religion stands for us for ever. We love Christianity for what it has brought us, now that we are no longer upon the cross. . . .

I worship Christ, I worship Jehovah, I worship Pan, I worship Aphrodite. But I do not worship hands nailed and running in blood upon a cross, nor licentiousness, nor lust. I want them all, all the gods. They are all God. But I must serve in real love. If I take my whole, passionate, spiritual, and physical love to the woman who in return loves me, that is how I serve God. And my hymn and my game of joy is my work. All of which I read in the anthology of *Georgian Poetry*.[6]

For Lawrence in March 1913, Hardy was nihilistic, hopeless, a writer in the forefront of the nineteenth century's demolition of traditional ideas of religion, of love, and, most interestingly, of a traditional 'faith in [human] endeavour'. Lawrence accused Hardy of having destroyed this particular humanism, probably because he found in the Wessex Novels a humanity almost totally at the mercy of chance and change and the whimsy of the gods. However, Lawrence's initial remarks about Hardy in the *Study* (ch. 3) suggest he made a significant change of mind between the review of March 1913 and the beginning of work on the *Study* in September 1914. The disdain, even disgust, registered in the review has softened into something very like admiration. In fact, the Hardy of the opening chapters of the *Study* might be one of the Georgian poets Lawrence so praised in the previous year. None of Hardy's heroes and heroines, Lawrence notes 'care[s] very much for money, or immediate self-preservation', for all are absorbed by the struggle 'to come into being'. Hardy's novels, like the poems in *Georgian Poetry* by Abercrombie, Masefield and others, exhibit 'the struggle into love and the struggle with love: by love, meaning the love of a man for a woman and a woman for a man'. Lawrence admires 'these people of Wessex' for 'always bursting suddenly out of bud and . . . always shooting suddenly out of a tight convention, a tight, hide-bound cabbage state into something quite madly personal'[7] 'The time to be impersonal has gone', Lawrence had announced in his praise of the poems of the Georgians just one year before: 'We start from the joy we have in being ourselves and everything must take colour from that joy.' Now he finds that Hardy's people, 'even the apparently wishy-washy heroines of the earlier books', all possess 'a real, vital, potential self, . . . and this self suddenly bursts the shell of manner and convention and commonplace opinion' (*Study*, p. 410).

A brief account of the composition of *Study of Thomas Hardy* is in order here, for it emerged at the same time Lawrence was writing and rewriting the narratives that later became *The Rainbow* and *Women in Love*.[8] In late December 1912, shortly before the appearance of the review of *Georgian Poetry*, Lawrence had abandoned a novel based on the life of Robert Burns and begun another titled *The Insurrection of Miss Houghton*, which was to become *The Lost Girl*. In March 1913 he set aside *The Lost Girl* and began *The Sisters*, which he completed in June, and which he would eventually divide to make into *The Rainbow* and *Women in Love*. In September 1913 he was at work again on *The Sisters*, and by January 1914 had retitled it *The Wedding Ring*. By May, he had completed it and at Frieda's request had retitled it *The Rainbow*. In July 1914, the month of his marriage to Frieda, Lawrence was reading Hardy's novels and Lascelles Abercrombie's *Thomas Hardy: A Critical Study* (1912) in preparation to write 'a little book on Hardy's people' for Nisbet and Co. In August, Methuen returned the manuscript of *The Rainbow* as unfit for publication; in early September Lawrence, 'out of sheer rage', began his book on Hardy. In November 1914 Lawrence was finishing the *Study* and at the same time beginning the fourth and last revision of *The Rainbow*. It was then, in a letter to Amy Lowell, that Lawrence called the *Study* 'a sort of story of my own heart'. In the first half of 1915, Lawrence realized that the novel he was writing (*The Rainbow*) was too long to be published in one volume. He finished the manuscript of *The Rainbow* in early March, revised it extensively, and resubmitted it to Methuen in early June. In April, he also began rewriting the second half of *The Rainbow*, the segment that would eventually become *Women in Love*. Also, in March, Lawrence seriously considered rewriting the *Study of Thomas Hardy*, a plan that eventuated in the essay 'The Crown', which he completed by October 1915. *The Rainbow* appeared on 30 September 1915 and was banned on 13 November of the same year. Between April and October 1916, Lawrence returned to the original *Sisters* and rewrote it in four drafts as *Women in Love*, which was published in 1920. The *Study of Thomas Hardy* remained unpublished until 1936.

Lawrence's strongest praise for Hardy in the *Study* emerges in his assessment of *The Return of the Native*, a novel whose central action, Clym Yeobright's tragic attempt to reconcile devotion to his mother with passionate love for the voluptuous Eustacia Vye, strongly resembles the private dilemma Lawrence had transformed into the struggle of Paul Morel in *Sons and Lovers*, only two years before. But Lawrence has relatively little to say about the 'son – lover . . . who is legion' in his remarks on Hardy's *Return* in the *Study*. Instead, he praised in *The Return* what many critics would later admire in *Sons and Lovers*, the close kinship between man and nature, what Mark Spilka has described as the 'active relation' between Paul, Mrs Morel, and the sun, moon, and especially the flowers, of 'a live and responsive universe'.[9] The 'real stuff of tragedy' in *The Return of the Native*, Lawrence urges, is Egdon Heath: 'the primitive, primal earth, where the instinctive life heaves up' (*Study*, p. 415). Clym Yeobright fails (unlike Paul Morel, one notes) because, though 'he was born out of the passionate Egdon to live as a passionate being whose strong feelings moved him even further into being', these feelings, subjected to 'business and to the greater system it represented' never flower into being. 'The dark struggle of Egdon, a struggle into being as the furze sturggles into flower, went on in him, but could not burst the enclosure of the idea, the system which contained him' (p. 416).

Out of this interchange between Clym and his native Egdon emerged what Lawrence called the 'constant revelation', the 'wonder . . . and . . . beauty' of Hardy's novels, the quality Hardy shared, in Lawrence's judgement, with Sophocles, Shakespeare and Tolstoy: 'this setting behind the small action of his protagonists the terrific action of unfathomed nature; setting a smaller system of morality, the one grasped and formulated by the human consciousness within the vast, uncomprehended and incomprehensible morality of nature or of life itself, surpassing human consciousness' (p. 419). This is high praise, and Lawrence would never essentially alter it. In 1916, for example, he would remark on the 'lovely, mature, and sensitive art' of the Wessex Novels; in 1917, on his preference for Hardy's novels over those of all Lawrence's contemporaries, excepting the early Conrad; in 1924, on Hardy as 'a last big one, [one who] rings the knell of our Oneness'.[10] In 1929, shortly before Lawrence's death, Hardy was, according to Barbara Weekley, the only writer she heard Lawrence speak of with respect, a fact confirmed by a recent study of Lawrence's debt in *Lady Chatterley's Lover* to Hardy's *Two on a Tower*.[11] Along with this enduring admiration, however, Lawrence retained a dislike for certain things in Hardy. Early in 1928, while writing the third version of *Lady Chatterley's Lover*, Lawrence was still taking the measure of his great precursor: 'What a commonplace genius he [Hardy] has, or a genius for the commonplace, I don't know which. He doesn't rank so terribly high, really. . . .'[12]

The source of Lawrence's uncertainty about Hardy is Lawrence's view that Hardy is an unrelenting pessimist and an intrusive moralist. Though Lawrence placed Hardy in the august company of Shakespeare and Sophocles, he insisted on a crucial difference between them:

> that whereas in Shakespeare or Sophocles the greater, uncomprehended morality, or fate, is actively transgressed and gives active punishment, in Hardy . . . the lesser, human morality, the mechanical system is actively transgressed, and holds, and punishes the protagonist, whilst the greater morality is only passively, negatively transgressed, it is represented merely as being present in background, in scenery, not taking any active part, having no direct connexion with the protagonist.
> (*Study*, pp. 419–20)

Lawrence's preference for characters capable of enacting 'the greater morality', characters such as Ursula and Gudrun Brangwen, is implicit in the following:

> Oedipus, Hamlet, Macbeth set themselves up against, or find themselves set up against, the unfathomed moral forces of nature, and out of this unfathomed force comes their death. Whereas . . . Eustacia, Tess, Sue, and Jude find themselves up against the established system of human government and

morality, they cannot detach themselves, and are brought down. Their real tragedy is that they are unfaithful to the greater unwritten morality, which would have bidden . . . Eustacia fight Clym for his own soul, and Tess take and claim her Angel, since she had the greater light; and would have bidden Jude and Sue endure for very honour's sake, since one must bide by the best that one has known and not succumb to the lesser good.

(p. 420)

Hardy's devotion to the 'lesser, human morality' explains also his at once having a *prédilection d'artiste* for the aristocrat', and 'at the same time . . . [a] moral antagonism to him'. Hardy, to Lawrence's despair, condemns the aristocrat to death at the same time as he is fascinated by his sexual energies. Lawrence attributes this to two causes: 'the community has come to consciousness in him' and he sees the 'germ of death' dwelling in those who can 'afford to *be*' (pp. 435–6). So a Manston, a Troy, a Eustacia or Wildeve, a Henchard, Tess or Jude must die. Hardy's inability to champion the sexual aristocrat, to stand with the exceptional spirit against the average, is, says Lawrence, the root of his pessimism. Hardy, out of moral timidity, cannot champion what he most values – the emotional, i.e. sexual, freedom embodied in an Aeneas Manston, a Eustacia Vye or a Tess Durbeyfield.

Lawrence deepens this censure of Hardy when he insists – particularly in his long discussion of *Tess* and *Jude* in chapter 9 of the *Study* – that Hardy is betrayed by his metaphysic. Though Hardy's 'feeling, his instinct, his sensuous understanding is . . . very great and deep, deeper than that, perhaps, of any other English novelist', his theory of being – that ' "the spirit of Love must always succumb before the . . . power of the Law" ' – is 'pitiable' (p. 480). It is 'the same cry all through Hardy, this curse upon the birth in the flesh, and this unconscious adherence to the flesh', Hardy has shown 'Love in conflict with the Law, and only Death the resultant, no Reconciliation' (p. 513). That Lawrence's dismissal of Hardy here is made on his own behalf as the struggling author of *The Rainbow* is clear from a letter he wrote to A. W. McLeod on 26 April 1913:

I am so sure that only through a readjustment between men and women, and a making free and healthy of this sex will she [England] get out of her present atrophy. Oh, Lord, and if I don't 'subdue my art to a metaphysic', as someone very beautifully said of Hardy. I do write because I want folk – English folk – to alter, and have more sense.[13]

With this confession of purpose in view, the function of Lawrence's ambivalence toward Hardy in the *Study* becomes clear: Lawrence is clearing imaginative space for himself as a novelist through his criticism of the novels of his major precursor among English novelists. He is in effect announcing the arrival on the English scene of the author of *The Rainbow*, the novel he was at that moment writing, and *Women in Love*, the novel that was soon to follow. This is surely the point of the closing paragraphs of the *Study*:

> Humanity does not continue for long to accept the conclusion of these writers [Dostoevsky, Hardy, Tolstoy, Flaubert], nor even of Euripides and Shakespeare always. These great tragic writers endure by reason of the Truth of the conflict they describe, because of its completeness, Law, Love, and Reconciliation, all active. But with regard to their conclusion, they leave the soul unsatisfied, unbelieving.
>
> *Now the aim of man remains* to recognize and seek out the Holy Spirit, the Reconciler, the Originator, He who drives the twin principles of Law and Love across the ages.
>
> *Now it remains* for us to know the Law and to know the Love, and further to seek out the Reconciliation. . . .
>
> . . . It has always been . . . either a wrong conclusion, or one forced by the artist. . . . *Now it remains* for us to seek the true balance, to give each party, Apollo and the Furies, Love and the Law, his due, and to seek the Reconciler.
>
> (p. 514; italics added)

But who is this Reconciler? It is, says Lawrence, the writer who knows 'the natural law of his own being', then seeks out 'the law of the female, with which to join himself as complement', and then, finally, shows that man and woman together are 'one within the Great Law, reconciled within the Great Peace'. And out of this final knowledge comes the supreme human art, the art 'which knows the struggle between the conflicting laws, and knows the final reconciliation, where both are equal, two in one, complete. This is the supreme art, *which yet remains to be done*. Some men have attempted it, and left us the results of efforts. *But it remains to be fully done*' (pp. 515–16; italics added).

This announcement of personal mission by way of conclusion to the *Study* suggests also the function of the harsh criticism of Hardy that occurs throughout the *Study*. Since Lawrence intends to depict 'fully' the drama of man and woman that Hardy has only 'attempted', has depicted only in part, then Hardy's abortive attempts must be handled roughly:

> Let it be said again that Hardy is a bad artist. Because he must condemn Alec d'Urberville, according to his own personal need, therefore he shows him a vulgar intriguer of coarse lasses, and as [a] ridiculous convert to evangelicalism. . . .
> This [depiction of Arabella] is only Hardy's bad art. He himself, as an artist, manages in the whole picture of Arabella almost to make insignificant in her these pig-sticking, false-hair crudities. But he must have his personal revenge on her for her coarseness, which offends him, because he is something of an Angel Clare. (pp. 488–9)

> *The Well-Beloved* is sheer rubbish, fatuity, as is a good deal of *The Dynasts* conception. (p. 480)

> The tiresome fact about Hardy is that, so often, he will neither write a morality play nor a novel. (p. 435)

This censure, because so often countered by high praise, is no ordinary expression of distaste, such as James and Stevenson's scorn for Hardy's style, Eliot's contempt for his unbelief, or Leavis's distrust of his intelligence. Lawrence's censure is more like George Moore's – an expression of anxiety and doubt by one very much in the grip of Hardy's example and influence. Lawrence and Moore are travellers following a guide they dare not trust entirely, and so the muttering, the backward glances, the careful study of signposts and of their own 'maps', as well as the concealed acceptance of the guide's choice of route, if not of destination. If they arrive at their destinations, and they both do – for who would question the authenticity of *Esther Waters* and *The Rainbow* – they must be able to proclaim, in spite of their guide, the independence of their journey. Lawrence's *Study of Thomas Hardy* is an example – perhaps the greatest in the language – of what Harold

Bloom has called the fusion of 'poetic history' and 'poetic influence' that occurs when 'strong poets' misread one another 'so as to clear imaginative space for themselves'. And Lawrence is one of the strong poets, an artist 'with the persistence to wrestle with [his] strong precursor, even to the death'. Lawrence does not 'idealize' Hardy; he appropriates him.[14]

Lawrence's 'creative misreading' of Hardy in the *Study* indicates that the *Study* is, at centre, a meditation on influence, on the incursion of the past on the present. And, in fact, Lawrence's method in the *Study* is consistently historical and his sense of history highly 'personal'. The history of art is for him here almost exclusively a succession of artists in their kinships with precursors; and it is his own position among the artists of the West – from palaeolithic times to the early twentieth century – that Lawrence seeks to discover and declare. A creative tension between the young and the old is apparent from the opening of the *Study*, where an old man at the door of a cave cautions the young men with him to imitate the squirrel and the ant and avoid the ways of the fiery poppy, 'that reckless, shameless scarlet flower' (p. 399). This tale of the dying elder – he scolds and reminisces, then compromises and dies, then makes a ghostly return to counsel the young – is but the first in a series of encounters between precursors and successors, between artistic sires and their progeny. In all these encounters the outcome is shaped by Lawrence's stubborn commitment to 'true individuality and . . . a sufficient completeness in ourselves', to liberation of the new from the old, of the present from the past (p. 405). The great 'self-preservation scheme' Lawrence so abhors is, in part, traditionalism, that millstone around the necks of the young who are 'struggling to come into being' (p. 410). If Hardy's people are admirable for their drive to 'explode out of . . . convention', Hardy is for Lawrence too often unfaithful to this volatility in his people (ibid.). Lawrence's preference for characters who resist to the death 'the push of tradition' undoubtedly emerges from his wish as a novelist to move beyond the achievement of novelists who, like Hardy, show 'Love in conflict with the Law, and only Death the resultant' (p. 513).

To move beyond his artistic parentage, Lawrence had to distinguish carefully between his undeniable debt to the past and his need to break with it. For example, he cannot accept completely his much-admired Carlyle's dictum that 'Work is All', but must reshape it (with the help of a German proverb) into this: 'One must work to eat, and eat to live.' And to live, for Lawrence, as for the American writers he would praise in *Studies in Classic American Literature* (1923), is to draw from the past and yet break with it. To live is 'to be free to be [oneself]', to be at liberty to create oneself (*Study*, pp. 425–6). Man he likens to 'a palpitating leading shoot of life, where the unknown . . . beats and pulses'. When a man thinks or moves he must retrace, unavoidably, 'some proved experience':

> He is as the leading-shoot which, for the moment, remembers only that which is behind, the fixed wood, the cells conducting towards their undifferentiated tissue of life. He moves as it were in the trunk of the tree, in the channels long since built, where the sap must flow as in a canal. He takes knowledge of all this past experience upon which the new tip rides quivering, he becomes again the old life, which has built itself out in the fixed tissue, he lies in line with the old movement, unconscious of where it breaks, at the growing plasm, into something new, unknown. . . .
>
> Such is a man at work, safe within the proven, deposited experience . . . ; he has only made himself one with what has been, travelling the old, fixed courses, through which life still passes, but which are not in themselves living. (pp. 424–5)

But this exploration of 'proven, deposited' experience is a prison, for, if a man is a growing tip and leading shoot of life, then 'his own body [is] a quivering plasm of what will be, and has never yet been'. and 'his own soul [is] a fighting-line, where what is and what will be separates itself off from what has been':

> Is not this his purest joy of movement, the indistinguishable, complex movement of being? And is not this his deepest desire, to be himself, to be this quivering bud of growing tissue which he is? He may find knowledge by retracing the old courses, he may satisfy his moral sense by working within the known, certain of what he is doing. But for real, utter satisfaction, he must give himself up to complete quivering uncertainty, to sentient non-knowledge. (p. 425)

In the fifth chapter of the *Study*, the chapter titled 'Work and the Angel and the Unbegotten Hero', Lawrence prefaces an acerbic description of Hardy's lack of sympathy for his 'aristocratic characters' with an account of what he calls the Janus-like nature of man. Man at once rejoices in his knowledge, which is 'that which has been, [and] . . . is revealed', and gives himself up to being 'in blindness and wonder and pure godliness, the living stuff of life itself, unrevealed' (p. 430). And so a man's work, and this must include the work of the novelist, is 'the repetition of some one of those rediscovered movements'. And these 'movements', it must be presumed, include the novels of one's precursors, which are 'repeated' or imitated up to a point, then departed from. For the final meaning of work is not only that one repeats or imitates things of the past, but that one extends human consciousness (p. 431). True extension of consciousness requires rebirth, which occurs for the man 'of twenty or thirty' (Lawrence was twenty-nine in 1914) not through 'knowledge' but through 'some utterance only':

> 'Ye must be born again', it is said to us. Once we are born, detached from the flesh and blood of our parents, issued separate, as distinct creatures. And later on, the incomplete germ which is a young soul must be fertilized . . . and we must be brought forth to ourselves, distinct. . . .
>
> So, when I am young, at eighteen, twenty, twenty-three, when the anguish of desire comes upon me, as I lie in the womb of my times, to receive the quickening, the impetus, I send forth all my calls . . . asking for the word, the Word which is the spermatozoon which shall come and fertilize me and set me free. . . .
>
> Give us a religion, give us something to believe in, cries an unsatisfied soul embedded in the womb of our times. Speak the quickening word . . . that will deliver us into our own being.
> (pp. 433–4)

What Lawrence immediately turns to in Hardy, directly from this reflection on how 'the new is not the resultant of the old, but something quite new, quite other', is Hardy's failure to sympathize with the aristocrat, the man who can 'afford to *be*, to be himself, to create himself, to live as he himself' (p. 436). Lawrence censures Hardy here for not making characters who conform to Lawrence's vision of how men of 'distinct being', men such as he, rise above the masses.

Lawrence's highly selective survey of the history of art, which makes up the greatest part of chapters 7 and 8 of the *Study*, is governed by a wish to trace artistic parentage: 'Botticelli develops to Correggio and to Andrea del Sarto, Andrea del Sarto develops forward to Rembrandt, and Rembrandt to the Impressionists. . . . But Botticelli, on the other hand, becomes Raphael, Raphael and Michelangleo' (p. 457). The farther forward in his survey of Western art Lawrence moves, the more clearly he sees that contemporaries, near-contemporaries, and even a pair of artists separated by many years, can struggle, each in his authentic way, with identical issues: 'Raphael and Michelangelo are men of different natures placed in the same position and resolving the same question in their several ways. Socrates and Plato are a parallel pair, and, in another degree, Tolstoi and Turgenev, and, perhaps, St. Paul and St. John the Evangelist, and, perhaps, Shakespeare and Shelley' (pp. 458–9).

That this pairing of artists over the ages is connected with the pairing of himself with Thomas Hardy that occasioned his *Study of Thomas Hardy* amidst his work on *The Rainbow* seems clear in chapter 9 ('A Nos Moutons'), where first he praises Hardy for his strength of feeling then roundly condemns him for the failure to show how to reconcile the eternal 'antinomy between Law and Love, between. . . . Flesh and . . . Spirit'. By the ninth chapter of the *Study*, Lawrence has worked himself into a position from which to define his kinship to Hardy, who, like Turner, the last (and only English) painter in Lawrence's survey, failed to 'mate body with spirit' (p. 474). Having announced Hardy's great shortcoming, Lawrence can now declare the basis for a new art, which must be new not *in toto* but in being independent from that which it in part imitates. And this independence will be achieved in its form, which 'must always be different':

> Artistic form is a revelation of the two principles of Love and the Law in a state of conflict and yet reconciled: pure motion struggling against and yet reconciled with the Spirit. . . . It is the conjunction of the two which makes form. And since the two must always meet under fresh conditions, form must always be different. Each work of art has its own form, which has no relation to any other form. When a young painter studies an old master, he studies, not the form, that is an abstraction which does not exist: he studies maybe the method of the old great

artist: but he studies chiefly to understand how the great artist suffered in himself the conflict of Love and Law, and brought them to a reconciliation. Apart from artistic method, it is not Art that the young man is studying, but the State of the Soul of the great old artist, so that he, the young artist, may understand his own soul and gain a reconciliation between the aspiration and the resistant. (pp. 477–8)

Having after great effort come to this understanding of the way the young artist schools himself in the 'State of the Soul' of the old artist, Lawrence can move, with brief glances into Shelley, Swinburne and Tolstoy, into some thirty pages on the state of the soul of the artist who wrote *Tess* and *Jude*. In particular, Lawrence describes the great division in Hardy between sensuous and metaphysical understanding, which originates in Hardy's cursing the flesh and at the same time adhering to it. Through this encounter with Hardy, Lawrence arrived at his own mission in the novel he was then writing. In the tenth and last chapter of the *Study*, he set forth, as has been noted, his programme as novelist: to reconcile Law and Love, 'to seek the true balance, to give each party, Apollo and the Furies, Love and the Law, his due, and so to seek the Reconciler' (p. 514).

To turn now to *The Rainbow* and *Women in Love* is to discover how two of Lawrence's greatest novels are marked by his study of Hardy's method and 'state of soul' in *Tess* and *Jude*. The affinities between *Jude* and *The Rainbow* have been much remarked on, and Ian Gregor's observation 'Where *Jude* ends, *The Rainbow* begins' is as enticing as it is acute.[15] But critics have virtually ignored Lawrence's strong sense of *Tess* and *Jude* as interconnected, dialectical works, as suggested by his observation that *Jude* is only *Tess* 'turned round about' (*Study* p. 488). Hardy's influence on *The Rainbow* and *Women in Love* is most interesting when seen with Lawrence's sense of the interrelationships of *Tess* and *Jude* in mind.

Lawrence was the first critic to note that Hardy went to some length in *Jude* to repeat and yet alter certain of the terms of *Tess*: 'Instead of the heroine containing the two principles, male and female, at strife within her one being, it is Jude who contains them both, whilst the two women with him take the place of the two men in Tess. Arabella is Alec d'Urberville, Sue is Angel Clare' (*Study*, p. 488). Lawrence's chief complaint about Hardy's handling of Angel Clare, Alec d'Urberville and Tess, as well of Sue Bridehead, Arabella Donn and Jude, is that Hardy did not go so far as he might have in showing the male and female impulses coexisting in each of them. Lawrence saw that, in making Jude a male Tess, Sue a female Angel Clare, and Arabella a female Alec, Hardy was reaching for new subtlety, new depth of ironic insight, in his treatment of human passions. But Lawrence also found Hardy inhibited by his personal attitude toward passion. As has been noted, he deplored Hardy's condemnation of Alec as 'a vulgar intriguer of coarse lasses', and was outraged by Hardy's 'personal revenge on [Arabella] for her coarseness' (p. 489). Lawrence also deplored Hardy's failure to understand that two kinds of love coexist in men and women: the 'selfish instinct' that says my mate is 'administered unto me and I am supreme'; the 'unselfish' instinct that says my mate is 'the unknown, the undiscovered, into which I plunge to discovery, losing myself' (p. 490). In sum, Lawrence insists throughout his remarks on *Tess* and *Jude* on something at which Hardy merely hints, that 'what is true of men is so of women' as well: 'If we turn our faces west, towards nightfall and the unknown within the dark embrace of a wife, they [women] turn their faces east, towards the sunrise and the brilliant, bewildering, active embrace of a husband. And as we are dazed with the unknown in her, so she is dazed with the unknown in us' (p. 492). One result of Lawrence's belief in 'the coexistence of male and female traits in every individual'[16] are observations – at once startling and revelatory – such as the following.

> [Arabella] sees in [Jude] a male who can gratify her. She takes him, and is gratified by him. Which makes a man of him. He becomes a grown, independent man in the arms of Arabella, conscious of having met, and satisfied, *the female demand in him*. This makes a man of any youth. He is proven unto himself as a male being, initiated into the freedom of life.
>
> (p. 493; italics added)

Arabella, says Lawrence, is 'unanswerably female' and in this parallels Alec; both are unable to change in themselves. Both have the will to remain where they are, 'static, and to receive and exhaust all impulse' received from their mates. Alec 'betrayed the female in a woman, by taking her, and by responding with no male impulse from himself. He roused her, but never satisfied her. He could never satisfy her. It was like a soul-disease in him:

he was, in the strict, though not the technical sense, impotent. . . . He was spiritually impotent in love. Arabella was the same' (p. 489).

Jude is like Tess in being 'bored, or *blasé*, in the body' – he as a result of hard study and intellectual yearning, she as a consequence of 'coming of an old family, that had been long conscious, long self-conscious' (p. 495). Out of this obsession 'to have nothing to do with his own life', Jude turns to Sue. And Tess turns to Angel for a similar reason: 'She wanted life merely in the secondary, outside form, in the consciousness' (ibid.). And so, Tess and Sue *and* Jude, the man as well as the two women, belong to the 'old woman-type of witch or prophetess, which adhered to the male principle ["consciousness [of] . . . mind only"], and destroyed the female principle ["experience in the senses"]':

> [Sue] was born with the vital female atrophied in her: she was almost male. Her *will* was male. . . .
> . . . Sue wished to identify herself utterly with the male principle. That which was female in her she wanted to consume with the male force, to consume it in the fire of understanding, of giving utterance. . . .
> Sue is the production of the long selection by man of the woman in whom the female is subordinated to the male principle. . . .
> . . . But Sue is scarcely a woman at all, though she is feminine enough. (p. 496)

If Sue is male in her devotion to the life of the mind, to the utterable, and to the Word, Jude is female in 'his blood' and 'his sensuous being', which he is obsessed to bring to the level of consciousness through study (p. 500).

> What he indeed wanted to get from study was, not a store of learning. . . . He wanted . . . to find conscious expression for that which he held in his blood. And to do this, it was necessary for him to resolve and to reduce his blood, to overcome the female sensuousness in himself, to transmute his sensuous being into another state, a state of clarity, of consciousness.
> (pp. 499–500)

Sue and Jude's relationship is doomed not because Jude demands and obtains sexual gratification of Sue, but because he wanted 'that deepest experience' that only a woman can grant a man, 'that penetrating far into the unknown and undiscovered which lies in the body and blood of man and woman, during life. He wanted to receive from her the quickening, the primitive seed and impulse which should start him to a new birth' (p. 503). But Sue, 'cut off from the source and origin of life' by centuries of religious knowledge, cannot respond to Jude. Their tragic failure, concludes Lawrence, is 'the result of over-development of one principle of human life at the expense of the other, an over-balancing; a laying of all the stress on the Male, the Love, the Spirit, the Mind, the Consciousness; a denying, a blaspheming against the Female, the Law, the Soul, the Senses, the Feelings' (p. 509). Why, Lawrence wonders, in the closing sentences of chapter 9 of the *Study*, was there no place for a Sue Bridehead in the social scheme of things? Why have we no 'reverence' for what human history has made of her, and of us? Particularly of those of us who, like Sue, are 'specialized', are neither woman nor man, but are 'almost neuter'? (ibid).

Lawrence found in *Tess* and *Jude*, then, both a new way of looking at persons caught up in sexual relationships and a remarkable variety of sexual feelings.[17] Angel and Sue were for him examples, male and female, of persons whose sex is crushed by religious knowledge. Alec and Arabella are the opposite: persons indifferent in their sex to religious or social restraint. Tess and Jude are an odd combination of restraint and licence: both capable of strong passion, both emotionally volatile. Tess has a dangerous temper, Jude has his melancholy, his lust, and his appetite for strong drink. Lawrence clearly perceived *Jude* as Hardy's sequel to *Tess*, an extension of the passional conflicts exhibited in *Tess*. He must also have seen that *Jude* is not just a male, but an austerely male, *Tess*. The lush lyricism of *Tess*, the moving scene-paintings that mark it, give way to the spare and bleak antithetical form of *Jude*. It is even conceivable that Lawrence's idea for two novels deriving from *The Sisters*, an idea he arrived at in early 1915, came to him as a result of his work with *Tess* and *Jude* for the *Study of Thomas Hardy*, which he had in mind in the summer of 1914. In *The Rainbow* and *Women in Love*, Lawrence does not, of course, simply attempt to repeat Hardy's exploration of sexual ruin from the point of view of the female and then the male victim. Marriage, rather than sexual ruin, is the dominant concern in both *Rainbow* and *Women in Love*. He uses not the story of seduction, but the family chronicle, the Brangwen saga, to shape his governing contrasts – between Ursula and her mother and grandmother, then between Ursula and Gudrun. But his concern, with remarkable frequency, is with the ambiguous sexuality of his people – the masculine qualities, especially the capacity for violence, in Ursula, Gudrun and Hermione; the feminine qualities, particularly the dependency in love, of Anton, Birkin and even Gerald. And between *The Rainbow* and *Women in Love*, as between *Tess* and *Jude*, there is a shift from a phasal to an antithetical structure, from a lyrical and descriptive mode to an analytic and dramatic one.

Ursula's career in *The Rainbow* is defined by her liberation of herself – through work and sexual adventure – from assumptions about a woman's role and nature deeply rooted in her society, her family history, and her own consciousness. At the end of the novel she stands poised, having escaped marriage and motherhood, and having brutally subdued Anton Skrebensky with her love-making, on the threshold of an unknown future. Her role in *Women in Love* is a logical extension of this – subdued, somewhat domestic – defined as much by her love for Rupert Birkin as by her sexual experiences, her work as a teacher and her loyalty to the past. She has the courage of her convictions and she speaks out memorably on important occasions – against Gerald for his harsh treatment of a mare he rides, against Herr Loerke and Gudrun and their defence of Loerke's egotistical idea of art, against Birkin (in spite of her love for him) and his highly intellectualized idea of love. Ursula is an altogether sympathetic figure, one who grows and ripens, and yet in *Women in Love* she is subordinated to Gudrun – the embodiment, like Hardy's Sue Bridehead, of a 'new' kind of femaleness.

Gudrun's view of love and womanhood are in their way as different from Ursula's as Ursula's were from the ideas of their mother and grandmother. Ursula's career describes a spiral. She begins life under the strong influence of a mother devoted entirely to husband and home, then rebels against domesticity by taking on the aggressive, violent manner of the male – both in her works as a teacher and in her affair with Anton. Finally, she returns to what can only be described as a domestic role, but newly conceived. Her flight from the nest begins when, uncertain of her affection for Anton and disgusted by a lesbian relationship with

Winifred Inger, one of her teachers, she leaves home (against her father's wish) to take a position at the rough Brinsley Street school. There she soon learns that 'it was power, and power alone that mattered', a lesson the mastery of which she demonstrates when she beats into total submission an insolent male student. The language of her triumph over the troublesome boy is not without sexual overtones: 'Nothing could touch her now; she was beyond Mr. Harby [the headmaster]. She was as if violated in death.' And later in the same episode: 'Something had broken in her; she had passed a crisis. Williams was beaten, but at a cost.' And again: 'she had paid a great price out of her own soul, to do this. It seemed as if a great flame had gone through her and burnt her sensitive tissue.'[18]

Ursula's domination of the rude boys and her defiance of Harby (and earlier of her father's wish that she not work) is followed by her rejection of Anthony Schofield's proposal of marriage. It is wholly appropriate that, when she departs from Brinsley School, her fellow teachers should give her copies of the poems of Meredith and Swinburne, for both had struggled mightily with the question of 'modern love'. Certain now that 'she [is] free', she can speak with scorn of Winifred Inger's marriage to Tom Brangwen, can turn with zest to the study of botany, and can throw herself into a passionate love affair with Anton, who has just returned from the Boer War. Ursula dominates and exploits Anton as ruthlessly as Alex had exploited Tess and Arabella Jude, though with mental as well as physical force. Ursula has, in her 'masculine' drive for freedom and power, moved beyond the knowledge of science and morality into the realm of 'another, stronger self that knew the darkness':

> She could see the glimmer of dark movement just out of range, she saw the eyes of the wild beast gleaming from the darkness, watching the vanity of the camp fire and the sleepers; she felt the strange, foolish vanity of the camp, which she said 'Beyond our light and our order there is nothing', turning their faces always inward towards the sinking fire of illuminating consciousness. . . .
>
> The darkness wheeled round about, with grey shadow-shapes of wild beasts, and also with dark shadow-shapes of the angels, whom the light fenced out, as it fenced out the more familiar beasts of darkness. And some, having for a moment seen the

darkness, saw it bristling with the tufts of the hyaena and the wolf; and some having given up their vanity of the light, having died in their own conceit, saw the gleam in the eyes of the wolf and the hyaena, that it was the flash of the sword of angels, flashing at the door to come in, that the angels in the darkness were lordly and terrible and not to be denied, like the flash of fangs. (*R*, ch. 15)

This fusion of the bestial and the angelic, the suggestion here that Ursula's adoption of a male manner has moved her to perceive a unity between even the most disparate things, is the basis for the mixture of tenderness and strength that is uniquely hers in *Women in Love*. Sexual intercourse with Anton strengthens Ursula's devotion not to him but to the undying creatures of darkness her encounter with him has wakened in her: 'The man, what was he? – a dark, powerful vibration that encompassed her. She passed away as on a dark wind, far, far away into . . . the dark fields of immortality' (*R*, ch. 15). She is enmeshed now not just with Anton, but with an essential maleness, with 'the undifferentiated man he was', and with a latent maleness, recently stirred, in herself. Consequently, she can refuse Anton's offer of marriage, with the near-comic result that he is suddenly thrust into a traditionally feminine role – that of the petitioner, of the trusting maiden who has been sexually mastered ('She had taken him') and now seeks to salvage respectability by marrying. In a sense, Anton begs Ursula 'to make him an honest man'. When she refuses his second appeal, he weeps profusely, like many another 'woman' disappointed in love. His weeping, like Ursula's decidedly dominant role in their love-making, 'cruelly, coldly defaced' his manhood (ibid.)

Not only does Ursula exhaust and dominate Anton, physically and psychologically: she also in the interim cultivates, in good 'male' fashion, an eye for other possible lovers. The 'full-blooded, animal face' of a cab-driver fascinates her; the 'intent animality' of a young Italian waiter attracts her. At least for the moment she is a virtual Doña Juanita, an erotic idealist seeking 'something impersonal' not in but through the man she takes. And, of course, a version of erotic idealism is what Rupert Birkin will offer her in *Women in Love*. In the meantime, she destroys poor Anton in one last searing embrace on a moonlit beach:

She lay motionless, with wide-open eyes looking at the moon. He came direct to her, without preliminaries. She held him pinned down at the chest, awful. The fight, the struggle for consummation was terrible. It lasted till it was agony to his soul, till he succumbed, till he gave way as if dead, and lay with his face buried, partly in her hair, partly in the sand. . . .

It was a long time before he came to himself. He was aware of an unusual motion of her breast. He looked up. Her face lay like an image in the moonlight, the eyes wide open, rigid. But out of the eyes, slowly, there rolled a tear, that glittered in the moonlight as it ran down her cheek.

He felt as if the knife were being pushed into his already dead body. . . .

He drew gradually away as if afraid, drew away – she did not move. He glanced at her – she lay the same. Could he break away? He turned and saw the open foreshore, clear in front of him, and he plunged away, on and on, ever further from the horrible figure that lay stretched in the moonlight on the sands with the tears gathering and travelling on the motionless, eternal face. (*R*, ch. 15)

As suggested by Anton's feeling that a 'knife were being pushed into his already dead body', Ursula is the phallic, the dangerously phallic, agent in this encounter. And Anton (resembling Hardy's deflowered Tess or deceived, humiliated Jude) can only wander off into marriage to his colonel's daughter. Though Ursula, like Tess, becomes pregnant, she is scarcely troubled by thoughts of social or moral ruin. The experience of sex is for her a way to knowledge, and a knowledge that enables her to face the future on her own terms and to preserve that which she values from her past. The 'flames' of pregnancy she finds 'good', and it is now that she recovers a deep, if temporary, regard for her mother Anna and that prolific woman's devotion to the marriage bed and the domestic hearth: 'Suddenly she saw her mother in a just and true light. Her mother was simple and radically true. She had taken the life that was given. She had not, in her arrogant conceit, insisted on creating life to fit herself. Her mother was right, profoundly right, and she herself had been false, trashy, conceited' (ch. 16). Ursula's acceptance of the possibility of motherhood is also, finally, her acceptance of the paradox that the glory and radiance of the rainbow emanates from the muck of common life.

Ursula's rainbow vision of 'the earth's new architecture . . . , the world built up in a living fabric of Truth, fitting to the overarching heaven', emerges not from a complete rejection of the past and its familial intimacies (this is to be Gudrun's way), but from a wish to reconcile the old intimacies with her new uprootedness and all its uncertainties (ibid.).

How like, yet unlike, Hardy's *Tess*. Setting aside for the moment the critical difference that Ursula's child is never born, Ursula is like Tess in that she encounters through work and sex the world beyond her rural origin. Unlike Tess, however, Ursula attacks that world of maleness and power; unlike Tess, she ends triumphant. The irony in this, which Lawrence must have fully recognized, is that Ursula triumphs, as Hardy's Alec and Arabella triumphed, at a high cost to someone. Ursula's visionary capacity to see the new emerging, phoenix-like, out of the blood and spirit of those 'sordid people who crept hard-scaled and separate on the face of the world's corruption' requires an almost inhuman detachment from the plight of those sordid people. Like Tess, Ursula is a creature of flesh, instinct with and radiant with spirit. Unlike Tess, Ursula survives, or is oblivious to, the human realities (including the moral law) that would curb, punish, even destroy this spirit. But her superiority to the moral law – an expression perhaps of Lawrence's wish to correct Hardy's 'error' in subordinating his people to the law – could easily make her an impersonal monster, something akin to Gudrun or Hermione Roddice, those power-mad women of *Women in Love*. Lawrence averts this in a masterful way.

The chief source of Ursula's spirituality is memory, for out of her memory of the Brangwen past flows her humaneness, as enduring as it is tender. This is revealed in Ursula's nostalgic reflections as she travels by night train with Birkin through Ghent on the way to the winter holiday at Innsbruck that will end in tragedy:

> Ursula saw a man with a lantern come out of a farm by the railway and cross to the dark farm-buildings. She thought of the Marsh, the old, intimate farm life at Cossethay. My God, how far was she projected from her childhood, how far was she still to go! In one lifetime she travelled through aeons. The great chasm of memory from her childhood in the intimate country surroundings of Cossethay and the Marsh Farm – she remembered the servant Tilly, who used to give her bread and butter

sprinkled with brown sugar in the old living-room where the grandfather clock had two pink roses in a basket painted above the figures on the face – and now when she was travelling into the unknown with Birkin, an utter stranger – was so great that it seemed she had no identity, that the child she had been, playing in the Cossethay churchyard, was a little creature of history, not really herself.[19]

The repetition of the word 'intimate' and that word's incarnation in the loving details of Ursula's memory of the servant Tilly and the furnishings at the Marsh Farm is a key; for in *Women in Love*, as in *Jude the Obscure*, intimacy born of family and memory is dying or dead. This is even more the case for Gudrun and Gerald than for Ursula and Birkin.

Ursula can never forget the affection and intimacy she knew at the Marsh Farm and at her home at Cossethay, and it is precisely her capacity for tenderness and affectionate intimacy that sets her off from Gudrun, Gerald Crich, and even from Birkin. She denounces Gerald's cruel handling of his Arab mare at the same time as Gudrun is attracted to his mastery of the animal. She rejects Herr Loerke's exclusively self-reflective art, again in the face of Gudrun's approval. Most important, she never tires of mocking Birkin and his intellectual loving. She rejects as 'an obstinacy, a theory, a perversity' his wish to be loved by Gerald as completely as by her. Ursula knows on her pulses that Birkin's yearning for an impersonal love is as destructive of human happiness as Gerald's devotion to detached and efficient ways of operating his coal mine and Gudrun's almost complete indifference to the ordinary human lives around her. Ursula is endowed with an almost-mystic sense of the spirit in the flesh, of the 'shadow-shapes of angels' that exist within mortal human forms. This poetic power shapes her encounter with the horses on Willey Green, near the end of *The Rainbow*.

Like Hardy's *Tess*, Ursula is responsive to the nonhuman powers about her. It is 'the hard, urgent massive fire' of the horses' flanks, 'the quiver and strain and thrust of their powerful flanks', that possesses her, both frightens and gratifies her; for she recognizes it as the fecundating principle of life itself, active here in animal, and strongly masculine, form (*R*, ch. 15). In her struggle with and break from her family, in her determination to be as tyrannical, and therefore as 'masculine', a teacher as Harby, in her rejection of one man's offer of marriage and her sexual humiliation of another man, and, finally, in her quiet determination to have Birkin, Ursula is consistently responsive to the life forces – physical and spiritual – working through her. She will not suppress or deny them in the name of morality, or of philosophy. She can love Birkin in spite of his stubborn perversity in matters of love. She can resist Gudrun and Loerke's defence of a self-reflective art out of her devotion to a life beyond the self. As daughter and teacher, as lover of plants, animals and men, as would-be mother and silent witness to nature's mysterious presences, Ursula is a Tess, but a Tess freed of killing guilt. Even more than with Tess, moral education has touched only the outer person. Ursula never ceases to be Tom Brangwen's granddaughter and Anna Brangwen's daughter. In Birkin she finds a compatible mixture of the old passions and new rage for freedom. In Gudrun, on the other hand, Ursula finds an almost complete antithesis. If Ursula can be seen as a Tess without shame, Gudrun is a Sue without guilt, a Sue, one might say, with all the selfish instinct of an Arabella and none of the vulgarity.

The difference between Ursula and Gudrun is encapsulated, too patly perhaps, on the first page of *Women in Love*, where one finds Ursula stitching and Gudrun sketching, and Ursula struggling at the same time to answer Gudrun's and the novel's, question: 'don't you *really want* to get married?' Ursula cannot at this point answer, though her stitching, with its hint at home-making, is as suggestive of her future in marriage to Rupert Birkin as Gudrun's sketching is of her future with Gerald Crich and then the artist Loerke. Ursula is twenty-six and a class-mistress at the Willey Green Grammar School, Gudrun twenty-five and an artist, recently returned to live at her parents' home after several years of art study and studio work in London. Ursula will eventually marry Birkin, an educator and artist who, like her, seeks lasting human attachments. Both are educators, and both are lovers of nature. Though their relationship is not a traditional one, their courting and marrying seems almost old-fashioned when set against the mad struggle between Gudrun and Gerald and the relentless pursuit of Birkin by Hermione Roddice. The pairing of Ursula and Birkin repeats, in its way, the pairing of Ursula's parents and grandparents.

Gudrun's man is to be Gerald Crich, the handsome, strong-willed, sinister heir to an industrial fortune. This is to prove a disastrous mating, for, if Gudrun's totem is the cat and her chief mode of speech bitter irony, Gerald's totem, as Gudrun eagerly notes, is the wolf, and his typical gesture is physical violence. The beasts of Ursula's circle of darkness (p. 50, above) have come, howling and slashing, into the light. Artist and industrialist are both portrayed as destroyers. Gudrun's barely repressed sadism is more than matched by Gerald's brutal and even murderous instincts. He had accidentally, or not so accidentally, shot to death a younger brother. He is merciless in his domination of the Arab mare he rides. He subdues with sheer strength of hand a struggling rabbit that Gudrun wishes to examine. He is ruthlessly efficient as manager of the mine he has inherited, coolly setting aside, in the interest of higher profits, his father's charity and indulgence toward the workers. He is a deliberate and successful philanderer. He can be tender, particularly in his friendship for Birkin, but finally he is as incapable of love for Birkin as for Gudrun. No small part of Lawrence's triumph in this novel, whose antithetic pairings recall Hardy's *Jude the Obscure*,[20] is his sympathetic, objective treatment of characters as repellent as Gudrun and Gerald. Their humanity – particularly their hunger for a tenderness their temperaments deny them – is never sacrificed to Lawrence's relentless exposure of their destructiveness and cruelty.

Ursula and Gudrun's talk about love and marriage in the opening chapter is, in a real sense, not completed until another conversation (really a quarrel) they have near the end of the novel. It is as if the conversation in chapter 1 had never ended. This second occurs at Innsbruck, where the two couples (Usula and Birkin have by now married) are enjoying a winter holiday. There Gudrun, angered by what she decides is Gerald's inability to love her, as well as by his interest in other women, falls in with a dwarfish German sculptor, Herr Loerke, whose distinctly 'aesthetic' view of art she embraces, much to Ursula's anger and disgust. Loerke has shown Gudrun a photogravure reproduction of one of his sculptures: a green bronze statuette, the image of a young girl, naked, sitting sideways on a horse, 'a massive, magnificent stallion, rigid with pent up power', its neck 'arched and terrible, like a sickle' (*WL*, ch. 29). Not just Ursula's encounter with the horses on Willey Green at the end of *The Rainbow*, but also Ursula and Gudrun's witness of Gerald's brutal treatment of his Arab mare at a crossing near Willey Green in *Women in Love* (ch. 9), is recalled by Loerke's statue, which Gudrun finds somewhat shameful but also fascinatingly beautiful. Ursula is as outraged by Loerke's rendering of the girl on the horse as she had been by Gerald's treatment of the mare, which Gudrun had found indefinably appealing. Ursula dismisses out of hand Loerke's defence of his statue as a 'certain *form*, part of a whole form . . . [with] no relation to anything outside that work of art' (ch. 29). Ursula will not accept this sophistry; she insists it is an image of a horse. To Gudrun's defence of Loerke – 'What do you mean by a horse? You mean an idea you have in *your* head, and which you want to see represented' – Ursula responds with what is for Loerke and his zealous defender an ultimate confusion of life and art: the accusation that Loerke's horse is a 'picture of himself' (ibid.) First Loerke, then Gudrun, flies out in reply to Ursula:

> 'A picture of myself' he repeated in derision. '. . . It is a work of art, it is a picture of nothing, of absolutely nothing. It has nothing to do with anything but itself, it has no relation with the everyday world of this and other, there is no connection between them, absolutely none, they are two different and distinct planes of existence, and to translate one into the other is worse than foolish, it is a darkening of all counsel, a making confusion everywhere. . . .'
> 'That is quite true', cried Gudrun, let loose in a sort of rhapsody. 'The two things are quite and permanently apart, they have nothing to do with one another. *I* and my art, they have *nothing* to do with each other. My art stands in another world, I am in this world.' (Ibid.)

Ursula gives as good as she receives:

> 'It isn't a word of it true, of all this harangue you have made me', she replied flatly. 'The horse is a picture of your own stock, stupid brutality, and the girl was a girl you loved and tortured and then ignored. . . .
> 'As for your world of art and your world of reality, . . . you have to separate the two, because you can't bear to know what you are. You can't bear to realize what a stock, stiff, hide-bound brutality you *are* really, so you say "it's the world of art". The world of art is only the truth about the real world, that's all – but you are too far gone to see it.' (Ibid.)

Gerald at first joins Loerke and Gudrun against Ursula and her fierce attack on an 'esotericism which gave man his last distinction'. But, upon closer questioning, Loerke's cruelty to the girl who modelled for the statue, as well as his almost-ghoulish preference for 'small and fresh and tender and slight' women, is exposed; this, and Gudrun's growing attachment to the artist, turns Gerald violently against him. Gudrun is by now as attracted to Loerke as Ursula (and Gerald) are repelled by him, and Ursula and Rupert Birkin soon leave the silent, frozen world of Innsbruck for the 'dark fruitful earth' of southern Europe. They return only after Gerald's suicide, brought about when his growing hatred for Gudrun and Loerke explodes into a physical attack on both, an attack from which he recoils in self-loathing to go off to his death by exposure to the cold.

The conversation between Ursula and Gudrun about marriage that opened the novel ends here, then, near the novel's end, with Ursula's declaration that 'Rupert is right – one wants a new space to live in, and one falls away from the old' (ch. 29). Ursula has married, and her answer to Gudrun's question in chapter 1 is, in effect, 'Yes, I *really want* to marry, if I can find in marriage a bridge over the abyss that divides my past from my present life.' Gudrun, in this the fatalist, does not believe it possible to reshape the old, especially the old idea of love, with its call for self-denial. If Gudrun and Gerald can agree on nothing else, they can agree that they are incapable of love in this traditional sense. But Ursula, speaking out of an instinctive knowledge of her power in love, speaking out of her trust in Birkin, knows a supernatural reality 'of which Love is only a little part' (ch. 29). This reality she has found with Birkin and she will continue to seek it with him. Gudrun cannot follow Ursula in this, and, as Ursula silently reflects, Gudrun cannot 'Because you never *have* loved' (ibid.).

Gudrun Brangwen, then, is as stricken as Sue Bridehead by her inability to love a man. And, just as Sue's tortured emotions bring about the deaths of her children, the ruin of Jude, and her own self-mutilating return to Phillotson, so Gudrun's taste for violence and cruelty brings about the fatal confrontation between Gerald and Loerke. Gerald and Loerke are oddly alike in their cruelty. Gerald's indifference to his employees is like Loerke's indifference to his model and his audience. Gudrun's fascination with Loerke's statuette is like her fascination with Gerald's cruel mastery of the horse and the rabbit. Industrialist and artist are alike in their inhumaneness, and Gudrun loves the inhumaneness in both, though she finally prefers Loerke to Gerald because she finds him superior in understanding. His cruel mental power she finds better than Gerald's cruel physical force. In a sense, Loerke is Gudrun's Phillotson, a man deficient in human qualities to whom a Gudrun or a Sue can attach her own deficient humanity. In the *Study of Thomas Hardy* Lawrence called Phillotson 'a human being as near to mechanical function as a human being can be', a 'reptile' belonging to the 'putrescent activity of life' (p. 502). In *Women in Love* Lawrence describes Loerke as 'a strange creature', a 'rabbit', a 'bat', a 'brown seal', an 'insect', a 'little dry snake' (WL, ch. 29). Though Lawrence honours both Loerke and Phillotson for being true to themselves, it seems clear that for Lawrence Gudrun's turn to Loerke, like Sue's to Phillotson, is a loathsome thing, a turn toward death-in-life.

Gudrun is also like Sue in motive. As repelled by Gerald's demanding sexuality as Sue was by Jude's, she in part clings to Gerald out of jealousy. His attractiveness to other women forces her hand, just as Jude's attractiveness to Arabella forces Sue to finally give herself to Jude. Gudrun insists to Gerald that she is interested in Loerke 'because he has some understanding of a woman, because he is not stupid' (WL, ch. 30). What Gudrun finds in Loerke, however, is a subdued sexuality. She turns to him because, unlike Gerald, Loerke is 'a free individual' who can offer her a Bohemian life free from 'so much hideous boring repetition of vulgar actions, vulgar pleasures, vulgar postures' (ibid.). Gudrun chooses a man in whom consciousness of mind dominates experience of the senses. Like Sue, Gudrun 'was born', to quote Lawrence in the *Study*, 'with the vital female atrophied in her: She was almost male. Her *will* was male' (p. 496). Gudrun's choice of Loerke is her choice of the mind over the senses, and Lawrence honours her choice at the same time as he deplores her for it.

I don't delude myself that I shall find an elixir of life in Dresden. I know I shan't. But I shall get away from people who have their own homes and their own children and their own acquaintances and their own this and their own that. I shall be among people who *don't* own things and who haven't got a home and a domestic servant in the background, who *haven't* got a standing and a status and a degree and a circle of friends of the same. O God, the wheels within wheels of people, it makes one's head tick like a clock, with a very madness of dead mechanical monotony and meaninglessness. How I *hate* life, how I hate it. How I hate the Geralds, that they can offer me nothing else. . . .' (Ch. 30)

This passage is the counterpart and antithesis of Ursula's reflection on the night train through Ghent (see p. 53 above). There Ursula was looking back to the days at the Marsh; here Gudrun is looking forward to Dresden. Ursula was savouring the old intimacies connected with the family home, its furnishings and servant; Gudrun is repelled by them. Ursula's 'My God, how far was she projected from her childhood' is echoed in Gudrun's 'Oh God, the wheels within wheels of people', the former suggestive of a need for the old intimacies, the latter of a need for detachment. Ursula's sense of time is captured in her affectionate memory of the 'grandfather clock' at the Marsh; Gudrun's in 'the mechanical monotony and meaninglessness' of life in respectable society. Ursula's consciousness is sensuous and retrospective, Gudrun's is mental and forward-looking; and when the consciousnesses of both are allowed to develop unhampered by society – as Tess's and Sue's *are not* – this is the result: Ursula and Birkin joined in unconventional marriage; Gudrun and Loerke locked in pursuit of self-gratification; and Gerald dead.

Gerald's self-induced death recalls Jude's similar end, just as Gerald's struggle with the lethal violence of his nature recalls Jude's hopeless struggle against his dream to rise in the world. Both are deeply flawed men who are unable to alter or cure a destructive tendency in their natures, and both perish as a result. Gerald's death is interesting in light of Lawrence's seeming insistence on preserving and honouring the views of Gudrun and Ursula. Ursula's survival of sexual violation is Lawrence's 'correction' of Tess's tragedy, just as Gudrun's avoidance of moral masochism is his 'answer' to Sue's ultimate wretchedness. Ursula's experience of sex is a move toward freedom; Tess's violation is a move toward death. Gudrun's choice of Loerke is a move toward freedom; Sue's return to Phillotson is an act of self-torture. Why, in light of these 'revisions', could Lawrence not honour Gerald as he had honoured these others, for being, in his phrase, 'true to themselves'? Is he here and for once following Hardy and Hardy's belief in the inevitable superiority and authority of the human law? The answer to this must be no, for Gerald's death differs from Jude's in being wholly self-induced, wholly free of nudging by conscience or society. Jude seeks to punish himself. Gerald entertains no such thought. As a result of his affair with Gudrun, Gerald is made to suffer nothing comparable to Jude's loss of Sue and their children. Gerald's liaison with Gudrun is as free from moral considerations as Jude's relationship with Sue is smothered by them. Gerald's self-induced end is a free act; Jude's hastening of his death is coerced by all the forces that have opposed him from the beginning. Gerald's choice of death over life, like Ursula's and Gudrun's choices, is a step into freedom. Sue, Tess and Jude have no comparable choice. Ursula is a Tess freed to develop in love; Gudrun is a Sue freed to develop in her profound unease with herself and her world. Gerald is a Jude freed to choose the moment of his own end. Lawrence's people, unlike Hardy's, develop according to the laws of their individual natures; to them Lawrence subjects the community and its morality.

3
'An Undying Underground Stream': Hardy and John Cowper Powys

> *To plagiarize from the great is always a sign of greatness.* . . . *Sophocles and Shakespeare were Hardy's models and his deliberate echoes of them are to me only another convincing proof that there is in literature an undying underground stream of tradition as to the kind of subject and even as to the kind of treatment of that subject which strikes deepest into the universal and unchanging such as binds all the really great writers together and leaves outside in each successive generation the clever 'originals' of the passing cults.* (Powys, 1938).

In the case of John Cowper Powys (1872–1963), novelist, as well as philosopher, poet and lecturer-*extraordinaire*, the decisive influence of Hardy is never in question; for Powys never tired of describing it – in poems, essays and letters, but most particularly in his novels, which appeared between 1915 and 1936. But how Hardy's influence manifests itself, especially in the five novels of 1925–36 set in Dorest and Somerset, is a complicated question, in part because Powys himself was so determined to provide an answer. The novels of Scott, Dostoevsky and Dickens, as well as the poems of Wordsworth, were by Powys's own admission as important as the Wessex Novels as purely literary influences. But then Hardy was much more than a purely literary influence on Powys; for, as Powys suggests in his *Autobiography* (1934), as well as in many other references to Hardy between 1915 and 1936, Hardy was a poetic father and mentor in an immediate and conscious sense. This can be said because in the *Autobiography*, as shall be seen, Powys makes repeated associations between his

Dorset-born and Dorset-bred biological father, the Reverend Charles Francis Powys, from whom he was estranged for much of his life, and the Dorset-born and-bred Thomas Hardy, whom he knew personally and on whom he in large part consciously modelled himself as a novelist. Powys re-explores these connections in fictional terms in his autobiographical novel *Maiden Castle* (1936), in which Dud No-Man, a novelist much like Powys himself, is writing his own version of Hardy's *Mayor of Casterbridge* in the form of the story of Mary Channing of Dorchester, a woman executed in Dorchester in 1705 for murdering her husband. In *Maiden Castle* Dud vacillates between the presence of Thomas Hardy and the presence of his biological father, a man of massive simplicity and imagination named Uryen Quirm. In his *Autobiography*, written two years earlier, John Cowper Powys is pulled in a similar way between the Reverend Charles Powys and the much-admired Thomas Hardy.

Though it seems Powys knew little or nothing of Thomas Hardy until about 1893, when he was twenty-one and about to leave Cambridge University for a career as a lecturer and writer in England and America, his exposure to Dorset and its traditions had begun much earlier; for, though he himself had been born (the first of eleven children) in Derbyshire, his father, a clergyman and the son of a Dorset clergyman, brought his family back to his native Dorset in 1879, when he accepted a curacy at St Peter's, Dorchester. The Powys family lived in Dorchester until 1885, and John called his first two years there, before he was sent away to school in Sherborne in 1882, 'the most important, most significant, and certainly most happy of my whole life'.[1] Conflict between the sternly traditional Reverend Francis Powys and his dreamy and emotional eldest son was unavoidable, and there is evidence that the strong appeal Hardy held for John Cowper Powys from the 1890s on lay in Hardy's representing to the young genius a splendid and imitable blend of traditional Dorset ways with powerful intellectual and emotional nonconformity. This will be examined in more detail later, with reference to *Weymouth Sands* (1934) and Hardy's *Well-Beloved*, *Maiden Castle* and Hardy's *Mayor*, and Hardy's prominence in the *Autobiography*. But first let us look briefly into Powys's copious record of his associations with Hardy.

Strangely enough, it seems that it was not until he had left Cambridge in 1894, at the age of twenty-two, that Powys first read one of the Wessex Novels – *Far from the Madding Crowd*. Where

Henry James had complained of this novel's factitiousness and insubstantiality, and though George Moore would deride it for its crude English, Powys found it nothing less than enchanting:

> Little did I realize what a stone circle of monoliths and trilithons, grey with the lichen of centuries of English tradition, I was entering, when I chanced on this volume; or what a memorable influence, calm, austere, noble – just the influence needed by a coward who loved colour more than form – I was submitting to when I got hold of this book. . . . It was a small, plain, brown volume in a very simple binding. I recollect reading nearly half of it in one single walk; and, as with all the books I have loved best, its actual substance, cardboard, paper, print, and the words 'by Thomas Hardy', passed and repassed into the gates against which I leaned, into the tree roots under which I sat, into the pond willows on whose branches I laid my hand, into the road-dust that blew up in my face as I moved forward step by step, turning pages that seemed to me – so full of ironies and pities were they – not pages of a book at all, but wind-shaken oak-leaves in some oracular grove of Dodona!
>
> (*Auto*, pp. 224–5)

Immediately following this praise for Hardy, but speaking now of his immense admiration for John Keats, Powys writes candidly of the role of his poetic precursors in the schooling of his genius: 'I knew I was a mere imitating copy-cat, repeating, repeating, repeating the rhythms of men of genius. But . . . I knew then [1893–4], just as I knew twenty years later . . . that I *was*, in some way impossible to prove, a great and for all my cringings and propitiations, a terrifyingly formidable genius!' (*Auto*, p. 225). By 'repeating the rhythms' of the great poets, Powys was seeking to free his own genius by finding 'rhythms' congenial to him. And in Hardy he found a novelist in whom 'form' – narrative structure, plot, a pervasive irony – was dominant. Hardy could therefore be a mentor against whom Powys could shape his optimistic sense of infinite human possibility and his need to explore and re-explore his own psychic life.

In 1896, Powys published his first book, a collection of twenty-nine lyrics titled *Odes and Other Poems*. Six of the twenty-nine are dedicated to writers: to William Cowper (a maternal ancestor), Swinburne, Lamb, Keats, Yeats and, of course, Thomas Hardy, to whom Powys boldly sent a copy. The author of the just-published *Jude the Obscure* responded with an invitation to tea at Max Gate. Bedevilled as he was in the 1890s by hostile reviewers, Hardy must have been grateful for the generous praise he found in Powys's 'To Thomas Hardy':

> Master of human smiles and human moan,
> Of strange soul-searchings, raptures, agonies,
> Passions that ask for bread and find a stone,
> Hopes hungered into madness like the seas,
> And Pity dumb with pleading like the wind:
> Prophet art thou of that mysterious tongue
> Wherewith our ancient Mother, deaf and blind,
> Her griefs immortal and her joys hath sung
> In the unheeding ears of human-kind.
>
> O Master, thine a special meed of praise
> From me whose heart is all thy sweet West's own,
> Hushed with the dew that dreams on orchard sprays
> With clover scents about the woodlands blown.
> Full oft in those enchanted solitudes,
> When fairy fingers ring the flowery bells,
> And make a thousand mystic interludes
> To the slow weaving of Hymettian spells,
> Cool-couched on mossy bank I've floated down
> The fair, swift currents of unnumbered dreams
> Plucked Amaranth blossoms by Elysian streams
> And kissed the starry skirts of Dian's gown.
>
> And there, in commune with thy mighty heart,
> I saw how life's light wreath of summer roses
> Remorseless Fate's inveterate frown discloses,
> And sullen Death's intolerable dart:
> Saw man's last hope beneath a soulless sky
> To live for Love, and for Love's sake to die.[2]

Apart from the lush, Keatsian sense of nature in the highly allusive second stanza, the first and third stanzas tell what Powys found so appealing in Hardy's novels: the mingling of irony and pity that marks Hardy's tragic view of things; the implacable natural process that spins on beneath the beauteous natural scene; the

West Country itself; and, finally, love as the all-consuming passion of human life. The reader of Powys's novels knows that some of the most characteristic elements of Hardy's fiction – the mingling of comedy and tragedy, the omnipresence of nature, the absurdity of human passion in the face of cosmic indifference – were also to be the stuff of Powys's novels, though with noteworthy differences. The first of these novels, titled *Wood and Stone* and dedicated to Thomas Hardy, would appear in 1915.

But in 1896 the twenty-four-year-old graduate of Cambridge and one-time resident of Hardy's Dorchester went back to Dorchester, to Max Gate, to visit the 'Master'. This visit resembled, at least in Powys's recollection of it, nothing so much as a laying on of hands. Powys was most kindly received by 'the great Thomas Hardy himself', taken into the study at Max Gate, shown the manuscript of *Tess of the d'Urbervilles*, presented with a copy of that great novel, and given tea on the lawn. And there the master and the disciple spoke of – of all things – poetic influence:

> I remember telling him how I detected in his work that same portentous and solemn power of dealing with those abstract-concrete phenomena, such as dawn, and noon, and twilight, and midnight, that Wordsworth displayed in his poetry. He accepted the comparison, I remember, as a just one, but he proceeded to animadvert in no measured terms upon Wordsworth's pious optimism. He called my attention to Edgar Allan Poe's 'Ulalume' as a powerful and extraordinary poem. In those days I had never read this sinister masterpiece, but following up Hardy's hint I soon drew from it a formidable influence in the direction of the romantically bizarre. (*Auto*, p. 228)

Powys responded to Hardy's kind reception with an invitation to the vicarage at Montacute, in south Somerset, since 1885 the Reverend Charles Powys's home. Hardy was quick to accept, and during that memorable visit Powys had the privilege of showing Hardy the church and the abbey farm. Powys was charmed to be told by Hardy, ever the church architect, that the builders of the ancient church had left the chancel 'a little askew in order to represent the manner in which the Redeemer's head sank upon one side as he gave up the ghost.'. He was amused by Hardy's quick response at being shown the house of the most beautiful girl of the village. The author of *Tess* and *The Well-Beloved* 'gave a curious little start. "We get back to humanity, back, back to humanity, Powys!" he chuckled' (*Auto*, p. 228). Powys was deeply pleased to find that Hardy shared his scruples about killing animals for human food. And Powys was strangely moved to note how like his father Hardy was in noticing 'imperceptible frostmarks that day in the road'. Powys seems to have perceived (in retrospect, at least) the irony that lay in a visit by the author of the often anti-clerical *Tess* and *Jude* to the son and the home of the vicar of Montacute:

> The longer I fix my mind upon this far-off day the more vividly it all comes back to me. . . . When . . . the train . . . finally drew up, and he, with the first Mrs. Hardy at his side stepped out, what did I not feel! Do you think I have forgotten even what he wore that great day? O most carefully was he dressed, consonant, in his Dorset-bred mind, with a formal visit to a Somerset Vicar. He wore a light tweed suit, with knickerbockers to match, and he had thin black stockings on, almost like those in which I had seen his friend, William Barnes, walking so stately down South Walk. Llewelyn [Powys], after his fashion, and in a manner that even I – John, the arch-imitator – cannot copy, has told how, when we took him down to the Robbers' Castle under the high garden-wall, and called upon him to write his name in the band's archives, he wrote, in that clear classic hand I had seen in the manuscript of *Tess*, 'Thomas Hardy, *a Wayfarer.*' . . . Frail as an elf Mr. Hardy was, but his hands were the hands of a master-craftsman. . . . (*Auto*, pp. 229–30)[3]

The lasting importance of Hardy's visit for Powys is suggested by his mentioning it nearly sixty years later in a letter to his friend Nicholas Ross: 'How well I remember Hardy talking to us when we got him to ourselves in the garden at Montacute.'[4] As Powys said in a letter of 1955, Hardy was one of the three greatest men he had met in his long and well-travelled life. He added, 'From Thomas Hardy I learnt, long long ago, to see all human feelings, gestures, actions, and everything else! – my own and everybody's – against the Inanimate Background of Nature, whether flat or mountainous or moorish or swampy and marshy or of desert sand.'[5] But this is to anticipate.

The year 1900, which found Powys completely in the swing of his wandering life as an Oxford University extension lecturer, found him also 'reading insatiably volume after volume, all the novels I could lay hold of, of Dickens and Thomas Hardy' and at the same time forcing himself to ponder, as he travelled, 'upon some confounded, never to be written romance of my own' (*Auto*, p. 307). So immersed had this scholar gypsy been in his reading of Hardy that he found it difficult 'to see a dwindling hill-road without thinking of Hardy' (p. 308). Writing some thirty-five years later, he would recall, in his inimitable fashion, ingesting Hardy and chocolate in almost equal portions – with the result a visitation by the Spirit of Hardy:

> I would retire at an early hour and find a noble great fire blazing upon my hearth; and for hours and hours I would sit up reading *The Return of the Native* or *Far from the Madding Crowd* or *The Woodlanders* or *Jude the Obscure*, while all the while voluptuously and luxuriously, more after the manner of a young woman than a young man, I would take piece after piece of chocolate out of my bag and nibble it in my absorption; till by degrees as I listened to the wind in the chimney the genius of Hardy would drive my demon away and some formidable Spirit from Stonehenge would come rushing out of the Magic West into this dark house and my whole inner being would change. Then I would sit with my bony knees close to the red coals and feel myself to be as formidable and as powerful as that south-west wind itself! I would feel myself to be what the great Magician Merlin was before he met his 'Belle Dame Sans Merci'.
>
> (*Auto*, p. 309)

That this reading of Hardy was decisive to Powys's decision to become a novelist is clear in Powys's introduction to his first book of criticism, *Visions and Revisions*, published in 1915, also the year of his first novel:

> What I might call my earliest 'writing-life', and the same could apply to my brothers and sisters,[6] is intimately linked with the life's work of Thomas Hardy. One of my earliest memories of Dorchester were [sic] encounters in its chestnut avenues with Hardy's own venerated schoolmaster, the dialect-poet William Barnes. . . . And if you, predatory reader, insist on holding me up to demand at pen's point exactly what 'hold', or 'fall', in the hard wrestling with life which we all have to practise, I picked

up from my contact with Hardy, I would reply at once: 'The Sophoclean power of transsubstantiating the burden of any victim's suffering, whether that suffering is mental or physical, till it becomes, by the sheer poetry of its identification with human suffering all the world over, the very bread by which we live and move.'

It is indeed that same grand Shakespearean trick by which our actor's sympathy, stirred to its depths by the whole world's tragedy, thrusts our special private grief back a little, not erasing it of course, but in the world-old mystery of an imaginative Secular Mass, in a sense redeeming it. Yes it is because Hardy was a poet before and after he used his architectural and sculptural eye for the shapes of people and things pilloried by chance or destiny against an infinite godless space that we can get from him the sort of calming and steadying for our distracted nerves that we derive, not so much from religion, which too often increases rather than relieves tension, but from the reiterated monotones of earth and sky.[7]

These remarks on Hardy, in this, Powys's first book of criticism, deserve comparison with D. H. Lawrence's *Study of Thomas Hardy*, which Lawrence was writing at almost exactly this time (see above, pp. 35–6). Like Lawrence, Powys is attracted by Hardy's rootedness in the English countryside. And as *Wood and Stone* (1915) shows – it deserves comparison with *The White Peacock* (1911) in this regard – Powys was as taken as Lawrence by Hardy's interest in the place of sexual passion in the lives of human beings. And Powys, again like Lawrence, sought to correct Hardy's vision by showing that human survival and even triumph lie with impassioned individuality. Though Powys does not follow Lawrence in the belief that in a right way of loving lies the reform of English society, he is like Lawrence in seeking the acceptance of the passional life, particularly the passional life of the deviant individual. Powys is less determined than Lawrence to identify and correct Hardy's weaknesses. As he said, he was the 'arch-imitator'; by contrast, Lawrence is the aggressive translator of Hardy's vision into the terms of his own. Powys is most unlike Lawrence in his fascination with the pre-English, even the pre-Roman, background of the Wessex Novels. It is the future author of *A Glastonbury Romance* and *Maiden Castle* who values Hardy's origins in a West Country where 'traditions of Saxon and Celt,

Norman and Dane, Roman and Iberian, have grown side by side into the soil': 'Tribe by tribe, race by race, as they come and go, leaving their monuments and their names behind, Hardy broods over them, noting their survivals, their lingering footprints, their long decline.'[8]

Even if it were not dedicated to Thomas Hardy, it would be adundantly evident from *Wood and Stone: A Romance* that in his first novel Powys put himself to school in Hardy, whom he describes in his dedication as 'the Greatest Poet and Novelist of Our Age' and praises in his Preface as the only one 'among all modern English authors . . . who brings with him an atmosphere of the large mellow leisurely humanists of the past – of the true classics'. Powys can not imagine planting his standard 'in the heart of Wessex without obeisance being paid to the literary overlord of that suggestive region'.[9] Pay obeisance he did, for *Wood and Stone* is nothing less than a Hardy pastiche.

Like the later and greater of Powys's 'Wessex Novels' – *A Glastonbury Romance*, *Weymouth Sands* and *Maiden Castle* – *Wood and Stone* centres on the struggle between two modes of life: a materialist one (represented here by a predatory businessman, Mortimer Romer), and a spiritual one (embodied in various persons, most of them Christian, whom Romer controls and torments). In itself, this is not a characteristically Hardyan set of concerns, and Powys in fact traces it to his reading of Nietzsche, in whom he found the perennial struggle between 'Power, Courage, and Pride' and 'Sacrifice . . . [and] Love' (*W&S*, Preface, p. vii). But, if Powys's theme is not overtly Hardyan, his setting and structure are. The novel is set 'between Glastonbury and Bridport, at the point where the eastern plains of Somersetshire merge into the eastern valleys of Dorsetshire' (ch. 1). Hardy's *Return of the Native* (1878) is in several ways Powys's model. Leo's Hill and its quarries dominate the geography of *Wood and Stone* in much the way Egdon Heath and Rainbarrow dominate the landscape of *The Return*. Powys's opening with a description of Leo's Hill echoes at several points the famous description of Egdon Heath with which Hardy begins *The Return*. The lives and destinies of the people of Nevilton, whose centre is Nevilton Mount (where the Holy Rood of Waltham was first found), are dominated by the quarries and their ruthlessly ambitious owner, Mortimer Romer. The people of Nevilton, like the people of Egdon, are less than their land; a spectator here, like one on Hardy's Egdon, quickly becomes aware 'of the fatal force of Inanimate Objects over human destiny' (*W&S*, ch. 1). This phrase anticipates Powys's remark of 1955, quoted above, that he had learned from Hardy 'to see all human feelings, gestures, actions, and everything else!! . . . against the Inanimate Background of Nature'.

Gladys Romer, daughter of the sadistic overlord and herself a cruel flirt, owes much to Hardy's Eustacia Vye of *The Return*. Hardy's depiction of Eustacia as a woman whose one desire was 'to be loved to madness' (bk I, ch. 7) is echoed in Powys's description of Gladys wanting Luke Anderson, an employee of her father's by whom she manages to become pregnant, 'to desire her as a girl; – to desire her to madness' (*W&S*, ch. 4). There are other Hardyan effects as well. James Anderson, brother to Luke, tells Lacrima, the novel's heroine and chief exponent of love and sacrifice, that he reads and enjoys the novels of Thomas Hardy (chs 4, 22). Lacrima, 'innocent of the darker side of literature', rejects the idea because she has seen Hardy's books 'in the hands of Gladys Romer'. Powys describes a sunset, in Hardy's manner, as resembling a bloodshot eye (ch. 5). One of Hardy's favourite techniques for counterpointing romantic sentiment with grim reality is copied in a scene in which the eccentric Maurice Quincunx thinks of his beloved Lacrima and at the same moment hears 'a thrush outside the window! . . . cracking a snail upon a stone' (ch. 6). Powys's description of Lacrima's meeting with the lustful John Goring echoes Hardy's reflection on Tess Durbeyfield's unfortunate meeting with Alec d'Urberville:

> What curious irony is it, in the blind march of events, which so frequently draws to the place of our exclusive sorrow the one particular spectator that we would most avoid?! . . . Who that has walked through life observingly has not been driven to pause with sad questioning before accidents and occurrences that seem as though some conscious malignity in things had *arranged* them? (ch. 6)

Tess is echoed again in Powys's commentary on Lacrima's futile pleas to the sadistic Gladys Romer (who reads Hardy) that she not be forced to bathe with her:

> But the daughter of the Romers vouchsafed no reply to this appeal. . . . The night-owls, that swept . . . over the village

brought no miraculous intervention from the resting place of the Holy Rood. What was St. Catherine doing that she had thus deserted the sanctuary of her name? Perhaps the Alexandrian saint found the magic of the heathen hill too strong for her; or perhaps because of its rank heresy, she had blotted her former shrine altogether from her tender memory.   (Ibid.)

Hardy had written with similar irony of the moment of Tess's violation by Alec: 'Where was Tess's guardian Angel? where was the providence of her simple faith? Perhaps, like that other god of whom the ironical Tishbite spoke, he was talking, or he was pursuing, or he was in a journey, or he was sleeping and not to be awaked' (*TD* ch. 11). Powys's hint that Lacrima's virtue is in danger of violation by a woman is an early indication of his increasingly explicit interest in homosexuality. It recalls perhaps the seemingly lesbian episode between Cytherea Graye and Miss Aldclyffe in Hardy's *Desperate Remedies* (1867).

Powys echoes the first chapter of Hardy's *Woodlanders* (1887) in his defence of domestic tragedy:

It is often airily assumed that the obstinate and terrible struggles of life are encountered abroad – far from home – in desolate contention with the elements or with enemies. It is not so! The most obstinate and desperate struggles of all – struggles for the preservation of one's most sacred identity, of one's innermost liberty of action and feeling – take place ... under the hypocritical calm of the domestic roof.   (*W&S*, ch. 6)[10]

Powys's use of rustic characters such as Mrs Fringe, who informs the Mr Clavering of both the grim and humorous realities of village life (ch. 9), recalls moments in Hardy's *Return*, *Far from the Madding Crowd* and *Mayor of Casterbridge*. A Hardyan exhibition of nature as an indifferent or cruel presence in human affairs is visible throughout, as when 'the distant expanse of the Milky Way, too remote in its translunar gulfs to heed these planetary conflicts, shimmered haughtily down upon the Wood and Stone of Nevilton – impassive, indifferent, unconcerned' (*W&S*, ch. 19).

Perhaps Powys's greatest debt to Hardy in *Wood and Stone*, particularly to *The Return of the Native*, is his imitation of Hardy's use of the unities of time and place. This was to become a structural practice in all but one of Powys's novels to 1936. After *Wood* and Stone, in *Ducdame, Wolf Solent, A Glastonbury Romance, Weymouth Sands* and *Maiden Castle,* Powys restricts the action – as Hardy did in *The Return* – to a single year and a single locale. Powys undoubtedly discovered this in Hardy's *Return* and found it congenial to his own passionate interest in the influence of environment on character. Powys also shares Hardy's interest in the homecomer as hero. Wolf Solent, John and Mary Crow of *A Glastonbury Romance,* and Dud Noman of *Maiden Castle* – like Hardy's Clym Yeobright of *The Return* and Grace Melbury of *The Woodlanders* – all return to a place they had inhabited earlier, struggle to reassimilate themselves and, in a sense, fail. Powys is as relentless as Hardy in his belief that return is impossible, that there is no turning back the clock, no recovery of things past.

But, if Hardy's influence is strong in *Wood and Stone,* if the novel is indeed a Hardy pastiche, equally evident is Powys's movement from pastiche to style, from imitation of Hardy to discovery of his own vision and method through his swervings from Hardy. For example, Powys is in this novel and others a candid psychologist. What Hardy merely hints at, Powys frankly shows and states. Gladys and Mortimer Romer's aggressive sexuality is linked to their sadistic teasing, their love of domination and cruelty. Similarly, the reclusive Mortimer Quincunx – resembling in several ways the John Cowper Powys we know from the *Autobiography* – is portrayed frankly as a sexual misfit, the first of Powys's several voyeurs and nympholepts, each of them obsessed with what in the *Autobiography* Powys would describe as his own 'hideous vice' of gazing at the limbs of women and girls. Hardy's treatment in *The Return* of Clym Yeobright's sexual timidity, Christian Cantle's sexual impotency and Eustacia Vye's sexual adventurism is oblique and uncertain in comparison. Also, Powys is a novelist with explicit political concerns, something Hardy never displayed, at least not after Alexander Macmillan warned him against the 'socialism' of his first and never published novel, 'The Poor Man and the Lady'. The clash between the industrialist Romer and the labour-organizers among his workmen is but the first of several clashes between capitalism and 'communism' in Powys's novels. Some of Powys's greatest rascals – Romer, Philip Crow of *A Glastonbury Romance,* Dog Cattistock of *Weymouth Sands* – are ruthless exploiters of labour and of the earth itself in their pursuit of profit. At the same time, some of Powys's greatest fools are the communists, anarchists and fascists of his novels: the communist

Red Robinson and the anarchist David Speare in *A Glastonbury Romance*; the fascist Dunbar ('Dumbell') Wye of *Maiden Castle*. In sum, *Wood and Stone*, like Lawrence's *White Peacock*, is an interesting though not a great novel, an authentic beginning amidst a flourish of Hardyan images, techniques, characters and settings.

Between 1915 and 1925, the year Powys published the Dorset-set *Ducdame*, with its striking resemblances to both *The Return of the Native* and *Jude the Obscure*, Powys was in occasional communication with Hardy. In April and June 1915, Powys wrote to Hardy expressing continuing admiration for his poems and novels. In 1916, in *Rodmoor*, his second novel, set in East Anglia and centred on the tragic life of an aesthete named Adrian Sorley who believes in an 'instinct of destruction' as the essence of life, Powys explores what he perceives as Hardy's pessimism.[11] Hardy is mentioned as a 'great writer' by the tragically doomed Renshaws of the novel, but Dr Fingal Raughty, an eccentric but hopeful man not unlike Powys himself, dismisses pessimists such as Hardy in favour of Rabelais and Montaigne. Like Lawrence in his review of *Georgian Poetry* in 1913, Powys saw in Hardy a demolition of trust in human endeavour. *Rodmoor* is Powys's first attempt to find an alternative to Hardy's pessimism, which was alien to Powys's romantic belief in human possibility. In Adrian Sorley, as later in the Reverend William Hastings of *Ducdame*, Jason Otter of *Wolf Solent*, and Dud Noman of *Maiden Castle*, Powys created a character in need of cure for a pessimism rooted in distrust of the powers of the human mind. But, if the humanism of Rabelais and Montaigne beckons, the example of Hardy remains insistent. *The Return of the Native* is recalled vividly in the November bonfires of *Rodmoor*(ch. 26) and in the deaths by drowning of the lovers Adrian and Philippa at the end of the novel. Hardy is recalled also in the repeated attempts to fuse the bleak East Anglian landscape with character and conduct, attempts founded in the belief that 'human beings, like plants and animals, are subject to all manner of physical influences' (ch. 12).

In July 1918, home for the summer from a lecture tour in America, Powys wrote Hardy asking permission to visit him at Max Gate. In the same letter he urged Hardy to recall his visit to Montacute, some twenty years before.[12] Letters to Powys from his brother Llewelyn between 1920 and 1927 were another source of information about Hardy for the ever-curious John, who was again on the American lecture circuit. Relations between Llewelyn Powys and the Hardys were not smooth during these years, mainly as a result of Llewelyn's slighting remarks about Hardy in an article in the *Dial* in 1922 and in the autobiographical *Skin for Skin* (1925).[13] In spite of these differences, for Llewelyn Powys Hardy's was 'the genius which more than that of any other worthy [in his *Thirteen Worthies*, 1923] has impressed itself upon my imagination'.[14] Intimate in so many other things – they co-authored *Confessions of Two Brothers* in 1916 – John and Llewelyn Powys were at one also in their reverence for Hardy, a fact that can only have encouraged John's bold use of Hardy in his third novel, *Ducdame* (1925).

As in *Wood and Stone*, in *Ducdame* Hardy's *Return of the Native* is an important source and analogue. The moon-lit November opening of *The Return* is recalled, as is the one-year time frame of that novel. Powys has even provided a map of Ashover and the surrounding countryside, much as Hardy had mapped Bloom's End and the surrounding Egdon Heath for *The Return*. And, like *The Return*, *Ducdame* is set in Dorset (Hardy's Wessex). But *Ducdame* is not the story of the return of a native. It is the story of the ill-fated attempt of Rook Ashover of the House of Ashover to provide an heir for the family fortune. It is also the story of the love between two brothers: the ailing but optimistic Lexie Ashover (drawn no doubt from the consumptive Llewelyn Powys) and the moody, mysterious Rook. Lexie is an important balance to Rook, for Rook's gloom, deriving from his conflicting devotion to his demanding mother and his several lovers, is survived by Lexie's love of life in the face of imminent death. *Ducdame* is the second of Powys's fictional renderings of the tragedy inherent in family conflict. This interest in domestic tragedy began in the ghostly relations between the Anderson brothers and their dead parents in *Wood and Stone*; it continued in the strained relations between Philippa and Brand Renshaw and their worrisome mother in *Rodmoor*. Family conflict dominates the hero in *Ducdame* as well, and will continue as one of the governing elements in the other 'Wessex' novels: in Wolf's communications with his dead father and domineering mother in *Wolf Solent*; in Sam Dekker's struggle with his father for the love of Nell Zoyland in *A Glastonbury Romance*; in the wide range of parent–child conflicts centred on Magnus Muir's troubled memories of his father in *Weymouth Sands*; and, most dramatically, in Dud Noman's search for a father – both a biological and an artistic one – in *Maiden Castle*.

The persistence of the parent–child motif in Powys's fiction between 1915 and 1936 – founded perhaps in the struggle between the stern puritan father and emotionally unconventional son to be depicted in the *Autobiography* – suggests yet another reason why Hardy's *Return* was so important a model to Powys. Before Lawrence's *Sons and Lovers* (1913), Hardy's *Return of the Native* is the only major English novel to exhibit, however obliquely, the Oedipal theme in its tragic significance. Even more striking, especially from Powys's point of view as a friend, neighbour and disciple of Hardy's, *The Return* was autobiographical, an undeniable if partial and covert portrait of the artist as a young man troubled by a sexual ambivalence he could not express as an English novelist of the 1870s. Clym's vacillations between what John Fowles, a hundred years later, in yet another autobiographical novel shaped by Hardy's self-probing fiction, would call 'femalenesses' – domineering mother, passionate wife, sympathetic cousin, maternal Nature – must have struck Powys as an account of human experience uncannily like the one he was equipped by private experience to depict. Powys's susceptibility to just such an example was great in these years, as he himself remarked:

> I suppose it would be impossible for any human being to be more absolutely under the dominance of Literature than I am. I think by books; I move in an atmosphere of books; I am an infatuated bookworm. To the influence of books I have come lately to add the influence of Art; but it is Art approached through books, interpreted by books, and loved for bookish reasons. This obsequious submission to Literature and Art follows naturally from the morbid receptivity of my nature. It follows too from my curious dislike of self-assertion, and my weary desire to 'lie back' upon something or other external to myself. I love books and pictures, just as I love Fate. They are something upon which I can lean; something in which I forget myself and lose myself; something in the presence of which my clumsy and turbulent identity melts and grows lucid, flowing, transparent. This 'too, too solid flesh' of mine 'thaws and resolves itself into a dew' when brought near to these delicate influences.[15]

Powys's Rook Ashover, even more dramatically than Hardy's Clym Yeobright, it torn by affection for three women: his mistress

Netta; Lady Ann Wentworth Gore, his cousin, seducer, eventual wife, and mother of his heir; and Lady Joan Ashover, his widowed mother, a domineering woman impatient for a grandson and heir but reluctant to lose her son to another woman. These parallels with Clym and Eustacia, Clym's cousin Thomasin, and his strong-minded mother are too striking to be accidental. But Rook differs from Clym in important ways. He is haunted by the memory of his dead father, especially through the presence of his father's bastard brother, Grandfer Dick, who is also determined that Rook shall produce an heir. Rook is haunted as well by his father's bastard sons, his stepbrothers, a pair of monstrous dwarfs Ashover senior had fathered on the daughter (now dead) of a gypsy who hovers about the edges of the novel's action seeking both blackmail and revenge. Rook's dilemma is re-enacted and amplified in the misery of William Hastings, vicar of Ashover and author of a book (like Adrian Sorley of *Rodmoor*) on destruction as the essential principle of life. Like Clym Yeobright, Hastings is a would-be intellectual married to a passionate woman (Nell) who, like Clym's restless Eustacia, longs for excitement in the arms of another man, namely Rook Ashover. In his gloom, passion and violent death (at the hands of Hastings), Rook recalls Damon Wildeve, Eustacia's lover in *The Return*, as sharply as he recalls Clym. If these splittings and displacements of Hardy's characters seem somewhat facile, they also suggest the freedom Powys enjoyed in his developing use of Hardy.

For, if Powys was open to Hardy's influence, he was bent also on altering the strategies and themes of his precursor. His love of 'melting' his identity into Hardy's, of leaning on Hardy's stories as he might lean on Fate, was not totally self-obliterating. New elements appear in his work, and Lexie Ashover, at once vibrantly alive and fatally ill, is a key to the kind of departure Powys was making from Hardy in his third novel. At the end of *Ducdame*, Rook is dead, murdered by Hastings. Netta has become an Anglican nun, Lady Ann (by seducing Rook) has conceived and borne his son and heir, Hastings and his mad book on destruction as life's essence have been set aside, and Nell and Lexie survive to enjoy a ride on a merry-go-round and a romp in the hay.[16] The House of Ashover lives on, though Rook is dead. Both the intellectual spite of Hastings and the lingering desire for revenge of the gypsy woman have been thwarted. It is as if Powys were shaping his own version of Hardy's ending to *The Return*, in which

Clym's tragic melancholy is mocked by being set beside Diggory Venn and Thomasin Yeobright's reunion in love on a bright day in May. Over against Hardy's realism, expressed in what Hardy himself called 'his original conception of the story' (see Hardy's endnote, bk VI, ch. 3), Powys was shaping his favourite bit of wisdom, the view that it is in the power of the individual not just to destroy but also to re-create the world (*Auto*, p. 25). A fusion of Hardyan doubt and Powysian trust exists in the following: 'We are ourselves the gods who create the values of our life . . . and it is left to chance to provide the occasions for the applications of these meanings and purposes' (p. 47). This remark suggests what Powys was called upon to do in his own novels of Wessex life if he was to follow and at the same time depart from the Wessex Novels of Thomas Hardy. He could be a receiver and imitator of Hardy and at the same time achieve authentic utterance by showing, in the words of the hero of his next novel, that 'there is no reality but what the mind fashions out of itself'.[17]

If one reads *Wolf Solent* (1929) with the question of Hardy's possible influence in mind, it soon becomes apparent that in this novel Powys chose to explore the question of influence by placing it at the centre of his hero's psychology. Here, as elsewhere, Powys employs the story of homecoming: he called his fourth novel 'a book of Nostalgia, written in a foreign country [America] with the pen of a traveller and the inkblood of his home' (*WfS*, Preface). Like Clym, Wolf is a returning native. Like Clym, Wolf works out the subtle dangers of homecoming after long absence during the turning of a single year in the Dorset countryside (Ramsgard). Like Clym (and Rook), Wolf is torn between three women: his demanding mother; his beautiful and sensual wife, Gerda; and his intellectual, epicene friend and 'lover', Christie Malakite. But as the Gerda-Christie contrast immediately suggests, Hardy's *Jude the Obscure* is also an important model. This is apparent not just in the placement of the sensual-intellectual Wolf between the passionate Gerda and the cerebral Christie, which recalls Jude's placement between Arabella and Sue, but in the book's Preface, which echoes Hardy's 1895 Preface to *Jude:*

> What might be called the purpose and essence and inmost being of this book is the necessity of opposites. Life and Death, Good and Evil, Matter and Spirit, Body and Soul, Reality and Appearance have to be joined together, have to be forced into one

another, have to be proved dependent upon each other, while all solid entities have to dissolve, if they are to outlast their momentary appearance, into atmosphere. (*WfS*, p. 9)[18]

Powys praises Hardy in the Preface to *Wolf Solent* as one of 'the greatest of all novelists', and at one point in the novel Wolf's mother is reading Hardy's *Trumpet-Major* and fretting under its effect. But more important than these allusions as a sign of Hardy's 'presence' in *Wolf* is a new device to accommodate Hardy's 'presence'. The hero Wolf Solent is himself a writer. Even more important, he is a writer in constant, dynamic conflict with an older writer, a poet named Jason Otter who writes pessimistic nature lyrics in which he curses God. Hardy's *Late Lyrics and Earlier*, *Human Shows* and *Winter Words*, all published in the 1920s, had been labelled 'pessimistic' by reviewers, a judgement to which Hardy objected angrily in both his 1922 'Apology' to *Late Lyrics* and in his 'Introductory Note' to *Winter Words* (1928). In *Jude*, of course, he had been accused of the same sin and worse. Powys was undoubtedly aware of this favourite epithet of Hardy's reviewers, as well as of the many poems in which Hardy censured, corrected or commiserated with God. In this novel, Wolf first rejects Otter's pessimism, then is brought by the lessons of experience to see the basis for that pessimism, though not to embrace it. Wolf ends a chastened meliorist, a stubborn believer in human possibility in spite of his knowledge that in human affairs evil must often prevail.

Wolf, at age thirty-five, is a former history-master turned writer. The novel opens upon his return from London to his native town of Ramsgard (Sherborne) in Dorset, after an absence of twenty-five years. His father, a one-time history master at Ramsgard School, is long dead. His mother, a woman of 'despotic affection', soon follows him from London. Wolf is tormented by a vision of human suffering he had encountered in the ravaged face of a man lying on the steps of Waterloo Station in London. It is a vision of evil, perhaps ineradicable and pervasive. Haunted by this spectre, Wolf is desperate to preserve the integrity of a private myth and vision of things in which evil has no place. Modern civilization, including modern literature, Wolf finds distressing precisely because in it evil is exhibited as being ineradicable and pervasive.

Once settled at Ramsgard, Wolf finds employment as private secretary and amanuensis to Sir John Urquhart, squire of King's

Barton (Yeovil), Dorset. Under Urquhart's supervision, Wolf is soon at work writing a Rabelaisian history of Dorset, a chronicle of the secret sexual lives of men and women of his native county. This unusual county history will prove to be in large part his history, for he will learn of the sexual intrigues in his own family: his father's love affair with Selena Gault, daughter of a former headmaster of Ramsgard School; his father's bastard daughter (Mattie) by the wife of a Ramsgard hatter; his father's corruption by the pornography provided him by Mr Malakite, who himself has fathered a child on one of his daughters. Wolf's own history will develop true to family form. After seducing and marrying Gerda Torp of Ramsgard, he will be cuckolded by Bob Weevil and Lord Carfax, the latter a former lover of Wolf's mother. And, while married to Gerda, he will attempt to seduce Christie Malakite and in this attempt discover himself suddenly incapable of the sexual act. Gerda, his passionate and beautiful wife, will be driven to Weevil and Carfax because Wolf now denies her the gratification of physical love. The novel ends with Wolf about to drink a cup of tea after having acknowledged that his fate is to repeat, more as comedy than tragedy perhaps, the life pattern of his father. This might be seen as a surrender before a Hardyan sense of destiny. But it is not that, for, where a Jude Fawley, for instance, is destroyed by his inability to escape a private dream of learning, love and piety, Wolf Solent can set aside his private myth of a world without evil and accept the often grim realities of history and heredity. Wolf's change comes about not just through his discovery of his personal past, but more particularly through his strange friendship with the poet Jason Otter, whom he meets soon after his arrival in Dorset.

Wolf first learns of Jason when, upon arriving at King's Barton, he is given a room by Mrs Otter, Jason's mother, a room previously occupied by the poet. When Wolf returns from his first visit to Urquhart – his personal myth much menaced by Urquhart's cynicism – he finds Jason in his room, among paintings by Landseer and Alma-Tadema the Otters have hung there. Jason departs hurriedly, mumbling apologies, and Wolf is furious at this invasion of privacy ('If I can't have my room to myself, I'll go somewhere else' – (*WfS*, ch. 3). This encounter is soon followed by a second meeting with Otter, a meeting which may recall Powys's first meeting with Hardy, for Otter puts Wolf at his ease and gives him a book, just as Hardy had welcomed Powys to Max Gate with a copy of *Tess* (see pp. 66–7, above). Otter's face expresses a 'kind of restless misery', a need 'for help without assertion or intermission'. His blue eyes are 'exposed . . . stripped bare; they seemed to peer forth helplessly from the human skull behind them, as though some protective filaments that ought to have been there were *not* there!' (*WfS*, ch. 4). Jason helps Wolf remove from the room the Alma-Tadema and Landseer paintings which Wolf despises. Invited by Jason to visit the room to which he has moved, Wolf felt 'the same uneasy sensations in this chamber as he had experienced the evening before' (ibid.). After protesting against the 'ceremonious piety' of Jason's Arundel prints, he proclaims, rather pointedly, 'I couldn't work in this room.' Jason now shows Wolf his statue of 'Mukalog, the god of rain', a Hindu deity he had discovered in a book purchased from Mr Malakite. Jason also introduces Wolf to his personal mythology, which contrasts sharply with Wolf's. Otter belives that God resides not in the blue heavens but *'In the mud'* of the earth and that 'in this world Truth flies downward, not upward!' (ibid.). Struck by the almost-palpable evil radiating from Mukalog and shaken by Jason's weird beliefs, as well as by his visit to Urquhart, Wolf departs, his private belief in freedom and goodness much threatened. Wolf, it seems, resists the claims of the physical side of his nature; he prefers intellectual love. But Urquhart, Otter, Gerda, and the daily life and scenes of Dorset past and present all insist on the folly of intellectual love. But, because Wolf is a writer, the presence of Otter, an older writer, is especially disturbing, and yet powerfully appealing. Otter and his bitter poetry constitute a most seductive sort of opposition.

During his next meeting with Otter, Wolf is shown the pond in which James Redfern, Wolf's predecessor as Urquhart's secretary, had drowned himself (ch. 6). Jason confesses his love for Redfern and, somewhat surprisingly, his hatred for Redfern's ability to inspire pity: 'I'd like to kill pity – . . . to make people see what madness it is' (ibid.). Otter's frustrated affection for Redfern moves him to berate the hapless T. E. Valley, vicar of Ramsgard and former lover of Redfern. In a riotous scene at the Three Peewits Inn (ch. 8), Valley is insulted by Otter and Wolf's scandalous past is exposed to all present. Wolf loses his temper and forces Otter into silence, but Otter rails bitterly against Valley and the Christian God Valley serves.

As these events may suggest, the odd relationship between Wolf and Otter becomes intelligible if one sees Otter, like Urquhart, as representing for Wolf a father figure with whom Wolf must make his peace, not by total acceptance or rejection, but rather through an antithetical discovery of self. The three 'fathers' of the novel – Urquhart, Jason and Wolf's dead natural father – force Wolf in different ways to acknowledge certain ugly truths about human life: death, failure, infidelity, human helplessness before the universal will. But Wolf is not a wholly passive student before these gloomy teachers. Just as he will come to reject Urquhart and his obscene history of Dorset *after* he has written that history, so Wolf will attempt to take the measure of his father's hedonism and to temper Jason's pessimism. And he will succeed. He will find a place for these competing views within his private myth, and at the same time preserve the essential optimism of that myth.

For example, Wolf offers to buy from Jason the rain god Mukalog, warns Jason against the folly of hate, then asks to read Jason's poems. By this request he begins to win Jason's regard. Wolf's reading of Jason's 'The Slow-worm of Lenty' (ch. 12) is preluded by the repeated use of one of Powys's favourite borrowings from Hardy, the sound of a thrush crushing a snail before devouring it. This striking image of one of nature's loveliest creatures consuming one of its lowliest appeared in both *Wood and Stone* and *Ducdame*. For Hardy, in *The Return* and *The Woodlanders*, for example, the image conveys the cruelty in nature that operates also in the sexual and economic struggles of the people of those novels. In this episode in *Wolf*, Powys uses the image no fewer than four times to frame and comment on Otter's bitter poem. But, equally important, he counters the cruel image of a thrush devouring a snail with the 'indescribable contentment' of the song of a wood pigeon. Otter is pleased that Wolf should wish to hear his poem, and perhaps for that reason the embittered poet reads it to Wolf in 'a voice almost as modulated as the wood-pigeon's own':

> The Slow-worm of Lenty curses God;
> He lifts his head from the heavy sod;
> He lifts his head where the Lenty willow
> Weeps green tears o'er the rain-elf's pillow;
> For the rain-elf's lover is fled and gone,
> And none curseth God but the Slow-worm alone.

'Slow-worm' is a poem of love lost in a godless, unpitying world – a world much like that in Hardy's poetry – whose beauties are a mockery rather than a consolation or delight, and whose poets (for the Slow-worm is the poet) are doomed to curse what they might wish to celebrate:

> And the Lenty Slow-worm curses God
> For the sake of the rain-elf's pitifulness.
> . . .
> And the newts and the tadpoles who where she lay
> Mocked her from bellies white, orange, and grey,
> Cry now to willow and water and weed,
> 'Lenty Pond had a prophet indeed!'
> For the rain-elf weeps no more to her pillow
> Woven of twigs of the weeping-willow;
> But her lover, come back to the laughing rain-elf,
> Cries, 'The Slow-worm of Lenty is God Himself!'

After reciting this hymn to shattered love and to a God who curses himself through his poets, Otter gathers the bits of empty snail-shell left behind by the thrush, while Urquhart and Selena Gault, watching him, remark on the possibility of life after the death suggested by the empty shell. For Selena there is no eternity; for Urquhart, the possibility exists. Otter says nothing to this; nor does Wolf, who now proceeds to purchase from Otter the statue of Mukalog, which he intends to destroy because he thinks it the cause of Jason's pessimism.

Wolf has moved to a peculiar position between Jason, author of Hardyan indictments of God, and Urquhart, co-author with Wolf of an obscene history of Dorset. Great tension exists between these two haters and writers, tension that unexpectedly finds release when Jason and Urquhart, with Wolf present, watch Lobbie Torp and Bob Weevil bathe naked in Lenty Pond. The sight of the unclothed boys 'seemed to have drawn out of both [of Wolf's] equivocal companions every ounce of black bile or complicated evil' (ch. 14). Like the Reverend T. E. Valley, Urquhart and Otter are homosexuals and, in Powys's terse phrase, 'cerebral sadists'. Lenty Pond is the site of Redfern's suicide, brought about apparently by the competition of Urquhart, Otter and Valley for Redfern's love. The tragedy of Redfern is thus before the two older men as they indulge their sensuality by viewing the boys. The obscene history of Dorset Wolf is co-authoring is being re-enacted, though not in its tragic form. Evil, but also the aversion of worse evil, stands before Wolf. His fate will not repeat Redfern's.

Wolf's troubled attachment to Urquhart and Otter forms part of the 'passionate dispute with his father' (ch. 15) that stems from the radical conflict between Wolf's subjective philosophy and what he calls 'objective truth'. The Squire in his love for human obscenity, the poet in his contempt for God, and the dead Solent senior in his sexual adventurism confront Wolf with realities he is fearful to admit into his system, realities nicely summed up in Jason's belief that God is indifferent to man and resides in the mud. In one astonishing episode, Wolf conducts a dream debate with the skull of his buried father. Standing beside his father's grave, this latter-day Hamlet imagines himself 'a lean worm. . . , in the darkness of [William Solent's] hollow skull, arguing with it':

> 'This world is not made of bread and honey,' cried Wolf, the worm, to the skull of his father, 'nor of the sweet flesh of girls. This world is made of clouds and of the shadows of clouds. It is made of mental landscapes, porous as air, where men and women are as trees walking, and as reeds shaken by the wind.'
>
> But the skull answered him in haste and spoke roughly to him. 'What you have found out today, worm of my folly, I had outgrown when I was in the Sixth at Ramsgard and was seduced by Western *minor* in the headmaster's garden. To turn the world again into mist and vapour is easy and weak. To keep it alive, to keep it real, to hold it at arm's length, is the way of gods and demons. (Ibid.)

Wolf's aversion for the physical realities his father here describes will ruin his marriage to the sexually expectant Gerda, drive her into the willing arms of Weevil and Carfax, and turn Wolf toward the epicene Christie Malakite. This fastidious abhorrence for 'material accidents' is what Jason undoubtedly has in mind when he calls Wolf a 'crazy fool' (ch. 16) and what Urquhart has in mind when he shouts, 'You nympholepts are all crazy' (ch. 19). Wolf is in love with an idea, a mind-fashioned reality, and for this reason he is as blind, in Jason's view, to the 'fact' that God is against him as he is to the 'fact' of Gerda's need for physical love. Though Wolf cleverly insists that Jason's rejection of Wolf's illusion is

simply another illusion ('Jason's stripping himself bare is *his* way
. . . that's all' – ch. 16), when he speaks to Jason again it is after
the 'reality' he had been warned against has been manifested:
Gerda has taken the repulsive Bob Weevil as her lover because
Wolf has neglected her. Wolf feels 'as though a mob of Urquharts
and Jasons had burst into the inmost sanctuary of his feelings –
of his inarticulate physical feelings – and were jeering at them. . . .
These were just the things – these physical feelings – that in his
pride he had hidden from everyone' (ch. 17).

But Wolf is not destroyed by his humiliation. Instead, he proves
himself capable of learning: '*This* is reality. . . . This is the kind of
thing that men returning home at a quarter past nine in Colorado,
in Singapore, in Moscow, in Cape Town, in New Zealand, see in
the darkness! . . . This is reality' (ibid.). Wolf has learned (and
this prepares him for his next interview with Jason Otter) that 'one
can't always get help by sinking into one's own soul. It's sometimes
necessary to escape from oneself altogether' (ibid.). At their
next meeting, Jason reads Wolf a poem titled 'White Seaweed' in
which the poet warns against lingering among the illusions of
boyhood (another favourite theme of Hardy's). This somehow
provokes Wolf to jealousy at what he perceives to be his mother's
growing affection for Jason. Wolf's poetic 'father' seems here to
be on the verge of supplanting his biological father, and Wolf feels
a queer 'mixture of physical repulsion with pleasurable masochistic
submission' (ch. 18).

Wolf's sudden unease at Mrs Solent's attention to Jason exposes
his Oedipal jealousy, the source of his fear of Gerda's passion,
and the source of his nympholepsy. In nearly every woman he
meets, Wolf loves the fleeting image of a maternal ideal. And now,
when he finds Gerda and Mrs Solent talking amiably together, he
is doubly disturbed, for by this time both have betrayed him –
Gerda with Weevil, and Mrs Solent not just with his father and
with Otter, but also with a Farmer Manley, with whom she has
taken up. Wolf will learn later that Lord Carfax, soon to be Gerda's
lover, had been his mother's lover as well. Though he loves both
Gerda and his mother, his love is peculiar; like Hardy's Jocelyn
Pierston of *The Well-Beloved*, Wolf loves an ideal his mother and
wife, as well as Christie, fleetingly embody. Like Hardy's Clym
Yeobright, Wolf is disabled in love by his competing devotion to
his mother and his wife. Thus the strong suggestion of sexual
impotence in Powys's description of Wolf at this juncture:

when he was with Gerda and his mother together, his personality shrank and dwindled until he felt his actual body grow limp and lumpish. The supercilious calmness of his mother's face under her green parasol, the angry defiance of Gerda's face under her simple school-treat hat, with its pale watchet-blue ribbons, seemed to paralyse him; so that all he could do was to bow down before the storm, like a horse with its rump turned to the wind and its forehead turned to the fence! The male animal in him felt quelled and cowed by those two opposed currents of feminine emotion. (*WfS*, ch. 18)

Wolf's flight now to Christie Malakite, whom he has admired from their first meeting, is, he hopes, a turn-away from the sensuality of Gerda and his mother; for Christie, epicene and bookish, a writer and thinker like Wolf, is even more repelled than Wolf by physical passion. Christie's state of mind is captured in the third poem that Jason reads to Wolf, a poem ('The Owl and Silence') whose language suggests a visceral and spiritual horror in physical love:

> When the mossy vistas call to the rain
> To ravish their fern-fronds green,
> Thro' the dripping hazels they dart again,
> These points of damascene!
> And each root holds blood in its amber cup,
> Holds blood in its emerald bowl,
> While the White Owl covers silence up
> As death covers up the soul.
>
> The great White Owl, he passes by
> Like a ghost among the guests.
> The woodmice watch him with frightened eyes;
> The birds crouch in their nests;
> And Silence asleep on her lichen bed,
> Asleep on her fungus sheet,
> Feels those feathers sink on her drooping head,
> And fall on her tender feet! (ch. 19)

The three stanzas that follow these complete the poem's depiction of physical love as a predatory descent of the strong upon the weak. Symbol of death and coverer of silence on a pillow of love wet with rain, the owl is a symbol also of the mystery surrounding Wolf. Driven to love and to be loved, Wolf cannot love as nature demands, and so he inevitably loses all his beloveds – his mother to Farmer Manley, Gerda to Weevil and Carfax, Christie to her intellectual pursuits. Like Hardy's Jude Fawley, Wolf is utterly undone. And yet, unlike Jude, for all these humiliations, he is not without resource, and not without pride and purpose. He enlists the aid of Lord Carfax to have Jason's poems published, thereby launching Jason on a career that will lead to fame. He drives himself to complete the obscene history he is writing for Urquhart. Most important, he retains the inmost life illusion that supports his private mythology – 'his taking the side of Good against Evil in the great occult struggle' that is nature. 'You Dorset!' he declares, thinking particularly of Urquhart, Mr Malakite, Otter, and the father who is buried in Dorset earth, 'You've not beaten me yet, you Dorset! Ay! I'll be a match for you yet, you dark rain-scented earth' (ibid.). If the name Thomas Hardy is synonymous with the name Dorset, as it was for Powys, then Hardy too is being challenged.

What Wolf means in this challenge seems clear. He can now accept the objective fact of ineradicable evil in nature as represented both by Mukalog, the god of earth, and by all he has learned about his county, his family and himself. This lesson in evil first offered by 'the face on the Waterloo steps' continues through Wolf's acceptance of his father's infidelities, of Mr Malakite's unnatural love, of Urquhart's perversions (which extend beyond pornography and obscenity to homosexuality and necrophilia), and of Otter's god-cursing pessimism. He can accept, as a result of one year's living in Dorset, the Hardyan view that 'the will of the power behind life was clearly that human nerves should be confronted by monstrous, hideous dilemmas' (ch. 20). He can now at once accept and protest the unavoidable, irremediable human misery represented by the ravaged face of the man at Waterloo Station. He can accept and protest the obscene significance of Mukalog, whom he finally removes from his bureau drawer and tosses into a Dorset meadow, as if he were returning the ugly god to its native place. So deep and genuine is Wolf's shift from total belief in a private myth of good to a sense of evil's objective existence that his very use of words is affected. The very style of his writing of Urquhart's obscene history changes.

Writing day after day from seven o'clock to ten o'clock, Wolf had come to hit upon a style of chronicling shameful events and disconcerting episodes that cost him less and less effort as the weeks advanced. What really gave him impetus was a trick he discovered of diffusing his own resentment against the Power behind the universe into his own commentaries upon these human aberrations unearthed by his employer! The more disgust he felt for his task, the more saturnine his style became and the faster he wrote! Some of his sentences, when he revised them in cold blood, struck him as possessing quite a Swift-like malignity. He astonished himself by certain misanthropic outbursts. His habitual optimism seemed to fall away at such times, and a ferocious contempt for both men and women lay revealed, like a sullen, evil-looking, drained-out pond!
(Ch. 21)

Wolf has finally got to the bottom of that pond where, according to his father in his dream, reality lies; he has finally got down into that mud in which Jason Otter locates God, down among the 'human aberrations' unearthed by Urquhart. Wolf becomes a writer, and a man, through his encounters with and partial submission to these 'fathers', biological and poetical, who shake him out of his nostalgic idealism and optimism. Unlike Redfern, his predecessor with Urquhart, he survives his introduction to the cruelty, perversion and deception that characterize both the Power behind the world and the world itself. But if Wolf has set aside certain childish illusions, he has not submitted wholly or abjectly to his mentors or to an Ultimate Cause:

> it was his own mind that was diseased . . . not Nature. Well, diseased or not, it was all he had! Henceforth he was going to take as the talisman of his days the phrase *endure or escape*. . . .
> Between himself and what was 'behind' the Universe there should be now a new covenant! The Cause up there could certainly at any minute make him howl like a mad dog. It could make him dance and skip and eat dung. Well, until it *did* that, he was going to endure . . . follow his 'road', through the ink-stains, and endure! (Ch. 25)

This Wordsworthian assertion of gain in the face of loss (Wordsworth's 'Intimations' Ode is indeed invoked a few paragraphs earlier) is as firm a break from Hardy's pessimism as it is from Otter's. 'And there suddenly came upon him . . . the memory of another blundering mystic, another solitary walker over hill and dale, who in his time, too, discovered that certain 'Intimations of Immortality' had to take a narrower, a simpler form, as the years advanced' (ibid). One wonders in fact if Powys is not recalling here the conversation with Hardy of over thirty years before in which Hardy had 'animadvert[ed] in no measured terms upon Wordsworth's pious optimism' (see p. 66, above). But it was by no means a complete break with Hardy, any more than Powys's departure from Somerset and England in about 1900 to become a wondering lecturer in America for nearly thirty years was a complete break with his family and his Dorset heritage. Powys, as has been seen, throve on imitation; and in *Weymouth Sands* (1934) and *Maiden Castle* (1936) Hardy's *The Well-Beloved* and *Mayor of Casterbridge*, are, respectively, the governing analogues. The prominence of the sage of Max Gate in the *Autobiography* (1934) was, then, for Powys, as much a matter of present influences as of past associations.[19]

Weymouth Sands (published as *Jobber Skald* in 1935) continues the autobiographical probings of *Wolf Solent*, and does so with the central support of Hardy's last novel, *The Well-Beloved*, which has, as shall be seen, enjoyed an influence – on Proust and John Fowles, as well as on Powys – beyond what its merits as a narrative might lead one to expect. *Weymouth Sands*, in its setting – Weymouth and the Isle of Portland – and in its central concern to exhibit the emotions of a 'platonic nympholept' is much influenced by Hardy's last and intimately self-probing work of prose fiction.[20]. One is not surprised to discover that late in the novel (ch. 13), Jobber Skald and Magnus Muir, two men deeply disappointed in love, sit beside a youth on a bench on Weymouth beach and watch him read Hardy's *Well-Beloved*, which is the story of an artist's forty-year pursuit of Ideal Love through his loves for three members of the same family, natives of the very Isle of Portland (Hardy's Isle of Slingers) visible to Jobber and Magnus from that bench on Weymouth Beach in Powys's novel.

Weymouth Sands is a Powysian version of Hardy's *Well-Beloved*, the story of not just one man, but of a whole circle of men, seeking ultimate happiness through sexual union of various kinds. Sylvanus Cobbold the mystic and prophet, Jobber Skald the sailor and tranter, Magnus Muir the Latin master, Dog Cattistock the businessman, Sippy Ballard the town clerk, Jerry Cobbold the actor and clown, Richard Gaul the philosopher, Rodney Loder the solicitor, even Larry Zed, a demented boy – all seek in the women they seduce, love from afar, jilt, touch, dream of or pursue a satisfaction not to be found elsewhere, not in religion, wealth or power, learning, or the beauteous forms of nature. Sylvanus is most like Hardy's Jocelyn Pierston in avoiding sexual possession of the women he loves. Like Wolf Solent, Sylvanus finds gratification in observing women, touching them, holding them, but not in sexual intercourse with them. And he lands in an asylum for the insane as a result. Jobber Skald is most unlike Hardy's Pierston. Cast in the gigantic mould of a Gabriel Oak or Giles Winterborne, and endowed with the sexual drives of a Sargeant Troy or Alec d'Urberville, Jobber exercises a powerful physical influence over Perdita Wane. Their love-making before the rock-sculptured love torso on Portland is the symbol of a raw, uninhibited sensuality whose result is not mere physical satisfaction. For Perdita's passionate love of Jobber transforms into mercy Jobber's murderous hatred for Dog Cattistock, whom he has sworn to bludgeon to death with a stone he carries about in his pocket.

Between the platonic longing of Sylvanus and the satyr's violent sensuality of Jobber are ranged various shades of eroticism: Magnus Muir's decorous devotion to Curly Wix with a respectable marriage its end; Sippy Ballard's selfish love for the same girl; Dog Cattistock's exploitation of Hortensia Lily, of the dancer Tossty, and then of Curly Wix; Captain Poxwell's imaginary incestuous love for his daughter Lucinda; Daisy Lily's tentative lesbian affair with Peg Frampton, herself the beloved of the philosopher Richard Gaul. The loves of this novel run the gamut, though the most touching and beautiful is the brief liaison between the lonely Perdita, before she finds fulfilment with Jobber, and the simple-minded Larry Zed.

Perdita has walked to Lodmoor, a marshy plain east of Weymouth where the simpleton Larry lives with Gipsy May in a lonely hut. Larry, like all the men of the novel, is driven by erotic fantasies. His well-beloved he calls his 'Nothing-Girl', with whom he associates Perdita immediately upon meeting her: 'She likes me Nothing-Girl, – . . . who do cuddle I to sleep! If only she'd let poor Larry do it, how he'd hold she close!' 'Never', remarks Powys's narrator, 'had young Zed made love to anyone in his life; and only with that presence at night . . . had he ever really known, even in his imagination, what a girl's body can do to drive away pain and suffering and anger and misery from the mind of mortal man' (ch.5). Perdita, to her own astonishment, is attracted to Larry: 'his green eyes . . . his blood-red hair, with a matted elf-lock hanging loose over his forehead . . . his white gleaming teeth . . . long bare forearms, as free from hairs as her own! . . . his brown knees beneath his ragged knickerbockers . . . his supple waist and his thin slouching body' (ibid.). When Larry leads Perdita to a secret spot in the marsh to see a great grey heron, and when they watch the beautiful bird fly off, there surges up within her, 'with a dark delicious trembling, a particular feeling she sometimes had when she thought of death – its release, its finality, its great escape' (ibid.). When he invites her to his bed in the loft of his hut, supposedly to study his collection of seaweeds, she goes knowing that she is fully capable of giving herself to this demented boy. But Zed, in his own way as much nympholept as Sylvanus, is incapable of physical love. His pleasure is found in an imagined substitute for physical love, and so he can only chant to himself, 'I've got a girl on me bed', 'I've got a girl on me bed', 'I've got a girl on me bed.' For Zed, thought and song of the simplest kind must stand in for the act of love. When he finally goes to Perdita, who has willingly reclined on his bed, it is to hold her hand and imagine, only imagine, possessing her. The result is one of the most poignant moments in Powys's 'Wessex Novels':

> Very gently, just as if she had been made of some material more precious than flesh and blood, he stroked one of her bare hands which lay cold on her lap with the tips of his fingers. Perdita had closed her eyes; but in a moment she opened them again, for she felt by his quick breathing that he had fallen on his knees by her side and had tightened his fingers over the hand he had touched. . . . Larry's whole soul gleamed in his green eyes as he hung over her. His brain felt dizzy; but it seemed to him as though touching her so, and while she lay there prone and still beneath him, that a veritable consummation of his desire was already taking place. To his fervid imagination, it was enough that their eyes clung together and that she knew he was ravishing her in his thought. Her bare hand, round which his fingers burned, was to him then her whole body. For this was the first time in his life that he had held a girl who knew what he felt and did not stop him. His green eyes, as

they clung to her soft brown ones, kept saying to her: 'I'm taking you! I'm taking you!' and it seemed to him that she yielded more and more, as he bent forward, his body pressed against the side of the couch; and it seemed to him that it pleased her that he should be seeing her bare figure – as he *was* now seeing it in his intense imagination – and that it pleased her to lie so hushed and still, so that he could the more easily enjoy her; and it seemed to him that this strange passivity, she knowing that he was taking her, was the ultimate essence of her Being offered up to him; and that her lying so still, with her bare hand in his, while he enjoyed her, was the ultimate sign of what it meant to be a real, live mysterious girl; and that this was the secret of all girls, that they could not know how exciting they were; and that this was their inmost nature that they stayed so quiet while they were loved.   (Ibid.)

Perdita, ironically, thinks only of Jobber while Larry 'enjoys' her, but Larry, forced by his 'madness' and isolation into primitive intimacy with fish, heron and marsh, engenders in Perdita 'a strange, half-mystical detachment from all the poignancies and confusions of life' (ibid.). There is no apologizing by Powys here for the strangeness of Larry's way of loving, and no attempt to argue its superiority to the love of a Jobber, a Dog, or a Sippy Ballard. A reader does not question its human reality. The entire episode, carefully shaped and orchestrated – the dialect speech of Larry is an almost-perfect vehicle for the child-like view that pervades – might have failed in a wretchedly sentimental way, or have succeeded in a riotously comic one. It does neither, but conveys instead a sense of this strange love's human reality because of Powys's sympathy and honesty – sympathy for the defective boy and the lonely girl, honesty about the limits of such a relationship. The treatment of love in this episode, and in the whole of *Weymouth Sands*, like Proust's treatment of homosexuality in *Remembrance of Things Past*, represents an enlarged understanding of the range of human love. If *Weymouth Sands* derives from Hardy's *Well-Beloved* and its exhibition of 'the tragedy of a nympholept',[21] it also departs from that novel's narrow focus on nympholepsy as a malady peculiar to the artist. For Powys, to yearn for an ideal love or beauty, to seek and fail to realize that ideal, is the plight not just of the artist, but of men and women of every station. Powys democratizes Hardy's view and thereby extends his humanism beyond that of his master.

Powys's attack on vivisection in *Weymouth Sands* is rooted in this same belief that the act of loving can waken a power of will and imagination as strong as any power in nature. Sylvanus Cobbold's debate with Dr Brush, the director of experiments on living animals, makes this precise point:

> Don't you see that the mere fact of your *being allowed* to do this – for your chatter about giving 'em anaesthetics is all my eye – it's those nicely manufactured straps that hold 'em so still – proves that we've given up trying to touch the secret of life by being just and righteous and pitiful. Good God! Given up the whole direction we've been making toward, from the beginning! How did it ever get into the world at all, this idea of *not* being cruel? But once in the world, *it has done it*. It's the only thing that has changed anything – changed Nature herself! (Ch. 14)

Though Dr Brush's conversion as a result of Cobbold's plea is perhaps too sudden to be convincing (Murphy, his chief 'technician', is sent off to cultivate watercress), Powys's attack on vivisection, like his attack on the intolerance that places a Sylvanus Cobbold, because of sexual deviancy, under the care of a Dr Brush, suggests how far Powys is moving beyond the vision of Hardy's *The Well-Beloved*. And by this time in Powys's career one expects no less, for his use of Hardy has from the start been catalytic. Powys's strength as a novelist stems in part from his fearlessness before his precursors, from his seeming immunity to the 'anxiety of influence'. In *Weymouth Sands*, as in *Wolf Solent* and *Ducdame*, Powys worked, in his own words, 'unconsciously as far as life and reality and nature and human character are concerned', but at the same time remained 'vividly aware of the particular books and . . . writers and . . . friends who [had] influenced [him] in [his] work':

> I am . . . a born book-worm turned novelist or fabulist. As a book-worm I have devoured with a greed beyond what anyone could call critical and with an enchantment and intoxication that was like being drugged all the novels of Scott and Dickens and Dostoievsky and Balzac, and Hardy and Henry James. These novels I have read over and over again and I know them only

a little less well than I know the poetry of Wordsworth and Keats and Matthew Arnold and Edgar Allan Poe, and Paul Verlaine and the essays of Charles Lamb and Walter Pater. . . .

Of all our Wessex writers I am the most hopelessly and incredulously bookish. Yes, I am an incorrigible bookworm with a desperate mania for trying to write the sort of long romances I have always loved so intensely to read.[22]

As much, if not more, can be said of the hero of *Maiden Castle* (1936), the last of Powys's Wessex novels; for in it Dud No-Man is not just a reader of novels, but a would-be writer of novels as well, and a would-be writer of novels much like the ones he reads. *Maiden Castle* is the first of Powys's novels whose hero is a novelist; and Dud No-Man's work on a novel about Mary Channing, the woman executed in the amphitheatre at Dorchester in 1705 for killing her husband, does not merely echo Hardy's *Mayor of Casterbridge*. It also recalls the actual circumstances of Hardy's writing of *The Mayor* in Dorchester in the 1880s. Just as Hardy had returned to Dorchester in 1883, after some twenty years spent in other English towns and cities, to write *The Mayor of Casterbridge*, so Powys returned to Dorchester in 1943, after more than thirty years in America, to write *Maiden Castle*. Hardy lived and wrote at 7, Glyde Path Road (now Shire Hall Lane), Powys at 38, East High Street. Powys's retracing of Hardy's movements is retained in the quite definite echo between the title of Hardy's Dorchester novel and the title of his own. What better way to 'rewrite' *The Mayor of Casterbridge* than to write *Maiden Castle* in the town in which the former was written and set?[23] Dud, therefore, is the first of Powys's heroes to embody, in a sense, Hardy himself. In so far as Dud is also the hero of an autobiographical novel, he embodies a Powys–Hardy meld that must have given Powys great confidence as he wrote and great pleasure to create.

Maiden Castle, unlike Hardy's *Mayor*, is set in an historical Dorchester. Powys retains the actual name; he creates no mythic realm even slightly comparable to Hardy's Casterbridge. The novel's time structure resembles Hardy's in *The Return of the Native* – one year, from November to November. Powys's theme is also that of *The Return* (and *Wolf Solent*) – a nostalgic man's search for self against the mystery and pressure of his family past. Powys's hero, Dud No-Man, is much like Hardy's Clym Yeobright in being a returning native who seeks to reconcile conflicting devotions to a passionate wife and to an inescapable maternal presence. Even Egdon Heath has its counterpart – in Maiden Castle, the hill fort which like the Heath influences the lives of nearly all the persons of the novel. But these striking resemblances to Hardy are not the most profoundly Hardyan aspect of this book. Nor are the many references to Hardy – as for instance when Dud invokes the name of 'the great Wessex author' to describe the River Frome, or when Dud sees on the outskirts of Dorchester 'the sacred clump of trees planted by Hardy himself that marked the great writer's home', or when Hardy's poem 'Afterwards' is quoted to describe Dud's habit of not noticing certain things.[24] The most interesting evidence of Hardy's influence in *Maiden Castle* is to be found instead in the similarity that emerges between Dud's explicit interest in Hardy on the one hand and Dud's relationship to Uryen Quirm, his natural father, on the other.

Maiden Castle opens upon Dud No-Man's return to Dorchester in November 1935, after an absence of ten years. Dud has returned to write a novel about Mary Channing and to visit the graves of his parents and his wife Mona, all of whom had died in an epidemic ten years before. Obsessed with his memories of his wife and mother, he visits their graves in the cemetery on the Weymouth Road. There he meets a woman, Nancy Quirm, whom is grieving beside the grave of her son. Nancy, with whom Dud will grow increasingly intimate, is, unknown to him, his stepmother, the wife of his natural father, Enoch (Uryen) Quirm, who Dud will soon meet. Quirm is an enigmatic, somewhat diabolical figure, Welsh in origin, who longs to communicate with the pre-Roman gods of Maiden Castle (Mai-Dun). Quirm in fact believes himself the reincarnation of these ancient spirits. The man in the grave beside Dud's natural mother is not Dud's father, as Dud will soon learn. In the meantime, Dud's loneliness and sexual longing cause him to do an impetuous thing: to purchase (for eighteen pounds) from a circus near Dorchester a young equestrienne named Wizzie Ravelston. He does this because her curvaceous body has a powerful 'sensual attraction' for him. Nancy Quirm assists Dud in this transaction, which recalls of course Michael Henchard's sale of Susan and Elizabeth-Jane for five guineas in *The Mayor*. Nancy also enables Dud to meet Quirm and the other members of Nancy's circle: Professor Teucer Wye, a half-mad devotee of Plato; Thuella Wye, a lesbian artist; and Jennie Dearth, a sister of Thuella living in platonic friendship with

Claudius Cask, a wealthy humanitarian, a lover of old Rome, and a communist.

Though Wizzie is willing to become Dud's mistress, she soon finds him unappealing; for she is a passionate woman eager to be loved, and he, like Sylvanus Cobbold and Wolf Solent, prefers intellectual love. The result is a weird sexual comedy in which Wizzie moves between Dud, Uryen, Ben Urgen (who had raped her and got her with child three years before) and the lesbian Thuella. Dud in turn moves between Wizzie, Thuella, Nancy Quirm, the ghost of his dead wife Mona, and the memory of his dear dead mother, in whose bed he still sleeps. A part of that bed is especially noteworthy; one of its posts is adorned by 'a grotesque head of heraldic carving' soon found by Dud to be connected with the dark mysteries of Maiden Castle and with Uryen Quirm, who bequeaths to Dud the companion piece to the bedpost figure. Like Wolf and Sylvanus, Dud is 'nervously incapable of consummating his marriage'. Inclined to 'cerebral lovemaking', Dud is 'the reverse of amorous'. He is indeed morbidly fastidious. And yet, his is a life devoted to women. One of them is Mary Channing, the story of whose brutal execution Dud seeks to burn into the conscience of Dorchester, just as he longs to arrive at a 'conception of our dumb human chances of immortality' through devotion to the spirits of his dead mother and wife (*MC*, pt I, ch. 1).

Dud approaches this conception, like Wolf Solent, by confronting and passing beyond the conceptions of his 'fathers': the platonist Teucer Wye; Uryen, who believes that the powers of Maiden Castle reside in him; and Thomas Hardy, whose *Return of the Native* and *Mayor of Casterbridge* are present in various ways in *Maiden Castle*, and whose statue, at the Top-of-the-Town in Dorchester, plays a most important role in Dud's quest. The folly of old Teucer's bloodless platonism is acknowledged by Teucer himself, when he scolds his daughter Jenny for her aversion to sex and tosses his copies of Plato into a fire. Uryen and Hardy, however, are not so easily disposed of.

It is while walking with Uryen Quirm on Maiden Castle that Dud learns from him that Quirm had been his mother's lover and is indeed Dud's father. Like Wolf Solent when confronted by the grim truths about his parentage, Dud is outraged, his 'life-illusion' violated. This revelation is followed by a conversation in which Quirm offends Dud's belief in a life after death, which Dud derives from his powerful sense that Mona and his mother still live. Based on the presence of the 'other world' in certain Welsh myths, Quirm argues for the existence of a 'living entity . . . that'll survive death and burial' (pt II, ch. 6). This should appeal to Dud's own intimations of immortality, but Dud will not accept his father's view of the matter:

> Because I feel myself in bones and skull . . . hostile to this man's nebulous talk, and because I don't believe in any of his ideas, *that* doesn't mean I'm a bigoted materialist. I believe, absolutely, in another dimension surrounding this one; and I believe in my power of becoming a 'medium' for the life of the generations. I believe in the truth of my book about Mary Channing! (Ibid.)

In his belief in the imagination, Dud is, of course, his father's true son; for Uryen believes himself to be the reincarnation of the powers of the old Welsh myths. Uryen believes in the truth of this private revelation just as surely as Dud believes in the truth of his art. But then Dud's antipathy toward Uryen is more than a mere clash of opinion; it is a profound psychological recoil from the Uryen in himself:

> There was . . . a lower level of his consciousness wherein, like an antediluvian creature confronting its progenitor, he made no attempt at articulating what he felt. He simply hated the man because the man was his father. . . .
> . . . He felt as if he and his father, isolated from all other living things in the mystic circle of Mai-Dun, were two prehistoric entities linked together by the invisible semen of paternity, but *for that very reason* destined to a struggle of measureless malignity, a struggle that could only end in the death of the one or of the other. (Ibid.)

Dud will indeed have a hand in Quirm's death when he arranges for the publication of Quirm's mystical beliefs before a sceptical and uncomprehending modern world. For now, however, he is capable of pity ('a sort of outraged pity') when he looks into his father's face, a gesture Powys likens to the sickening experience of 'lifting a scab from an unhealed wound' and seeing there 'the foul blood and yellow pus' (ibid.). Uryen pleads for his son's sympathy and in doing so exacts from Dud a soul-wrenching apology:

'Why do you hate me so, lad? . . . I don't ask you to like me. Why should you? But what – have – I – done to you that you should look so stern at me, that you should harden yourself so against me?' . . .

. . . There came into our friend's consciousness a queer emotion. . . . It was an emotion of pure, blind, desperate awareness of the infinite pathos of another's identity – a feeling as if he were one kind of substance – stone, let us say – sending forth a tragic vibration that beat against a different kind of substance – iron, let us say – in a struggle to get at the heart of its alien being.

'I'm sorry – *Father!*' murmured Dud in a low voice. These words cost him a violent effort. Never indeed since his boyhood had he uttered anything that so tore at his vitals. (Ibid.)

But Dud's pity turns to violent antagonism when Quirm – in urging that only the pain of 'unfulfilled love, love turned to hate' enables one to 'break the bonds of life's natural law' and see the spirit behind material reality – insists that mental pain is far worse than physical suffering. Dud's humanitarian sympathies are outraged and he screams his rebuttal. But no sooner had he screamed it

than he became aware that he was catching the very rhythm of his father's tone. He was refuting him, but he was talking to the wind, just as he did! But, though he knew all this, he seemed compelled to go on. It was as if this contact with his father were forcing him to become like his father even in the act of denouncing him. (Ibid.)

What follows is a remarkable account of the uncanniness, if not the anxiety, of influence, both literary and biological:

his words were not his own. He was his father, arguing with his father. The harsh nervous eloquence, the curious spiritual anger, the wild ruggedness of the words he used, all belonged to this man of his mother's.

. . . They might differ over this mystery, but it was the same nerve, the same wolf's howl from the navel of life, the same obliviousness to every 'sense of proportion'.

Quite unaware of what he was doing Dud began plucking

both hands at the grass beside him. As he did this his whole lean frame began rocking itself up and down as if he had been a mechanical doll wound up to bow before his father. What he began to feel now was indescribable. Not only was he compelled to talk *like* his father, but he began to feel as if the Powers of Mai-Dun were fusing him with his father. (Ibid.)

It is difficult not to recall, when reading these sentences, John Cowper Powys's troubled affection for *his* father, an affection he had only recently re-examined in the *Autobiography*, published just two years before *Maiden Castle*. The Reverend Charles Francis Powys, who had died in 1923, is the unquestionable hero of the *Autobiography*. He is also the unquestionable (and unnamed) villain. He was, in his eldest son's words, a man of 'volcanic intensity of earth-feeling' and of simple, profound, unwavering belief – a description that fits Uryen Quirm in this episode on Maiden Castle and elsewhere in the novel. But the stern Christianity of Charles Powys was also the standard against which John Cowper was obliged to measure his peculiarly erotic temperament and his religious scepticism. Powys was deeply devoted to his father at the same time as he was hopelessly estranged from him. But Dud and Quirm's struggle in the novel, and John Cowper and Charles Powys's in the *Autobiography*, are given another analogue. As Dud and Quirm return from Maiden Castle to Dorchester, they pass the cemetery on the Weymouth Road in which Dud's wife, mother and stepfather are buried. As they walk, Dud thinks of Mary Channing, the heroine of his novel, and of his vow to burn the horror of her death 'into the bones of Wessex' (*MC*, pt II, ch. 6). As they pass the amphitheatre, the scene of Mary Channing's execution, the scene also of Michael Henchard's secret meeting with his wronged wife Susan in Hardy's *The Mayor*, they pass the circus ground where Dud had purchased Wizzy. Dud remembers his meeting with Nancy Quirm, a year earlier, on the first day he had entered Dorchester: ' "How like a figure in Hardy", he said to himself, "poor Nance looked that day staggering against these rails! It's funny how I began my life in Dorchester just as the mayor [Hardy's Michael Henchard] began his, only Trenchard [*sic*] sold *his* woman and I bought mine!" ' (*MC*, pt II, ch. 6).

This reference to Hardy is soon followed by another, for, as Dud and his father proceed up Trinity Street, then turn left unto High West Street and then right unto Glyde Path Road toward the Hangman's Cottage, Mr Quirm calls to the attention of his novel-writing and novel-reading son 'a curious waterspout or gargoyle-head, that had been placed above the old brick entrance to what seemed . . . like a Quaker meeting house. He had come upon a mention of this head in Hardy's book, but apparently it occupied in poor Trenchard's [sic] time a different position from what it did now' (ibid.).[25] Dud's return from Maiden Castle with his father has taken him into the very street where Hardy had lived when he wrote much of *The Mayor* in the early 1880s, perhaps before the very house in which was 'born' the novel lying behind the novel, about Mary Channing, that Dud is writing, *and* behind the novel, *Maiden Castle*, of which Dud is the hero.[26]

As these details suggest, Dud's struggle against Uryen, his natural father, is made to parallel his engagement with Hardy, his poetic sire. Though the struggle with Hardy is fierce, it is not, as with Quirm, a struggle to the death. And this is so because Hardy, unlike the myth-haunted Quirm, points Dud toward the future rather than the past. Hardy, as shall be seen, is 'modern' in a way that appeals to Dud. With Uryen, Dud's 'words were not his own' (pt II, ch. 6). Similarly, in *Maiden Castle*, Powys can 'argue with' Hardy's *Return* and *Mayor*, but not without echoing those novels, not without slipping into their rhythms, patterns and characterizations. Just as Dud forms his metaphysic against Quirm's, and his story of Mary Channing against the story of Michael Henchard, so Powys shaped his beliefs against the beliefs of his father on the one hand and the tragic philosophy of Hardy on the other. Powys's simultaneous acceptance and rejection of influence is like No-Man's ambivalence toward Uryen atop Mai-Dun:

> there came to be presented to him one of those searching glimpses into his intrinsic self that come so seldom to mortal men. 'I could never give up my life [to communist ideology] like old Claudius, . . . but I *could* struggle, like this man of Mother's, after the Secret. Not in his way, not by magic of course – but I *could* drop the entire world and live for the Spirit, as long as I was allowed my imaginative lusts!'
>
> (*MC*, pt II, ch. 6)

This would be, of course, no more than an ingenious hypothesis if it were not for Powy's determination to make it central to his purpose in this novel depicting Dud No-Man's discovery of the actuality behind his life illusion.

After a second visit to Maiden Castle, this one focusing the attention of all the major characters on some statuary recently exhumed there, Dud returns to Dorchester and pauses before Hardy's statue by Eric Kennington at the top of the town. Here Thuella, the painter of clouds and by this time the would-be lover of Dud, proposes to show the group something she has 'discovered in the Hardy Statue': ' "Look at 'Thel", whispered No-Man [to Wizzie]. "She's taken off her hat. Look at the sun on her head against old Hardy's knee! I wonder which he'd have been most interested in – you or her?" ' (pt II, ch. 8). Dud's strange question is addressed to himself as much as to Wizzie, for Thuella in her epicenism is not without appeal to him. Dud's question also suggests Hardy's connection in Dud's mind with Uryen, for Uryen wishes to possess *both* Wizzie and Theulla – both physical and intellectual love. Dud's question may suggest also that the nympholepsy and sexual impotence of Powys's autobiographical heroes – Wolf, Sylvanus and here Dud – is something he also associates with Hardy, perhaps with the Hardy implied in certain pages of *The Well-Beloved*, and quite possibly the Hardy of *The Early Life* (1928) and *Later Years* (1930), the autobiography published as a biography of Hardy by Hardy's second wife. Powys's *Autobiography* of 1936 is as candid on the question of his sexuality as Hardy's disguised autobiography was secretive. But Powys's portrait of himself as a man caught up in the practice of 'cerebral eroticism' (p. 119) has a counterpart in Hardy's remark (in *The Early Life*) that 'a clue to much of his [Hardy's] character and action throughout his life is afforded by his lateness of development in virility, while mentally precocious' (*Life*, p. 32). Robert Gittings's recent portrait of Hardy as a mother-fixated son pursuing a maternal eidolon in woman after woman suggests what Powys may have discerned in Hardy: not just another Dorsetman who wrote novels, but a Dorsetman and novelist who shared, projected in his fiction and thereby legitimized for Powys's narrative art what Powys repeatedly called, thanks perhaps to the stern censor that stood over him in the form of the Reverend Charles Powys, his 'viciousness'. Powys (and his Dud No-Man) found in Hardy a kindred soul.

A curious feature of the *Autobiography* is the way Powys senior, described repeatedly as the greatest human being in Powys's life, and Thomas Hardy, held up as the greatest writer of the time, are seen to be similar. Powys seems to wish to fuse them, to blend somehow the contradictory mixture of heterodoxy and orthodoxy – religious and emotional – they to him represent. They are first alike for him in their Dorset heritage. Charles Powys, himself the son of a Dorset clergyman, 'had imbibed from his Wessex childhood certain West Country words and intonations which he would occasionally make use of . . . upon occasions when solemn or poetical issues were involved' (p. 4).

> [It was] the tone with which my father always spoke of cuckoo flowers, rather than anything he said in praise of them, that made these pale growths the very epitome of romantic poetry for me. . . .
> . . . It was by a thousand slight touches, and sideway thrusts, and casual hints, and inarticulate directions, that my father . . . would indicate *the absolute inferiority* . . . of Derbyshire ways, scenery, people, customs, dialect, flora, to those of his native Wessex.
> It was this fierce, inarticulate, irrational loyalty *to his own*, to all the old things, the old ways, the old people, the old battle cries, the old causes, the old customs, that my father had the power of communicating to me without direct speech of any kind. (pp. 31–2)

If Powys found himself deeply estranged from his father, he also discovered the source of his poetic temperament in his father. His praise for his father's power of communicating to him the greatness of the old recalls his praise for Hardy in *Far from the Madding Crowd* for ushering him into that 'stone circle of monoliths and trilithons, grey with the lichen of centuries of English tradition' (see p. 64, above). Similarly, his father's love for the flora and fauna of the West Country recalls his tribute to Hardy's love for the 'sweet West' in his poem to Hardy of forty years before (see pp. 65–6 above).

This pleasure Powys took in connecting Thomas Hardy with the Reverend Charles Powys produced such sentences as this: 'Blackmore Vale, in the heart of which my father, like Tess of the d'Urbervilles, first saw the light, bears many resemblances to Somerset' (*Auto*, p. 152). When Hardy visited Montacute in the

1890s (see pp. 66–7, above), Powys noted the Dorset poet in both his father and his new master:

> It happened that there were imperceptible frost-marks that day in the road, making those odd little creases and criss-cross wrinkles in the mud that my father always loved to see, and these minute tokens of the processes *he* knew so well, were not missed, though I had missed them, by the hawk's eye of this other Dorset-born noticer of such things. (*Auto*, pp. 228–9)[27]

The sentences of the *Autobiography* immediately following this one suggest that during Hardy's visit to Montacute John Powys had, face to face before him, two fathers: one ministering to his earthly wants, the other to his spiritual. And it was, amusingly enough, the Reverend Charles Powys who sliced the bread, and the writer Hardy who is likened to 'the Pope-God':

> That morning I remember announcing to my father and to all the family that the greatest writer *then living on this earth* was coming to visit us! All the while my father was praying, in that noble deliberate way he had, using naturally, easily, and quite *extempore*, the very language and accent of the old Tudor founders of our Church . . . I was saying to myself: 'He is coming! He, *He* is coming!' just as though I were Homenas talking to Pantagruel about the great one, the unique one, the Pope-God. All the while my father, with the whole-wheat brown loaves from Stoke-sub-Ham and the great pat of yellow butter from Mr. Cole's dairy before him, was filling the nine mouths left to him . . . I was thinking to myself with beating heart: 'He will be here at our next meal, *He* will be here!' (p. 229)

At the same time as Powys can see in himself and his father an identical personal pride and dislike for society, he can associate his own eyes with those of Thomas Hardy. He admires Hardy's 'great greenish-black eyes, dark as those of Leo XIII, gleam[ing] forth like the eyes of a gar-falcon' (p. 230). Shortly after, he describes himself, the hapless nympholept, walking in Brighton 'with eyes like the eyes of a ger-falcon [sic]' looking for 'some soft, receptive feminine form whose ankles I could at least pretend belonged to a sylph-like body' (p. 240). In a passage that anticipates Robert Gittings's account of Hardy's pursuit of the Sparks sisters, as well as of Pierston-Hardy's and Cobbold-Powys's pursuit of their beloveds, Powys recalls that he 'slept at different times with three sisters of the same family' in his own tireless pursuit of the 'eternal feminine' or 'ideal sylph' (p. 242).

Powys's 'abnormal eroticism' possibly contributed to his father's momentous decision to make Littleton Powys, and not John, the eldest son, the executor of the family will. In spite of the offence to him in this, John Powys remained devoted: 'My whole philosophy is based upon my father's monumental simplicity; and towards this I strive as Christians strive toward Jesus' (p. 429). At the same time, he cultivated the antithesis to his father represented by Hardy, as in the following:

> What happiness from life we can attain, what revelations about life we can reach, what beauty in life we can respond to, must always have as their background . . . an awareness of the terrible necessity of forgetting the unthinkable things which the cruelty of the First Cause has prepared both for those who accept Him and those who reject Him. (p. 463)[28]

These competing loyalties depicted in the *Autobiography* are reenacted in *Maiden Castle* in Dud's vacillation between Quirm, whose peculiar beliefs based on ancient Welsh myth Dud sets aside, and his poetic father, Thomas Hardy, who appears in the novel in the only 'personal' form possible in the Dorchester of 1935–6, Eric Kennington's statue, which, as has been noted, suddenly becomes the centre of attention when Dud and the others return from Mai-Dun and the unearthing there of two statuettes, one of Caridwen, the earth goddess of Samothrace, and other of the Devil. It is with this recent discovery fresh in mind that Dud and Wizzie watch Thuella rest her head against the bronze knee of Hardy's statue. They resolve that they will have nothing to do with her foolery.

> When, however, they reached the statue they found it harder than they had expected to follow this . . . resolution. Straight towards the barracks as if he were acting as umpire in some invisible aerial tournament gazed with fixed stare the great sculptor in words. His bronze legs in their serviceable stockings, were crossed restfully at the knee, and his compact head, poised above his upright shoulders, was held as alert and as raptorial

towards the cunning masks of the Immanent Will, as it had been held in life for the best part of a century.

'Hullo! you look as if you were all gathered round the figure-head of a ship!' cried No-Man in his abrupt way, as they joined the others; and though as a rule Wizzie deliberately closed her mind to his offhand imaginings, this time . . . she gave herself up completely to this fancy of his. Their friends were too occupied to bother about the way he greeted them, so that she had time to feel as if the old town lying round them were actually and indeed some huge phantasmal ship, loaded to the bulkheads with the perilous cargoes of the generations, and voyaging to its unknown port behind that forward-gazing bronze figure. (Pt II, ch. 8)

This reverie is crudely interrupted by the voice of Thuella's brother Dunbar, a crack-brained fascist (his nickname is 'Dumbell') sketching something on the flyleaf of a Blackshirt tract he is holding against the back of the bronze Hardy. Dunbar is in fact making a striking replica of what Quirm had identified as Caridwen, 'the headless Unknown', 'the Great Goddess Caridwen' (ibid). Wizzie, forgetting for a moment her dislike for the sexless Dud, watches with astonishment as Dud takes the pencil from Dunbar's hand and writes the name 'Mona' across the sketch of the goddess. This is the beginning of the end of Dud and Wizzie's marriage, for Wizzie now sees that Mona, Dud's dead first wife, still holds Dud's devotion. Dud's mother-worship, the cause of his impotency with both Mona and Wizzie, Dud can now associate with the sex myth of his father, with Uryen's bizarre notion that one perceives the secret of life's law only when one's love is unfulfilled, turns to hate, and the frustrated lover becomes a seer through the pain of sexual despair. 'Stir up sex *till it would put out the sun*', Uryen has counselled Dud during their visit to Maiden Castle, 'and then keep it sterile':

> Now, lad, you must know it is not given to everyone to feel what I'm talking about. At its intensest it comes when love and hate are one. It is terrible then. It is a feeling so terrific that it often ends in madness; but if it doesn't end that way, it ends in *breaking through*. You must know, lad, that there are secrets only revealed to magic. . . . And this only comes when the emotion of love-hate gathers to a point that's terrible. And you

must know too that it only comes when the passion remains sterile. Any fulfilment dissipates its power. Nothing but unfulfilled love, love turned to hate, can beat hard upon the barrier of life, can beat hard enough upon what separates us from the secret, till it breaks through! (Pt II, ch. 6)

It was at the moment of rejecting this view of genius that Dud felt as though the Powers of Maiden Castle were 'fusing him with his father' in the most abominably painful way. But now, before Hardy's statue, Dud accepts this derivation and attempts to associate it and its possible origin in his unbreakable attachment to his mother with the Thomas Hardy preserved in Kennington's statue. In short, Hardy's statue is for Dud an even more powerful totem than the statue of Caridwen unearthed at Maiden Castle, and his inscription of the word 'Mona' against it suggests what indeed has been the case with Dud, and with Powys, from the beginning: Hardy, as man and writer, is the figure 'against' whom he writes. Hardy is both a paternal support and a creative antagonist. Thuella nestles her head against Hardy, as against a father or lover, because the creator of Sue Bridehead would understand well a woman for whom sexuality is a torment and a trial. This is conjecture, for Thuella never does tell what she has found in Hardy's statue. But, in the context of *Weymouth Sands*, *Wolf Solent* and the *Autobiography* (that self-portrait 'without women'), choosing between a fleshly and an intellectual way of loving is constantly under study. As in the case of Lawrence in *Women in Love* and Proust in *Remembrance of Things Past*, John Cowper Powys makes sexual varietism a subject for serious fiction. And each does this, in different ways, with the help of Thomas Hardy.

This seems to be the point of this climactic gathering of highly diverse individuals – the myth-haunted Quirm, the platonist Wye, the fascist Dunbar, the communist Cask, the homosexual Dud and Thuella, the sensual Wizzie and sexually repressed Jenny – around the 'forward-looking bronze figure' of Thomas Hardy. From the beginning, as has been seen, the mixture of ironies and pities in Hardy's novels had represented a supreme wisdom to Powys, a way of accepting and even loving the cruelty of the world, and of fighting against it. Hardy was for Powys the master of 'strange soul-searchings', of 'passions that ask for bread and find a stone', just as he was the voice of an indifferent nature whose unending griefs and joys, but for a Hardy, would be unknown to the world. If Hardy is leading man anywhere, it is not, in Powys's view, toward a single, all-embracing vision of truth or happiness, such as that held out by the fascist, communist, platonist or Christian. In the immediate terms of the novel, Hardy's wisdom does not point, for example, toward a robust life of the body for Dud and Wizzie. Jennie Dearth can give herself to Cask and end the sterility of her sexless life. But Dud, incapable of consummating either of his marriages, devoted to the memory of his dead, virginal Mona, unable to relinquish his mother's bed, can only live in fear that he will betray his Mona-mother-ideal if he loves another woman. And so he pours his passion into his story of Mary Channing. But this will also fail, for his manuscript will be rejected by a publisher. Wizzie, with Thuella, will flee to America and the freedom to pursue there her equestrian art and enjoy the devotion of Thuella. What Jenny has found in Cask, Thuella has found in Wizzie. But for Wizzie (as for Lawrence's Rupert Birkin in *Women in Love*) Thuella's love is only one possibility. She also loves her child Lovie, the product of her rape by Ben Urgen, the circus-master from whom Dud had purchased her. She even cherishes the memory of 'that wild struggle [with old Ben] in the caravan' because it 'ended in giving her Lovie' (*MC*, pt III, ch. 9). Like Gerda in *Wolf Solent*, like Hardy's Tess, Eustacia, and Elfride, the passionate Wizzie is the victim of a 'cerebral' lover, a lover rendered impotent by nostalgia stemming from devotion to an ideal associated with the mother. But where in Hardy tragedy is the result of such mismating, in Powys revitalization is the result. Gerda, Wizzie and Thuella live on, seeking that love that has eluded them.

Dud too is beyond defeat. An Angel Clare or Clym Yeobright must live with irreparable loss and unpardonable guilt. But Dud, though scorned and humiliated, is somehow invulnerable, like Wolf Solent and Sylvanus Cobbold before him. Wizzie's flight with Thuella does not anger him. The death of Uryen – in part as a result of the publication of his theories about Maiden Castle – does not leave Dud guilt-stricken. Dud has learned from Quirm that 'unreturned love' is 'the strongest magnetic force in the world', because, ironically, the sufferer from unrequited love is free of the ties that weigh as well as bind, the love of wife, brother, parent, or friend that can snuff out one's ability to 'live . . . in the great cosmic forces' (*MC*, pt III, ch. 9). If to live thus is a torture, it is also a triumph, because for Powys it is the necessary condition of the creative artist, the one who – if he is to be great – must look both at and through the lives before him.

Maiden Castle ends where it began, with Dud and Nancy (the re-embodiment of his lost mother) in the cemetery on the Weymouth Road – he to pay homage to his mother Mona, his stepfather, and now Quirm; she to pay homage to her dead son. She has found a son, he a mother. Like Michael Henchard of *The Mayor*, Dud is a deeply flawed individual no magic or medicine can heal. But Dud's end is not Henchard's, for, where Henchard is destroyed by his defects, Dud is in living pursuit of the beloved that has eluded him. Or, in the Wordsworthian phrase Dud now invokes (one recalls Wolf Solent's turn to Wordsworth at a similar moment), he is in pursuit of those intimations of immortality that his mother, then Wizzie and Thuella, and now Nancy represent to him.

From *Wood and Stone* in 1915 to *Maiden Castle* more than two decades later, Hardy was Powys's constant model and touchstone: in his use of Dorset settings, characters and speech; in his interest in the psychology of cerebral love. But, if Powys chose to walk in Hardy's footsteps in the first half of his fiction,[29] he also, particularly in his rejection of tragedy, his strongly self-revelatory narratives, and his candid treatment of abnormal sexuality, cleared a path distinctively his own. Wolf Solent, Sylvanus Cobbold, Dud No-Man, the John Powys of the *Autobiography* are blundering and blighted individuals. It is impossible to forget Powys's description of himself as 'a weak, cowardly, fastidious degenerate' (*Auto*, p. 184). But all these astonishing figures remain fiercely and comically human in their degeneracy. Wolf will not abandon entirely the private life illusion he pits against the unholy facts of his past and present. He must remain what he was. Sylvanus is arrested, jailed, humiliated, but he perseveres in his wish to make love prevail over cruelty in the world. Dud is no less a believer in the wisdom and value of his follies and perversions: 'He must go on as best he could in his own way' (*MC*, pt III, ch. 9). Powys's humanism derives from the tragic vision of the Wessex Novels and moves beyond it. Without the hatred for the conventional that too often mars the vision of Lawrence, with astonishing sympathy for those who deny and punish his benighted protagonists, Powys, through Wolf, Sylvanus, or Dud, exhibits the struggle to love and be loved among those usually described as degenerates. Like Hardy, Powys found it possible to write out of a keen sense of his deepest personal shortcomings, and to champion in his writings those unfortunates who suffer as a result of similar shortcomings in those they love. In both novelists, autobiographical fiction becomes fictional biography, and fictional self-study becomes an admirably objective portrait of the other.

4

Three 'Nostalgicians': Hardy, Marcel Proust and Alain-Fournier

There is no better way to begin to realize what one feels oneself than to try to recreate in oneself what a master has felt. In this deep effort it is our own thought as well as his that we bring to light.
(Marcel Proust, *On Reading*, tr. Milton Hindus)

When you read, you quickly extract from those authors you admire what you consider essential or novel because you have your masterpiece to write, and this so preoccupies you that you look on everything in the world around you as so much raw material.
(Jacques Rivière to Alain-Fournier, tr. Robert Gibson)

In the late summer of 1909, as an oft-told story goes, Marcel Proust secluded himself in his rooms at 102, Boulevard Haussmann, Paris, to devote himself to the writing of *Remembrance of Things Past*, the masterpiece he had begun some two years before, would essentially complete by 1912, and would continue work on until his death in November 1922. It is now clear that, in various forms, *Remembrance* had been under way well before autumn 1909: in the never-completed novel *Jean Santeuil*, written between 1896 and 1900; in several of the pieces collected under the titles *Pleasures and Days* in 1896; in Proust's translations (and prefaces to the translations) of John Ruskin, completed in 1904 and 1906; and in *Against Sainte Beuve*, a long critical essay written in 1908.[1] In the years between the publication of *Pleasures and Days* and the completion of the first version of *Remembrance* in spring 1912, Proust, in a wide and varied course of reading, had found especially attractive three English writers: Ruskin, whom he for a time championed for his devotion to art and his love of the past; George Eliot, the English novelist whose treatment of time and memory, particularly in her autobiographical *Mill on the Floss*, Proust found instructive to his own effort at the recovery of time past; and, somewhat surprisingly, Thomas Hardy, who in the 1890s, when Proust was getting under way as a novelist, was bringing his own career in fiction to a most impressive end – with *Tess of the d'Urbervilles*, *Jude the Obscure* and *The Well-Beloved*.

I say 'somewhat surprisingly' because at first glance Thomas Hardy and Marcel Proust seem worlds and not just nations apart: the writer of tragic chronicles about rural English life would seem to hold little of interest for the probing observer of Parisian high society. The writer of serial fiction and the author of *Remembrance* would seem to exist at opposite ends of the novelistic spectrum. Proust had explicit reasons for admiring and imitating Hardy, as shall be seen. But in part his interest and delight in Hardy must be attributed to the keen interest certain of the Wessex Novels provoked in France from as early as 1875, when Léon Boucher, in the *Revue des deux mondes*, praised Hardy's *Under the Greenwood Tree* (1871), *A Pair of Blue Eyes* (1873) and, in particular, *Far from the Madding Crowd* (1874). Where Henry James, one recalls, had in the December 1875 issue of the *Nation* (New York) found *Far from the Madding Crowd* little more than an occasion for ridicule, Boucher found in it shrewd observations on human society, subtle analyses of human passion, and a most intelligent adaptation of the ancient genre of pastoral romance to the demands of realistic fiction. Boucher praised highly what Virginia Woolf would also praise in Hardy's fiction some fifty years later, a rare gift for bringing the resources of poetry to the writing of prose and a genius for creating fascinating characters of both sexes. Boucher's conclusion about his young English novelist was cautious but firm, and the future was to prove him correct: 'If Mr Hardy continues to give to his art the same care and the same virile elegance, one predicts that he will always be celebrated by serious readers.[2] *Far from the Madding Crowd* was translated into the French in 1891 (as *Barbara*) and reached a third edition by 1901, in which year Hardy's *Tess* and *Jude* were also translated. But even earlier, in 1882, *The Trumpet-Major*, Hardy's Napoleonic novel, had appeared in French.[3] In April 1903, Henri Davray could write with confidence in the *Mercure de France* that Hardy's reputation as a novelist was on the rise in France.[4] Hardy's reputation was undoubtedly enhanced by the praise accorded *The Dynasts* (1903–8) by French reviewers, Davray among them. In 1906, Firmin Roz, translator of *Jude the*

Obscure, in a lengthy article in the *Revue des deux mondes*, praised Hardy to the skies as a realist and ironist comparable to Flaubert, Daudet and de Maupassant, and as the greatest English delineator of the mysteries of the human heart.[5] Even more significant for the history of French fiction in the early twentieth century, in the winter and spring of 1905–6 Proust's younger contemporary Alain-Fournier was deeply affected by his reading of Hardy's *Tess* and *Jude*. This was to have important results for both Fournier's personal life and for the form of his autobiographical masterpiece, *Le Grand Meaulnes* (1913). But more about Alain-Fournier later.

Proust cannot have been unaware of the attention Hardy was receiving in the French press. Prompted by his friend Èmile Blanche's praise of Hardy,[6] also perhaps by Roz's stirring tribute in the *Revue des deux mondes*, Proust wrote to Georges de Louris in November, 1906, asking to borrow a copy of *Jude*, probably in Roz's translation.[7] In autumn 1908 Proust was reading Hardy's story 'A Tragedy of Two Ambitions' ('Deux ambitions'); in late 1909 or early 1910 Hardy's *Well-Beloved;* and in late 1910 *A Pair of Blue Eyes*.[8] Immersed as he was at this same time in the writing of *Remembrance*, Proust was particularly affected by what he found in Eve-Paul Marguerite's translation of *The Well-Beloved*, as he remarked in a letter of January 1910 to his friend Robert de Billy:

> I have just read a very beautiful thing that unfortunately resembles a very little (though it is a thousand times better) what I am doing myself: *The Well-Beloved* by Thomas Hardy. it does not even omit the slight element of the grotesque that accompanies all great works. When you speak with Lister, ask him if he knows Thomas Hardy and Barrie, what kind of men they are, lovers of society, fanciers of women, etc.[9]

If Proust was struck by the way Hardy's *The Well-Beloved* anticipated *Remembrance of Things Past*, he was equally taken by the parallels and repetitions he detected between the *The Well-Beloved, Jude the Obsure* and *A Pair of Blue Eyes*:

> I observe in *A Pair of Blue Eyes* this admirable geometrical parallelism, those tombs alongside one another, those people seated on the tombs thinking of Sothway [Jethway], that boat placed parallel to the hill on which Knight and Elfride are standing, and those adjoining cars bearing Knight and Smith, while a

third car is carrying the corpse of Elfride. And the irritating, slow-moving story of Smith followed by the story of Knight, as in *The Well-Beloved*, though here it is the woman who loves three men. And always, as in *Jude the Obscure*, the bit of sculpture, sculpted from stone. What a role stone plays in these books. Tomb, church, quarry. Marcia marries Pierston, as Arabella remarries him [Jude]. There is a little of *Denys l'Auxerrois* by Pater in Pierston and the island. The novels of Hardy are constructed thus superimposingly, the tombs, the stories, one upon the other. A little corner of land and all upright, the one upon the other as on the island where the houses are built one atop the other.[10]

As these remarks suggest, the novels by Hardy Proust read between 1906 and 1910 attracted him for at least three reasons: because Hardy's *Well-Beloved* resembled *Remembrance of Things Past*; because *A Pair of Blue Eyes*, *Jude the Obscure* and *The Well-Beloved* revealed certain repetitive symmetries at work in Hardy, the result of Hardy's tendency to write and rewrite the same story (a tendency wholly typical of genius, in Proust's view); and, finally, because Hardy's temperament and experience seemed to Proust to have shaped Hardy's fiction. This last attraction is probably Proust's reason for asking Robert de Billy if Billy's British associate in Tangiers, Sir Reginald Lister, knew anything about the personal lives of Hardy and Barrie, whether they were men of society and fanciers of women. If this seems an unexpected concern in the author of *Against Sainte-Beuve*, in which literature is said to be in important ways a thing apart from the life of the writer, it is wholly understandable in the author of *Remembrance*, in which the life of the writer is central, both as subject and as metaphor. Proust is asking Billy if he (Proust) has not perhaps discovered an English *alter ego* in Hardy. Though I have not discovered Billy's reply, it seems fair to suggest that Proust perceived what Anglo-American criticism virtually ignored for sixty years – that *The Well-Beloved* is a highly original portrait of the artist (as an aging man) and an attempt to exhibit the connection between the artistic and the erotic temperament in the artist.[11] Even more than John Cowper Powys, Proust – at work when he read Hardy on his own autobiographical masterpiece, marked by an enormous concern with the connection between the rhythms of the passional life and the origins of literary creativity – sympathized with the attempt at sexual and artistic self-portraiture he detected in *The Well-Beloved*. After all, Proust had found in Hardy a living novelist who enjoyed the respect of a friend and artist such as Blanche, a novelist who had been treated with high regard in the pages of some of the leading literary journals of France, and a novelist who – in *Blue Eyes*, *Jude* and *The Well-Beloved* – had negotiated successfully the narrative path on which he himself was just entering. As George Painter has remarked,

> Proust . . . detected in Hardy's plot [in *The Well-Beloved*], in which the hero loves at different periods of his life a girl, her daughter, and her daughter's daughter, an affinity with his own; for *A la Recherche* was to be the story of three related loves in three separate epochs, Swann's for Odette, and the Narrator's for Gilberte and Albertine, a structure of which a more primitive form had already appeared in *Jean Santeuil*. Hardy's view of love, according to which we pursue not a person, but a fleeting image of our own creation which is the same in all objects of our desire, was equally Proustian . . . *The Well-Beloved*, together with *Jude the Obscure* and *A Pair of Blue Eyes*, remained in Proust's mind throughout the writing of his novel.[12]

As Painter also notes, Proust would bring Hardy to the fore again, in the late pages of *The Captive*, where, in a conversation between Marcel and his mistress Albertine, Hardy appears, this time in the distinguished company of Dostoevsky and Stendhal, as an example of a master novelist who wrote and rewrote 'a single work' expressive of a unique beauty that he and he alone brought into this world. This passage is a revision of Proust's note of some fifteen years before on *The Well-Beloved*, *Jude* and *Blue Eyes*, quoted above (pp. 112–13). But in the novel it is made part of the one-sided conversation between Marcel and his vacillatory, enigmatic Albertine, the second of his great loves. Though the passage is always mentioned by critics interested in Proust's use of Hardy, it is usually treated as an isolated allusion. Little or no attention has been given to its function in Marcel's and Albertine's history.[13] This episode is more, however, than a passing allusion. It deserves to be seen for its dramatic significance because Proust makes it quite clear that Albertine has been reading the novels of Hardy and others while residing in Marcel's apartment in Paris, reading in fact while Marcel sleeps. Proust makes it equally clear that

Marcel speaks to Albertine about Hardy (as well as Dostoevsky) when he is on the threshold of two of the most crucial events of his own life: the commencement of his own literary career (his first article in *Figaro* is soon to appear); and the sudden flight (and death) of Albertine, in part because of Marcel's suspicion that she has taken lesbian lovers.

The acceptance by *Figaro*, is, of course, the beginning of the career in letters Marcel has long sought. The flight and death of Albertine cast Marcel adrift, free him on the one hand to move before the urging of his genius, confirm him on the other in his essential isolation, in his growing perception that all human love is laced with treachery, and in his deepening understanding that time is a process of decay that only art can reverse. In sum, Albertine's death forces Marcel to embrace and declare his vocation as a writer of timeless narrative, narrative in which the past can be recovered – that fading past associated with his grandmother and mother, his native Combray, the steeples of Martinville, and the tea and madeleine served him by his Aunt Léonie. Proust here calls upon, in a sense appeals to, Hardy – author of a narrative strongly resembling his own – at that moment in Marcel's career when Marcel finally realizes that love for a woman is not the timeless solace he needs and seeks.

One is naturally led to wonder if Marcel's remarks about Hardy at this crucial moment in *his* life do not reflect the circumstances surrounding Proust's reading of Hardy between 1906, when Blanche urged him to read *Jude*, and January 1910, when he wrote Robert de Billy about his admiration for *The Well-Beloved*.[14] These important years in Proust's creative life had been ushered in by the death of his father in November 1903, and of his mother two years later. After six weeks (December 1905 – January 1906) in a nursing home at Boulogne-sur-Seine, he began in autumn 1907 the reclusive nocturnal existence at 102, Boulevard Haussmann, that was to continue for another dozen years. His sexual relationships, which before this time had involved both men and women of the upper classes, now took the form of homosexual relations with young men of the working classes (Alfred Agostinelli entered Proust's life in August 1907). In January 1907 his reflections on his treatment of his doting mother over the years were poured into the essay 'The Filial Feelings of a Matricide', in which by arguing the universal nature of the matricidal impulse he in a sense countenances the actual murder (in Paris) of a mother by her son. In late 1907 Proust revisited Cabourg, the resort he had visited with his mother some years before, and while there was nearly prostrate with sorrow for the loss of his companion and comforter of many years. In 1908, through the writing of *Against Sainte-Beuve* and his attack there on Sainte-Beuve's practice of assessing a writer's work by the facts of his life and character, he sought to clear the path for the autobiographical *Remembrance*. A book, Proust insisted, in a highly tenuous argument, is the product of a self other than the one the writer reveals in his habits, vices and social affiliations. (One thinks of D. H. Lawrence attempting about this same time, to lay the ghost of maternal influence in *Sons and Lovers*, and attempting to open the way to *The Rainbow* through the writing of the highly irreverent *Study of Thomas Hardy*.) In January 1909 occurred the eating of the toast and tea that wakened Proust's recollection of the garden at Auteuil, nearly thirty years before, where he, as a child, had been served a similar repast. In July 1909 Proust began to write *Remembrance of Things Past*.

These were some of the major events, personal and literary, surrounding Proust's reading of Hardy – *Jude* in 1906 at Blanche's urging, 'A Tragedy of Two Ambitions' in 1908, *The Well-Beloved* in late 1909 or early 1910, *A Pair of Blue Eyes* later in 1910. As has been suggested, what reading Hardy provided Proust at this important juncture of his career was the example of another novelist, a much-praised novelist, who had exhibited in fiction states of feeling much like those Proust felt compelled to exhibit in his emerging novel. It may even be the case that Hardy's interlocking narratives acted as a catalyst. In this connection a paragraph from Painter's meticulous record of Proust's progress toward *Remembrance* is worth quoting here in full:

> All the material of his novel had long been available to him. He had known its characters and experienced its plot – except for certain episodes which were still in the unknown future – in a period of his life which was now long past. He had even written it twice, in *Jean Santeuil* and in the novel of 1905–7 [now lost], and much of it (counting the new draft of 1908 and *Contre Sainte-Beuve*) four times over. But the identity of the last catalyst, which would fuse the whole and crystallize its meaning, its metaphysic and its secret structure, remained an impenetrable mystery. The story he had told so often could only display the vanity of human desire; it could only tell the terrible half-truth, that desire

is vain not because it is frustrated but because it is fulfilled, and the people and places we love turn to ashes when we possess them. Comparison between *A la Recherche* and the fruitless efforts of Proust's past twenty years of ceaseless writing will show the nature of the revelation which came to him in July 1909. In *A la Recherche*, although he mapped the desert of experience more bitterly and minutely than ever before, he showed that it leads, except for those who stay in it, to the recovery of innocence, that the joy of our vision is not cancelled by the disillusion of its attainment, that the truth of salvation everywhere underlies the truth of sin and despair. Proust had entered, at last and once for all, into Time Regained.[15]

It is altogether plausible that Proust's reading of Hardy, particularly of *The Well-Beloved* in 1909–1910, contributed significantly to the crystallization of *Remembrance* of which Painter writes – not only because of the striking similarity of form but also because of the even more striking difference of viewpoint. For Hardy's people there is no time regained, no recovery of innocence. In *A Pair of Blue Eyes*, the sacrifice of Elfride to Knight's puritan conscience is irreparable. In *Jude the Obscure*, the sacrifice of Jude to his own idealism, to Arabella's brutal sensuality and to Sue Bridehead's epicenism is beyond correction. In 'A Tragedy of Two Ambitions', the death of the drunken father as a result of his respectable sons' refusal to rescue him from drowning cannot be undone. And, in *The Well-Beloved*, Pierston's return to his natal place and attempt to resume there his love for Marcia, the first incarnation of his well-beloved, is doomed to failure. And with that failure to recover the ideal in the actual comes the failure and death of Pierston's art. Proust cannot, Marcel cannot, embrace this harshness, this grim sense of the unique, unreturning nature of things. At the same time, the adventures of Hardy's nympholepts – Knight, Sue Bridehead, and especially Pierston – fascinated Proust, as they apparently fascinate Marcel and Albertine.

Marcel's remarks about Hardy in *The Captive* do seem then to reflect some of the circumstances surrounding Proust's reading of Hardy between 1906 and 1910, and perhaps the key to this parallel is in Marcel's use of Hardy (and other novelists) to define narrative genius and thereby define his own devotion to the writing of narrative. If art – not society, not human love – is to be Marcel's salvation and home, then the importance of preparing himself for that vocation is evident. He does it here through reference to Hardy, Dostoevsky and others, and elsewhere in the novel through contact with the actress Berma, the painter Elstir, the novelist Bergotte, and the composer Vinteuil. Marcel (and Proust) evidently found in Hardy's fiction something strongly congenial to him. It was not what Lawrence, for example, would find: men and women struggling against the powers of an indifferent universe. Nor is it what Powys would find: a spirit out of Stonehenge and other ancient places impregnating his soul with dark mystery. Proust found, instead, the transformation of a sexual nostalgia similar to his own into narrative strategies resembling those he was in process of discovering.

Speaking to Albertine of the music of Vinteuil, the music he had first heard as a boy at Combray and been haunted by ever since, Marcel attempts to describe 'the mode by which [Vinteuil] "heard" the universe and projected it far beyond himself'.[16] The best he can offer Albertine in this difficult task is analogies. The pleasure derived from hearing Vinteuil, Marcel says, is like 'the peculiar pleasure which I had felt at certain moments in my life, when gazing, for instance, at the steeples of Martinville, or at certain trees along a road near Balbec, or, more simply, at the beginning of this book, when I tasted a certain cup of tea' (*RTP*, III, 381). Fearing perhaps that Albertine does not understand this analogy, Marcel presses yet another on her: the sounds and colours sent us by Vinteuil 'for the world in which he composed' resembled 'something that I might compare to the perfumed silkiness of a geranium' (ibid.). Still not satisfied that he has fully explained, Marcel turns to examples of other artists, Hardy among them; for Albertine, he knows, has been reading Hardy. As noted above, his remark is a revision of a note of 1908 on Hardy's novels:

> Another example of Vinteuil's key-phrases is that stone-mason's geometry in the novels of Thomas Hardy. . . .
> . . . Do you remember the stonemasons in *Jude the Obscure*, and in *The Well-Beloved* the blocks of stone which the father hews out of the island coming in boats to be piled up in the son's workshop where they are turned into statues; and in *A Pair of Blue Eyes* the parallelism of the tombs, and also the parallel line of the boat and the nearby railway coaches containing the lovers and the dead woman; and the parallel between *The Well-*

Beloved, where the man loves three women, and *A Pair of Blue Eyes*, where the woman loves three men, and in short all those novels which can be superimposed on one another like the houses piled up vertically on the rocky soil of the island.
(*RTP*, III, 382–3)

Hardy's 'stone-mason's geometry', like Stendhal's 'certain sense of altitude symbolizing the life of the spirit' and like the 'Dostoievski woman . . . with her mysterious face', is the identifying quality in *all* Hardy's novels because in essence 'the great men of letters have never created more than a single work, or rather have never done more than refract through various media an identical beauty which they bring into the world' (III, 382).

Not only did Proust use Hardy to illustrate his theory of the essential likeness of all the works of any great artist, but, as Painter has pointed out, he also employed certain themes of *The Well-Beloved* in *Remembrance*, particularly at the Duchesse de Guermantes's *matinée* (in *Time Regained*). Marcel suddenly realizes that he has aged, much as Hardy's Pierston does when he sees his wrinkled face in a mirror. Like Marcel before he feels the uneven paving-stones beneath his feet, Pierston, for whom there can be no recovery of time past, finds it impossible, in Hardy's words, to 'attach a definite sentiment to images of beauty revealed from the past'. Marcel mistakes Gilberte for her mother, Odette, just as Pierston mistakes Avice the second for Avice the first, or Avice the third for Avice the second. Odette's attempt to preserve the appearance of youth, like Marcia Bencomb's in *The Well-Beloved*, is the result of 'beautifying artifices'. Gilberte's offer to introduce her daughter, Odette's granddaughter, to Marcel, recalls Avice the second's saying to Pierston of Avice the third, 'I wish you would speak to her – I'm sure you would like her.'[17] At the same *matinée*, Marcel sees standing side by side Odette, Gilberte and Mlle de Saint-Loup, the mother and daughter he has loved and the granddaughter he will come to love. Alongside these three beloveds the reader is inclined to place – so insistent is this novel's passion for parallels and repetitions – Marcel's grandmother, mother and Albertine, equally beloved by him. The reader, with Marcel, observes yet another parallel in Saint-Loup's love for Rachel, then for Gilberte, then for Morel; and in Charlus's love for Jupien, Morel and many another young man; and in Albertine's love for Marcel, Andrée and others. The repetitions of love seem endless in *Remembrance* for, as not in Hardy, they can be heterosexual, as in the case of Marcel; homosexual, as in the case of Charlus; or bisexual, as in the case of Saint-Loup, Morel and Albertine.

This brings us to consideration of Albertine's apparent reading of Hardy while Marcel sleeps. One must assume, since Marcel speaks of *Jude* to Albertine, that she has read this novel, whose heroine, Sue Bridehead, bears certain resemblances to her. Hardy himself had described Sue, quite accurately, in a letter of 1895, as sexually abnormal in a certain sense: 'there is nothing perverted or depraved in Sue's nature. The abnormalism consists of disproportion, not in inversion, her sexual instinct being healthy so far as it goes, but unusually weak and fastidious.'[18] Albertine is of course attracted to both men and women as lovers. When Proust has Albertine read *Jude* while Marcel sleeps, he has her contemplate the career of another young woman struggling to live an unconventional passional life, and a young woman attached, as she herself is attached, to a man much tormented by her sexual impulses and his own. Proust has Albertine contemplate, or invites his reader to imagine her contemplating, the fact that Sue, like her, lives a tragic existence, one in which defect, the defect of inversion, or epicenism, for example, is visited upon a person within a society strongly intolerant toward it. And for Albertine, as for Sue, there is no hope of recovery or cure. Albertine would also have sympathized with Sue's plight as a virtual orphan seeking to support and advance herself by her talents. Albertine too is an orphan, and Marcel is her hope, much as Phillotson and Jude are Sue's. Albertine is rejected by Marcel for her lesbianism just as Sue is finally alienated from Phillotson and Jude by her unconventional, vacillatory, ideas about love and marriage. Albertine's throwing her window up in the middle of the night shortly before she flees from Marcel recalls Sue's leap from the window of Phillotson's house, where she too is a prisoner, even though (indeed because) she is Phillotson's wife. When Albertine reads *A Pair of Blue Eyes*, one imagines her finding that Elfride Swancourt, like her, cannot please the man she loved and is consequently driven to other lovers and eventually to her death. When Albertine reads *The Well-Beloved*, she can be imagined learning that she, like any one of Jocelyn Pierston's beloveds, is but one in a series of loves for Marcel – before her, Gilberte (with whom she also has been intimate), the Duchesse de Guermantes, and the many nameless girls whom the yearning Marcel pursues obsessively. In short, if Albertine is depraved and at times ruthless in her depravity, she is also fatally driven, the victim of desires she cannot control. Albertine is the prisoner of Marcel, to be sure, but she is no less the prisoner of her own sexual degeneracy and therefore, like Sue Bridehead, a tragic and sympathetic figure. Like Lawrence's Ursula and Gudrun Brangwen, like Powys's Christie Malakite, Proust's Albertine cannot easily love a man. To suppose Albertine reflecting on Hardy's novels in this way is not so whimsical as it may seem; for, as Walter A. Strauss has pointed out, Proust was a literary critic of astonishing sensitivity who discovered his own narrative manner through the writing of pastiches. Literary allusion and analysis such as one finds in this episode in *The Captive* is integral to Proust's narrative pattern and his characterizations. Proust, as Strauss says, 'uses literary references frequently to "deepen" his characters'.[19]

It seems fair to say that Proust's use of Hardy, particularly of *The Well-Beloved*, was both a matter of discovery and imitation and of having existing tendencies stirred and encouraged. In both *Pleasures and Days* and *Jean Santeuil*, which Proust wrote before he read *The Well-Beloved*, the idea of subjective love is present: the 'passionate adoration of a particular beloved, inevitably followed by "l'indifférence et l'oubli", followed as inevitably by adoration of another, and the repetition, in recurring phases, of the process'.[20] And in Hardy Proust found associated with the idea of subjective love a characteristic Proustian sentiment: that time destroys love. 'Love frequently dies of time alone – much more frequently of displacement', Hardy had written in the first sentence of chapter 27 of *A Pair of Blue Eyes*.

It seems highly probably, as L. A. Bisson has argued, that between 1914 and 1922 Proust incorporated into *Remembrance* some of these Hardyan elements. Proust's description of the aging Duc de Guermantes, a late addition to *Time Regained*, may derive from *The Well-Beloved*.[21] A passage from *Within a Budding Grove* echoes a passage in *Jude*:

On construit sa vie pour une personne et quand enfin on peut l'y recevoir, cette personne ne vient pas, puis meurt pour vous et on vit prisonnier dans ce qui n'était destiné qu'à elle.[22]

Somebody might have come along that way who would have asked him his trouble, and might have cheered him by saying that his notions were further advanced than those of his grammarian. But nobody did come, because nobody does; and under the crushing recognition of his gigantic error Jude continued to wish himself out of the world. (*JO*, pt III, ch. 4)

Bisson suggests that another passage in *Within a Budding Grove* may contain an oblique reference to Hardy ('un romancier') and *The Well-Beloved* ('la vie de son heros'):

> Si, en ce goût de divertissement Albertine avait quelque chose de la Gilberte des premiers temps, c'est qu'une certaine ressemblance existe tout en évoluant, entre les femmes que nous aimons successivement, ressemblance qui tient à la fixité de notre tempérament parce que c'est lui qui les choisit, éliminant toutes celles qui ne nous seraient pas à la fois opposées et complémentaires, c'est-à-dire propres à satisfaire nos sens et à faire souffrir notre coeur. Elles sont ces femmes, un produit de notre tempérament, une image, une projection renversée, un négatif de notre sensibilité. De sorte qu'un romancier pourrait au cours de la vie de son héros, peindre presque exactement semblables ses successives amours, et donner par là l'impression non de s'imiter lui-même mais de créer, puisqu'il y a moins de force dans une innovation artificielle que dans une répétition destinée à suggérer une vérité neuve.[23]

Two interpolations in *Time Regained* on the theme of subjective love strengthen the view that *The Well-Beloved*, *Jude the Obscure* and *A Pair of Blue Eyes* were before Proust as he wrote and revised *Remembrance*:

> L'amour nous montre la beauté fuyant la femme que nous n'aimons plus et venant résider dan le visage que les autres trouveraient le plus laid. . . . Mon étonnement à chaque fois que j'avais revu aux Champs-Élysées, dans la rue, sur la plage, le visage de Gilberte, de Madame de Guermantes, d'Albertine, ne prouvait-il pas combien un souvenir ne se prolonge que dans une direction divergente de l'impression avec laquelle il a coincidé d'abord de laquelle il s'éloigne de plus en plus.
>
> Si notre amour n'est pas seulement d'une Gilberte, ce n'est pas parce qu'il est aussi l'amour d'une Albertine, mais parce qu'il

est une portion de notre âme plus durable que les mois divers qui meurent successivement en nous.[24]

Though parallels and echoes such as these are not irrefutable evidence of Hardy's influence, it is difficult, in the words of Bisson, 'to resist the conclusion that the finding of a kindred perception in a living English novelist strengthened Proust's consciousness of his particular strand in the queer web of human destiny'. Bisson even suggests that in his last years of concentrated work on his masterpiece Proust took on some of Hardy's pessimism and endowed his Marcel with some of Jude Fawley's frustration.

P. E. Robert, advancing the work of Bisson and Painter, describes yet other parallels between Proust and Hardy.[25] Noting Proust's powerful attraction to Hardy's use of repetition and parallelism, Robert also suggests there are similarities between Hardy's views on friendship in *A Pair of Blue Eyes* and Proust's in *The Guermantes Way*. The troubled relationship between Stephen Smith and Henry Knight, like that between Marcel and Saint-Loup, illustrates, in Robert's view, the disenchantment with friendship of both Proust and Hardy. In *The Well-Beloved*, in Jocelyn Pierston's sequestering of Avice the second in his London apartment, Robert sees a parallel with Marcel's 'capture' of Albertine; and Avice's admission to Pierston that she had had other lovers recalls for Robert Albertine's similar admission to Marcel. In *Jude*, in the young Jude Fawley's admiration for the schoolmaster Phillotson, Robert detects a parallel to the young Marcel's attraction to Swann. Marcel's pursuit of Gilberte and Albertine repeats Swann's pursuit of Odette, just as Jude's pursuit of Sue repeats Phillotson's pursuit of Sue. One episode from *Jude* Robert believes has been wholly transposed in *Remembrance:* Arabella's neglect and desertion of the dying Jude so that she can attend the Remembrance Day festivities 'becomes' the Duc de Guermantes's refusal to acknowledge the death of a cousin in order that he can return to a ball.

Robert, Bisson and Painter might have added that Proust, for all his interest in *The Well-Beloved*, must have been encouraged by the slightness of Hardy's novel. Pierston's search is schematic to a fault, Hardy's attitude toward Pierston wavers between sympathy and scorn, and, perhaps most important, Hardy – out of fear of the Grundyites – was less than candid in his presentation of his central theme of subjective love. Hardy did not practise the candour of Proust in his treatment of abnormal states of emotion.

In short, if Proust found *Remembrance* anticipated in *The Well-Beloved*, he also found *The Well-Beloved*, by his own standard, a pale approximation of a novel depicting the pursuit of Ideal Love. 'Une tres belle chose qui ressemble . . . *un tant petit peu* . . . a ce que je fais' – these are the words he had used in his letter to Billy (italics added). Hardy's treatment of the idea – given not just his fear of the censors but his reluctance to work openly the autobiographical vein inseparable from the idea – lacks 'the note of acutely felt and personal experience' found in Proust's treatment of it. Hardy's exhibition of love in *The Well-Beloved* never gets beyond the theoretical; Proust's treatment of love, even when most theoretical, is always, one feels, expressly personal. Also, as suggested by the enormous difference in length between *Remembrance* and *The Well-Beloved*, Proust's treatment is much more analytic; for Proust the life of the human spirit in search of its emotional home is 'a key to the whole life and death of the affections'.[26] With Hardy, Pierston's way of loving is merely one possibility, one expression of his [Hardy's] tentative, impressionistic way of viewing things. Hardy was ever divided between the wholehearted loving of a Gabriel Oak, Giles Winterborne or Tess Durbeyfield, and the intellectual love of a Henry Knight, Sue Bridehead or Jocelyn Pierston.

If Proust found in *The Well-Beloved* an intention and design markedly similar to his own in *Remembrance*, he also – when he contemplated the parallels between *The Well-Beloved*, *Blue Eyes* and *Jude* – discovered something else: an awareness of the characteristics of both sexes expressive of a sexual temperament much like his own. This is in part the purpose of his request in the letter to Robert de Billy (p. 112 above) that Billy approach his English colleague at Tangiers for information about the private life of Hardy, 'apparently wondering', remarks Painter, whether Hardy shared 'his two intellectual vices': society and women. But, as Painter remarks elsewhere, Proust also had a hobby of collecting information on 'all the prominent, undiscovered inverts of Europe', and he frequently appealed for aid in this to his old schoolmate de Billy, 'who assisted him in this hobby with inside information gained in his career as a diplomat'.[27] Pierston's express preference for intellectual over carnal love in *The Well-Beloved* probably led Proust to wonder about Hardy's private preference. And Proust's curiosity here about the temperament behind the work is the basis for his own and his narrator's interest in 'the parallelism between *The*

Well-Beloved, where the hero loves three women, and *A Pair of Blue Eyes*, where the heroine loves three men'. Like Lawrence and Powys at about this same time, Proust found in the novels of Hardy a bisexual awareness unusual in the fiction of the day. In his circumspect way, Hardy was exhibiting in his fiction the for-the-time revolutionary idea that male and female sexual behaviour can be remarkably similar. As he had remarked in an essay of 1894, 'the spider is not invariably male and the fly invariably female'. Jacques Émile Blanche, the painter of both Hardy's and Proust's portraits who in 1906 recommended to Proust that he read *Jude the Obscure*, had noted a similar phenomenon in *Remembrance:* 'It seems to me that sometimes, and in your most beautiful pages, you borrow from one sex the features of the other; that in certain of your characters there is a partial substitution of gender, so that one might read "he" where you say "she".'[28] As Proust knew, much the same was true in *Blue Eyes*, *Jude* and *The Well-Beloved*. Thus an Elfride Swancourt, in her love for three men, is to Proust's delight, a female version of Pierston in his love for three women, just as Albertine is a female version of Morel or Saint-Loup in her interest in persons of both sexes. If Proust had read Hardy's *Tess* (translated, like *Jude*, in 1901) he would have discovered an even more remarkable example of sexual transposition in Hardy's work: Alec ruining Tess on the one hand, and Arabella ruining Jude on the other; Tess seeking redemption through love of the fastidious Angel on the one hand, Jude seeking renewal through love for the epicene Sue on the other. If for Lawrence '*Jude* is *Tess* turned roundabout', then for Proust *The Well-Beloved* was *A Pair of Blue Eyes* turned roundabout.

Proust's interest in Hardy was, it seems, a temperamental as well as a purely literary one. Proust possibly caught glimpses of himself as well as of his literary designs in Hardy, and perhaps this was so because Proust, already a lover of English literature when he first read Hardy, discovered in him a nostalgic idealism akin to his own. Proust's and Hardy's interest in subjective love may derive from an emotional conviction that the best, happiest times were the forever-lost times of their childhoods, childhoods coloured for both by powerfully affectionate, protective and intellectual mothers. Hardy, like Proust, was born after a difficult labour, and again like Proust was a delicate, in many ways a sheltered, first child and elder son. Hardy did not begin school until he was eight, and Proust at age nine had suffered the first attack of the asthma that would plague him to the end. Women were numerous and prominent figures in the early years of both: Proust's maternal grandmother, the servants Françoise and Ernestine, as well as Mme Jeanne Weil Proust; Hardy's paternal grandmother and maternal aunt, as well as Jemima Hardy, her nieces in the Sparks family a few miles away, and Lady Augusta Martin, the childless mistress of the local manor house, who doted on Hardy and with whom Hardy remained infatuated until he was well into his thirties. Both Mme Proust and Mrs Hardy had strong literary tastes that they passed on to their sons: Mme Proust's devotion to the writings of Mme de Sévigné recalls Jemima Hardy's love of *The Divine Comedy*. Both boys were devoted to music and painting as well as to literature, and the kinship between the arts became a distinctive element of their literary styles. Both were less drawn to their active, virile fathers than to their mothers; and both were deeply attached to the countryside surrounding the places of their earliest experiences: Hardy to the heath and woodlands that he transformed into the Mellstock of *Under the Greenwood Tree* and the Egdon Heath of *The Return of the Native*; Proust to the gardens of Auteuil and Illiers, the regions that became Combray in *Remembrance of Things Past*. Each was deeply attached to the sibling born immediately after him: Proust to his brother Robert, Hardy to his devoted sister Mary; and both seem to have struggled with a sense of illicit affection for this sibling. The argument has been made that Proust's homosexuality stems in part from his repressed affection for his brother.[29] That Hardy may have transferred his devotion to his mother unto his sister, and then unto a long line of other beloveds, has been suggested by Robert Gittings in his recent life of Hardy. Gittings argues that Hardy, much like his own Jocelyn Pierston, loved in succession his three maternal first cousins, Martha, Rebecca and Tryphena Sparks, all of whom bore a striking resemblance to Jemima Hardy. Hardy, like Proust, fell in love easily and frequently throughout his life. If Pierston–Hardy's pursuit of the well-beloved through three generations of the Caro family resembles Hardy's attachment to a mother image traceable in three cousins, then Marcel's pursuit of an elusive affection through his mother and grandmother, the Duchesse de Guermantes, Odette and her daughter Gilberte, Albertine, and Mlle de Saint-Loup (daughter of Gilberte), as well as through many other, unnamed, women, resembles Proust's own situation after 1886. As George Painter has shown, from age fifteen on, life for Proust was a kaleidoscope of loves.[30]

In *Nostalgia: A Psychoanalytic Study of Marcel Proust*, Dr Milton M. Miller, noting that Proust's nostalgia 'provides the matrix of his work', suggests that the same was true of Hardy and that *The Well-Beloved*, like *Remembrance*, is an expression of a 'man's search for a lost mother-image in three generations'. In 'the clarity of Hardy's story', Miller argues, 'Proust recognized a directness which the vagaries of his own book's roundabout search for a return to a past happiness did not permit'. Miller continues,

> Both Hardy and Proust make very clear in their novels . . . that a man's deepest love may very well be for a nostalgic phantom which inhabits the bodies of a series of individuals and provides artistic inspiration. . . . Ultimately, Proust and Hardy conveyed many of the same impressions: that our emotional paths are laid out to follow because of past events which are veiled from consciousness. Freud explored the role of the unconscious in determining human behaviour and the development of insight as related, not to aesthetics, but to therapy. Proust and Hardy indicated awareness of oedipal forces, as a result of their aesthetic sensibilities.[31]

Miller has identified several shared techniques and themes deriving from this common concern: the use of spying as a narrative device; the interest in a love carried on over several generations of the same family; the background and symbolism of the sea in both *Remembrance* and *Well-Beloved* ('coloring those loves with a regressive element'); and the connection between 'the original incestuous love . . . and . . . the wellsprings of artistic talent'.[32]

Proust and Hardy are nympholepts, pursuers through their fictional art of 'the unattainable Perfect in female form'.[33] And both are, in their nympholepsy, nostalgic idealists: the feminine ideal they pursue, because first perceived in the mother, is associated with a childhood felicity and an Edenic locale – the gardens at Illiers and Auteuil that became Combray, the tiny isolated community between woodland and heath that became Mellstock and Egdon. This pursuit of the well-beloved, of a lost joy and innocence, exacts of both the repeated discovery of a trace of the Original in each copy, of Love in the abstract in love for a particular woman, or man. The prominence of repetition, re-enactment, parallelism, the fondness for the 'anniversarial' occasional in their novels are perhaps explainable by their failure – more complete presumably in Proust than in Hardy – to separate themselves from the mother-ideal, with the result an inescapable pattern of feeling, projected in the form of their novels, that forces 'every important subsequent step . . . to be taken in the same terms, with the same strategy as that which first failed, no matter how inconsistent'.[34]

If Proust's vision is more unified and more intensely focused than Hardy's – since Proust exhibits the career of a single character in his quest for transcendence through love and art – the similarities that certain of Hardy's most important characters bear to one another suggest that, like Proust, Hardy was telling and retelling the same story, refracting through his stories of Wessex life a beauty he brought into the world. With the career of Marcel in mind, one sees new significance in Hardy's return again and again in his novels to the problem of a hampered sexuality: not just in Jocelyn Pierston of *The Well-Beloved*, but also in Henry Knight of *A Pair of Blue Eyes* and Angel Clare of *Tess*, men who ruthlessly condemn the impurity they find in the woman they love; in Farmer Boldwood of *Far from the Madding Crowd*, a man traumatized by the display of aggressive female sexuality at work behind Bathsheba Everdene's proposal of marriage via a playful valentine; in Clym Yeobright of *The Return of the Native*, a homecomer who cannot reconcile the conflicting claims on him of wife and mother; in Edred Fitzpiers of *The Woodlanders*, a wolf in the sheep's clothing of a platonic lover; in Sue Bridehead of *Jude*, a woman who can love three men but has no taste for the love of a man. With the exception of Fitzpiers and Pierston, all are victims of their repressed sexuality and become, as a result, victimizers of others. Their thwarted sexuality is the source of the emotional cruelty they inflict on those they love or would love. Knight's insistence that he be the first in Elfride's affections destroys Elfride, just as Clare's fanatical love of purity destroys Tess. Boldwood explodes into violence when the woman who had disturbed his monklike existence gives her affection to another man. Clym's neglect of Eustacia drives her toward adultery and then to her death. Sue's inability to give herself to Jude drives him to drink, back to the bed of Arabella, and eventually to a self-induced death. The imposition of motherhood on Sue is also, of course, the certain, albeit the indirect, cause of the death of her children.

Pierston and Fitzpiers differ from these others in that they translate sexual impulses into philosophical and artistic terms. Fitzpiers is a comic version of this, for he is merely justifying his philandering when he mouths sentiments about subjective love from Shelley, Swinburne and Schopenhauer.

Pierston is a more refined, more subtle, Fitzpiers. A genuine artist, he sees that the matrix of his art is his hopeless love for an ideal that flits from one member of the Caro family to another. And, like Proust's Marcel, Pierston's compulsive loving is tied to recollections of his natal place: Pierston's Isle of Slingers is Marcel's Combray. Pierston (as his name suggests) shapes the stone of his native isle; Marcel shapes the human histories of his native Combray and its two ways. In the end, Pierston returns to his native isle just as Marcel returns to Tansonville, as the guest of Gilberte, now the wife of Saint-Loup. For Proust, as has been noted, return is as nothing beside recollection, for, where return reveals that change is decay, recollection is re-creation – reinstatement of the sounds, tastes and sights of things as they once were. The human mind is for Proust (as it was for John Cowper Powys) a preserver and redeemer of things past, an enemy to time passing, in a way it was not for Hardy or his Pierston. Pierston's return to the Isle of Slingers and his reunion there with an aged Marcia (an old lover contemporary with Avice the first) is also the death of his art. Marcel's recollection of time past is also the *recovery* of time past, and with that recovery his art is born, his vocation as novelist confirmed.[35]

Proust finally parted ways with Hardy for much the same reason Moore, Lawrence and Powys found him difficult – unease with what each saw as Hardy's pessimism, an attitude rooted in Hardy's stubborn belief that all decays. By no stretch of the imagination is Proust an optimist about human nature or the human condition. Cruelty, selfishness, loneliness, greed and depravity abound, and even prevail, in the world of his novel; and his conviction that this is rooted in the nature of things is as strong as Hardy's. The Duc de Guermantes cannot bear to miss a party simply because a cousin is dying. The actress Rachel revels in the humiliation that time has forced upon the aging Berma. Morel and Albertine collaborate in the procuring of virgins: he to deflower them, she then to initiate them into the ways of Sappho. Marcel's love for various women, as he comes to see, is not in the ordinary sense love at all. It is, rather, like the homosexuality of Charlus, an unhappy expression of an unconscious urging. The lovingkindness or the sanity of traditional ways that endures and even prevails in Hardy's Wessex has no counterpart in Marcel's world. The servant Françoise, for example, a figure who in a novel by Hardy might be found to be a repository of traditional wisdom, is as cruel and designing as her betters. However, in the face of all this, Proust can assert with conviction that through art the artist (and his audience) can transcend the defective actualities of the world, can recognize and embrace the unchanging, the beautiful and the true. This is Proust's astonishing faith, and, if it seems incongruous beside the grim realities of his portrait of a depraved and heartless French society, it is genuine – though strikingly different from Hardy's view of a wholly unredeemable world, in which by inexorable law *all* decays, including that art of the world's greatest artists. What survives in Hardy is what he values above art – that is, humanity and certain human powers: endurance, patience, humour, acceptance, and, finally, perception of that severe beauty emanating from the truth that all decays. Hardy's attempt to formulate a philosophic optimism – the evolutionary meliorism of *The Dynasts* (1903–8) – was slowly achieved and quickly killed. It did not survive the First World War. Proust's faith in art did survive the war that devastated his native land. Faced with Hardy's stern judgement on things, Proust could embrace the preserving and redeeming powers of art, which were for him, as he said in a famous passage in *Time Regained*, 'a faithful recomposing of life', the 'only means of recapturing the past', and the beauteous container of life's truths. Hardy allowed no comparable relief. If Proust opted for art, Hardy chose tragic humanity. Among Hardy's legatees, only Henri Alain-Fournier (and Theodore Dreiser, as shall be seen) seemed able to adopt his tragic view of things.

Before leaving Proust to examine the debt of Alain-Fournier to Hardy, it is worth noting Hardy's awareness of Proust's debt to him, both because Proust is the only one of his 'disciples' Hardy openly acknowledged, and because Hardy suggested an origin – in the poetry of Swinburne – for the androgynous awareness Proust valued in *The Well-Beloved*, *Jude* and *Blue Eyes*. Writing sometime after 1917 of the attack by reviewers on *The Well-Beloved* in 1897, Hardy described his last novel as a 'fantastic tale of a subjective idea . . . exemplified also by Proust many years later', the 'theory of the transmigration of the ideal beloved one, who only exists in the lover, from material woman to material woman' (*Life*, p. 286). In July 1926, three years after publication of Proust's *The Captive* in France, Hardy made the following note:

> It appears that the theory exhibited in *The Well-Beloved* in 1892 has since been developed by Proust still further:
>
> 'Peu de personnes comprennent le caractère purement subjectif du phénomène qu'est l'amour, et la sorte de création que c'est d'une personne supplémentaire, distincte de celle qui porte le même nom dans le monde, et dont la plupart des elements sont tirés de nous-mêmes' (*Ombre*, i.40).
>
> 'Le désir s'élève, se satisfait, disparait – et c'est tout. Ainsi, la jeune fille qu'on épouse n'est pas celle dont on est tombé amoureux' (*Ombre*, ii.158, 159).   (*Life*, p. 432)[36]

The length of Hardy's entry about Proust suggests he was pleased by the thought of having influenced him, in part because such influence was an implicit rebuke to the taste of reviewers who had scoffed at *The Well-Beloved* in 1897. Almost triumphantly, and not altogether inaccurately, Hardy attributes to himself 'the introduction of the subjective theory of love into modern fiction' and traces its presence in his own fiction to his reading of Swinburne. Hardy does not state explicitly that Swinburne was his mentor in this. Rather, he places immediately after his remarks on Proust the words of a letter he had written Swinburne about *The Well-Beloved* in April 1897. Though never stated, a line of descent from Swinburne to Hardy to Proust is being strongly implied here. Hardy's letter is worth quoting in full, for it extends farther back into English literature the sources of Proust's masterpiece. It is also an interesting addition to the literature of literary influence:

> I must thank you for your kind note about my fantastic little tale, which, if it can make, in its better parts, any faint claim to imaginative feeling, will owe something of such feeling to you, for I often thought of lines of yours during the writing; & indeed, was not able to resist the quotation of your words now & then.
> And this reminds me that one day, when examining several English imitations of a well-known fragment of Sappho, I inter-

ested myself in trying to strike out a better equivalent for it than the commonplace 'Thou, too, shalt die' etc. which all the translators had used during the last hundred years. I then stumbled upon your 'Thee, too, the years shall cover', & all my spirit for poetic pains died out of me. Those few words present, I think, the finest *drama* of Death & Oblivion, so to speak, in our tongue. Having rediscovered this phrase, it carried me back to the buoyant time of 30 years ago, when I used to read your early works walking along the crowded London streets, to my imminent risk of being knocked down. . . .

P. S. I should have added that *The Well-Beloved* is a fanciful exhibition of the artistic nature, & has, I think, some little foundation in fact. I have been much surprised, & even grieved, by a ferocious review attributing an immoral quality to the tale. The writer's meaning is beyond me.   T.H.[37]

Hardy's placing himself and his 'fanciful exhibition of the artistic nature' between Swinburne and Proust in this way, his expression of interest in the lesbian poetess Sappho, and his (implicit) suggestion that there exists a line of development from Swinburne's poems, through his own last novel, to Proust's twentieth-century masterpiece (with its extensive treatment of sexual inversion) reveals his awareness of himself as a revolutionary in the depiction of love in fiction. Of course, he was also always eager to disclaim any such design or content in his novels.

For example, just one week before he wrote the letter to Swinburne, Hardy had written to Lewis Hind, editor of the *Academy*, refusing the invitation to reply to a hostile review of *The Well-Beloved* in the *World* several days earlier, a review which had condemned the novel as, in Hardy's phrase, 'sexual and disgusting'. Hardy defied 'any sane person to see immorality or impropriety in an applied Platonic Idea – a phantasmal narrative of the adventure of a Visionary Artist in pursuit of the unattainable Perfect in female form – a man repeatedly stated to be singularly free from animalism'.[38] This is disingenuous to an extreme, for Hardy, by openly associating himself from time to time with Swinburne, must have known that he was leaguing himself with a poet deemed, at least during his early career, immoral, improper and possessed by 'sex-mania'. We have seen that Hardy readily compared himself with Swinburne when *The Well-Beloved* was under attack. Even earlier, he had chosen to view critics' attacks on *Jude* as comparable in viciousness to critics' attacks on Swinburne's *Poems and Ballads* in the 1860s (*Life*, p. 270). He was as deeply flattered by Swinburne's praise of *Jude* as he was by his praise of *The Well-Beloved* (*Life*, pp. 270–1, 287). He visited Swinburne at Putney in June 1899, and again in June 1905, and at the time could chuckle with the aging poet over a remark Swinburne had discovered in a Scottish newspaper: 'Swinburne planteth, Hardy watereth, and Satan giveth the increase' (*Life*, p. 325). In the poem 'A Singer Asleep', Hardy's tribute at Swinburne's death in 1909, Hardy recalled his own reading of *Poems and Ballads* on 'that far morning of a summer day' (in London in the 1860s), praised the 'passionate pages of his [Swinburne's] earlier years' that had survived the 'brabble and roar' of Victorian detractors, and marked especially Swinburne's discipleship to Sappho, to the point even of imagining a ghostly reunion between the supreme poetess of lesbian passion and her 'Disciple warm and true'.

That Hardy knew that the treatment of the platonic Ideal in fiction was open to just the kind of interpretation made by the reviewer for the *World* is evident in yet another way. In *The Woodlanders* (1887), Hardy himself satirized Edred Fitzpiers for being a platonic pursuer of the ideal whose idealism is repeatedly undermined by his lust. In this novel Hardy actually anticipated the objections of his reviewer of a decade later by portraying Fitzpiers's intellectual love as nothing less that 'sex-mania' in disguise. Just as relentlessly as Pierston (or Marcel), Fitzpiers preys on woman after woman after woman. Unlike them, however, he is a potent lover, leaving one pregnant, one broken-hearted, one (his wife) enraged by his philandering, which he justifies with quotations from Shelley, Schopenhauer and Swinburne. Had Hardy thought of it, he might well have altered the remark from the Scottish paper he had chuckled over with Swinburne: 'Sappho planteth, Swinburne watereth, and Hardy and Proust give the increase.' As well, one might add, as Lawrence, Powys and Alain-Fournier.

I turn briefly to Alain-Fournier (born Henri-Alban Fournier in 1886) for two reasons. First, he was, like Proust, a French novelist deeply affected by Hardy, particularly by Hardy's treatment of love in *Tess* and *Jude*. In this, however, he differs instructively from Proust, who was attracted mainly by the form of certain of the

Wessex Novels, in particular the varying repetition of certain elements of that form. Second, he was to be (along with Hardy) an important influence on John Fowles (born 1926), himself a formidable novelist of love in its relation to art, and perhaps the most prominent disciple of Hardy among living English novelists. Fournier died on the battlefield near Verdun at the age of twenty-eight. This apart, his life, like Proust's, possesses a certain resemblance to Thomas Hardy's, a resemblance that may in part explain the strong and even determinative effect on him of *Tess* and *Jude*.

Fournier was born, like Hardy, in a rural home: the village of La Chapelle-d'Angillon in the Sologne, a quiet region of marshes, ponds, and decayed châteaux. He moved to Épineul, another village in the same region, while still a youth. Again like Hardy, he broke with the quiet of rural surroundings at a tender age. Just as Hardy by the age of sixteen had left the secluded cottage at Higher Bockhampton to work as an architect's assistant in Dorchester and then in London, Fournier by the age of thirteen had left his beloved village of Épineul for three years of study at the Lycée Voltaire in Paris, after which, in 1901, he entered training at Brest for a career in the navy. He was happy at neither school. Nor would he ever be happy when away from his native Sologne. Like Hardy, he belonged to the literate and rising peasantry. Hardy's mother, as has been noted, was unusually well-read for a woman of her station, and his father was a successful rural builder. Fournier's parents were both teachers in rural schools. As the first-born of their respective families, Hardy and Fournier were expected to excel and to rise out of their lower-middle stations. Possibly for this reason, both preserved to the end of their lives a powerful nostalgia for the closely knit family life of their early years and that life's associations with rural scenes and rural ways. Hardy built his permanent home (Max Gate) within walking-distance of his birthplace and family at Higher Bockhampton and maintained close ties to his family throughout his life; Fournier resided with his parents until his death. Each also had a loving and much beloved sister immediately his junior (Hardy's Mary and Fournier's Isabella) who was first playmate, then confidante and loyal admirer. The greatest fiction of both – like that of Proust – enacts a sense of loss connected with both the rural scene and certain youthful intimacies and innocences.

The rigours of Brest and the prospect of a naval career held little appeal for Fournier, and in 1903, without completing the training at Brest, he left to enter the Lycée Lakanal near Paris to prepare for admission to the exclusive École Normale Supérieure in Paris. After two years at the Lycée Lakanal, in the summer of 1905, he visited England, where he worked (in London) for a manufacturer of fabrics and at the same time studied to improve his English. At this time he read the novels of Wells, Kipling, Dickens and Hardy. Unlike Proust, who at about this same time was reading Hardy in French translation, Fournier read Hardy in English, as his letters to Jacques Rivière, a schoolmate at Lakanal, make clear. He turned to Hardy in 1905–6 at the suggestion, earlier, of M. Camille Melinand, a teacher of philosophy at Lakanal. His account of Melinand's enthusiasm for Hardy is preserved in a letter to Rivière of 16 November 1905, a letter that anticipates Jacques Émile-Blanche's advice to Proust in 1906. 'Read *Jude the Obscure*' Blanche would counsel Proust in response to Proust's inquiry whether Hardy was like Balzac, or the Goncourts or Anatole France. 'Don't live, don't live a month longer! without having read *Jude the Obscure* and *Tess of the d'Urbervilles*', Melinand advised Fournier. 'It is better than the best of Annunzio, better than the best of Tolstoy. . . . Unfortunately there seems to be no equal to him in France.'[39] As Robert Gibson has pointed out, Melinand's advice was to prove crucial, for Hardy's *Tess* appealed 'not only to [Fournier's] love of the countryside, but to his haunting sense of a happiness forever tantalizingly just beyond reach'.[40] Hardy's *Jude* was to have an equally strong appeal, particularly as an expression of the emotional chaos that can follow in the wake of a too-strictly observed puritan morality.

On 22 January 1906, Fournier sent Rivière a detailed response to *Tess*. This response is strongly, and enigmatically, personal. But there seems little doubt that he was profoundly marked by Hardy's novel:

Tess of the d'Urbervilles. If I were logical, I should say only, it can be useful to you – that is to say, in so far as I can judge, to give you some feelings that will be precious to you – and I should stop there.

I add that, during all the first part, I am saying to myself: 'agreeable and well-constructed, like a French novel, with all the power of the complete creation of a world and a life – proper to English novelists'.

But this ending of the first part and this second part (now so appropriately connected with the beginning of my last Sunday afternoon shut up in the school), what divine emotions have they given me!

In the mind of the adorably romantic and yet believable Tess, this drama, which moves from anguish to anguish, to a crescendo, across the endless sweetnesses of love, up to the day of the marriage – when, suddenly, without warning, after the last torments, the last terrible presages (oh, there, the most beautiful pages), suddenly, without warning, all collapses. And the sadness begins.

Certainly, I dislike the ending a little, the black drapery that is raised over the city – in order to say what will become of this Tess so beautiful, so sweetly unreal – I dislike the traitor–tyrant farmer (I exaggerate), who is little more than a sketch, and the two immense seduction scenes are to me very blameworthy.

But those three amorous farm girls, so simply unreal in spite of the thousand delicious precise details.

And the happiness of the ending, concisely expressed, this happiness after *too much* sadness and after the offence, this happiness that one holds in his hand, but that one *cannot* touch and that, all the same, one is immensely and silently happy to know there.

Read it.

And then he passes on also in time to another of those storms that violate our morals, even ours.

I am still under the influence of *Tess*. The course of my future ideas has been changed some little bit by it. And now the personage of Tess is someone for me, around me, in my life.

The philosophical ideas, on a first reading (outside of the great idea expressed by this story), appeared to me simple enough.[41]

Fournier found agreeably well-made Phase I of *Tess*, in which Tess, a lovely and pure maid, is violated by Alec d'Urberville upon going to work for d'Urberville's mother in order to aid her destitute family. He found equally attractive Hardy's ability to evoke a rural world and way of life, particularly the people of that world. He found deeply moving, the source even of the rarest emotions ('emotions divines'), Hardy's account in Phase II of *Tess* of the changes Tess undergoes as a result of her violation, and seems to have been positively swept away by Tess's movement (in Phases III and IV) toward apparent happiness in marriage to Angel Clare, a movement doomed from the outset by her fierce honesty and Clare's fanatical love of purity. Like many a reader before and since, Fournier both admired and disliked the ending of *Tess*, and was ambivalent toward Angel Clare ('the traitor-tyrant farmer'). Hardy's philosophy in *Tess*, notably the working of 'the President of the Immortals', he found simple enough, except for the leading idea ('le grande idée'). It is this idea that apparently changed the course of Fournier's thinking by making Tess's experience somehow his own. Precisely what this idea is must be inferred, but it seems clear that it is connected with Fournier's sense of a palpable and yet elusive happiness, a happiness that one can hold and yet not touch, a happiness that is precious because it is unattainable.

Here it is important to note that Fournier read Tess about six months after the decisive event of his personal and artistic life – his encounter in Paris, on 1 June 1905, with a tall blonde woman of striking beauty whom he had never seen before and with whom he fell immediately and permanently in love. Her name, he was to learn later, was Yvonne de Quièvrecourt, and she was to become his Avice, his Albertine, his Beatrice – in his own phrase, 'my destiny, all my destiny'. She was to become as well the inspiration for his masterpiece *Le Grand Meaulnes*, where she is present in the figure of the heroine, Yvonne de Galais. Fournier's encounter with Yvonne de Quièvrecourt was permanent in a way that, for example, Hardy's encounter with Lady Augusta Martin, or Proust's with Jeanne Pouquet, was not. Both Hardy (and his Pierston) and Proust (and his Marcel) observed their love attach itself to other women. Fournier, though from time to time enamoured of others, found the real and the ideal permanently resident in the same woman. He in fact maintained a discreet connection with Yvonne after her marriage and at the same time was bestowing his affections on other women.[42] This is worth noting because one strong attraction of Hardy's *Tess* and *Jude* for Fournier lay in his discovery that for Tess and Jude, as for him, there had been an all-too-human lover in addition to the all-surpassing one. He, like Tess and Jude, had been compromised by sexual passion.

Before the 1 June meeting in Paris, there had indeed been another woman (also named Yvonne), just as for Tess there had been Alec before Angel and for Jude Arabella before Sue. In August 1905, just two months after his meeting with Yvonne de

Quièvrecourt, Fournier demanded of this first Yvonne that she return his love letters. His ostensible reason was to avoid possible scandal at the Lycée Lakanal if the contents were ever made public. But there seems to have been another reason as well – his highly idealistic view of love, particularly of first love, and his fear, intensified and confirmed by his reading of *Tess* (and later *Jude*), that his earlier, romantic love would taint his later, spiritual one. Just as Tess's ruin by Alec destroys Angel's love for her, just as Jude's love for Arabella compromises him in the eyes of Sue (and in his own eyes), so Fournier feared his love for Yvonne the first had soiled his transcendent love for Yvonne de Quièvrecourt. In January 1907, at the same time as he was reading *Jude the Obscure*, he wrote as follows to Rivière:

> I've very recently met the first Yvonne again. I had nothing prepared in advance. I behaved admirably, all the more so because I was dreading this meeting. I treated her like some indifferent school chum whose health you politely ask after, and whom you ask if they've had a nice time in England. Then 'Good evening.' This was much better, much more than contempt.
>
> I've looked deep within myself but I can't find a glimmer of regret. Just for a moment, Hardy made me afraid. But, honestly, all it ever amounted to was a few kisses, and the whole agonizing adventure and the complete idyll took place in my mind, and in my mind alone.[43]
>
> In spite of myself I am like 'The Other who has come' – to whom I think I have attained, at times, and to whom I have not yet attained because I am *not lofty enough*, because she *is not beautiful enough*.
>
> If I have been childish, if I have been weak, if I have been conventional, if I've been silly, if I've been maudlin, then one must pardon me for having had this strength amidst the infamous city to create thus, by moments, *my life*, as if it were a wonderful story.

Fournier suggests here that he is trying to shape his personal life in accord with a story in his mind in which a hero models his life and love on an ideal. What frightened him in Hardy ('Un instant, Hardy m'avait fait peur') was Hardy's severe moral idealism – the belief, exhibited in Angel Clare's rejection of Tess, that the experience of carnal love is ruinous, corrosive enough to permanently mar one's emotional and spiritual capacities. Angel rejects Tess because she has borne Alec's child, just as Sue eventually spurns Jude, at least in part, because he had been Arabella's husband and lover. And both Tess and Jude accept these judgements against them. Fournier seems to judge himself in a similar way, and in his self-condemnation under the influence of Hardy's Tess and Jude we find an important quality of Augustin Meaulnes, the hero of the autobiographical *Le Grand Meaulnes*. Though Meaulnes does not invoke Hardy, like Fournier he despises himself for being careless in love. Earlier in this same letter to Rivière, Fournier had written as follows:

> When I think of *Jude the Obscure*, it is decidedly as important as I know not what. It ravages the heart. Someone has called Hardy the 'puritan anarchist'. That's the truth. I find now that it [*Jude*] is more profound, more vast, less particular than *Tess*. 'Puritan': with what terror is first love not encircled, this first marriage, which must be, inevitably, as if by a mysterious will, unique.

Fournier read *Tess* and *Jude* with unusual depth of feeling because he found in them both a terrifying resemblance to his own emotional experience, and these similarities persuaded him, as Robert Giannoni has persuasively argued, that he could turn his own experience to the ends of narrative art.[44] If *Tess* moved him to the depths through its depiction of irretrievable spiritual loss in a woman, *Jude*, which he apparently went on to read with Rivière's encouragement, disturbed him because it exhibits the sexual and spiritual ruin of a man. Like Proust and Lawrence, Fournier found Hardy's reversal of sexual roles in *Jude* both illuminating and inspirational.

Giannoni suggests several quite specific reasons for Hardy's strong appeal to Fournier. First, Fournier, upon reading *Jude* in 1906–7, found that Jude's first meeting with Sue, at the 'cross in the pavement' in Broad Street, Christminster [Oxford], resembled his first meeting with Yvonne on the Cours-la-Reine, before the Grand Palais, in Paris. When he read of Jude's first sight of Sue – at work in a religious-articles shop engraving the world 'Alleluia' in Gothic characters, and later at prayer in the cathedral – Fournier detected an uncanny resemblance to his second view of Yvonne, at prayer in the church of Saint-Germain-des-Prés, a week after the first meeting. 'Such a similarity of situations', observes Giannoni, 'made him see that his own history might . . . furnish him material for a work of literature. Was he not allowed to transpose his old adventure into a novel? Hardy had become for him a kind of mentor'.[45] Fournier also noticed that, like him, Hardy's Jude was smitten by the spiritual character of his beloved. For Jude, Sue is 'so ethereal a comrade that her spirit could be seen trembling through her limbs'.[46] For Fournier, as he wrote in a letter to Rivière, 'When near her [Yvonne de Quièvrecourt] one does not think of her body.'[47]

Still other aspects of *Jude* fascinated Fournier. Jude's rural upbringing, his loneliness and ambition, recalled Fournier's own boyhood (as they recall Hardy's). As a boy, Fournier had been happy but often misunderstood; and both Augustin Meaulnes and Frantz de Galais of *Le Grand Meaulnes*, in their loneliness and fear of the coming of adulthood, recall the youthful Fournier as well as the Jude who 'did not want to be a man' (*JO*, ch. 2). Also, Sue's words to Jude at their first meeting – 'You mustn't love me. You are too like me – that's all' – recalled to Fournier Yvonne's words to him on the Pont des Invalides: 'We are two children, we are behaving foolishly.'[48] This affinity between him and Jude caused Fournier to 'imitate' Jude in certain of his personal relationships. We have noted Fournier's fear that his liaison with the first Yvonne might taint his love for Yvonne de Quièvrecourt. This fear seems to have continued, for, several years after the break with the second Yvonne, Fournier came to view a love affair he was having with a working-class girl, Jeanne B. (the original of Valentine in *Le Grand Meaulnes*), as an enactment of Hardy's view in *Jude* that to obey one's physical instincts is to betray one's ideal. Fournier viewed Jeanne B. quite as Jude had come to view Arabella Donn. Jude's thought – 'The one affined soul he had ever met was lost to him through . . . marriage' – came to life for Fournier in his liaison with Jeanne B., whom he abruptly abandoned. As Giannoni remarks. 'The attitude of Hardy's hero towards his woman seems to have been for the lover of Jeanne B. a justification for his conduct.'[49]

Both *Jude* and *Tess* led Fournier to contemplate the theme of lost purity that was to govern *Le Grand Meaulnes*, where it is connected not just with Meaulnes's misfortunes in love but also with the setting and ways of a traditional rural world. The farmers, artisans and shopkeepers of Hardy's Wessex and of Fournier's Sologne are exemplars of a simpler social order from which both writers had removed themselves in their rise in the world. Thus the prominence of the theme of the 'happy home' ('la maison bonheur') threatened by change and intrusion. Hardy and Fournier developed this theme of loss in a tragic manner by urging the irretrievability of the lost paradise. Whether it be loss of purity, of childhood's joys, or of a cultural simplicity, this loss is permanent. This is the source of the overwhelming sadness of *Le Grand Meaulnes*, in which Augustin Meaulnes's great misfortune is not his inability to rediscover the festive house of Frantz de Galais and the love of Yvonne de Galais, but his refusal (presumably out of honour) to retain this lost happiness and love once he has recovered it. For Meaulnes, as for Angel Clare, love withers on contact with the beloved.

The story of Meaulnes is told by François Seurel, the son of rural schoolteachers. Seurel lives in central France and resembles at several points the young Fournier. The school of Seurel's parents is in the village of Sainte-Agathe, and one of their students, a classmate of François's who becomes his closest friend, is Meaulnes, an enigmatic boy of seventeen who, soon after his arrival at the school, rules the play of the other boys by sheer force of personality. Thus his designation on 'the great Meaulnes'. Off on a journey to meet the grandparents of Seurel (against the wish of the schoolmaster), Meaulnes loses his way in the Sologne countryside, falls asleep, and upon waking wanders by accident unto the grounds of a decaying manor house (Les Sablonnières). There he observes joyous preparations being made by a group of children for the marriage of the son of the house, Frantz de Galais. Meaulnes joins in the festivities and is suddenly struck by the presence of a beautiful fair-haired girl playing a piano. She is Yvonne de Galais, sister to Frantz, and the susceptible Meaulnes soon imagines her as his wife. He speaks to her then and later (in words that recall vividly Fournier's words to Yvonne de Quièvrecourt), revealing his plans for the future. Though she seems to doubt him, she promises to await his return. Soon after, the party is disruped by Frantz's announcement that the wedding has been cancelled. Valentine, his wife-to-be, has balked at the idea of someone of her modest origins (she is a dressmaker) becoming the wife of a de Galais. As Meaulnes departs with the other guests, he hears a gun-shot and sees a man bearing off an injured man. The wounded man will prove to be Frantz, whose break with Valentine has driven him to attempt suicide. Meaulnes now falls into a deep sleep and awakes to find himself once more at Sainte-

Agathe. Once back at school, however, he is obsessed with the desire to find his way back to Les Sablonnières, to Frantz, and especially to the beautiful Yvonne.

At this juncture, Seurel joins Meaulnes in his search for the lost beloved, and the two become so absorbed in their quest that the leadership of the school boys is assumed by a stranger who has arrived with a group of wandering players. Though Meaulnes does not yet know it, the usurper is Frantz de Galais, who one evening extorts from Meaulnes the map with which he is attempting to locate the lost manor house. Circumstances dictate an alliance between Meaulnes, Seurel and de Galais when the latter confesses that he too is seeking to recover the lost place. When Meaulnes finally discovers that the stranger is Frantz, brother to Yvonne, he is eager to speak to him. But he is thwarted when Frantz flees Sainte-Agathe to avoid arrest on suspicion of theft. In despair, Meaulnes leaves Sainte-Agathe for Paris in the hope of finding Yvonne, but he fails and gives up hope when told by a woman he meets that Yvonne has married. This woman, who is in fact Valentine, Frantz's lost fiancée, becomes Meaulnes's mistress – a turn of events that leads directly to the story's tragic ending. In any case, Meaulnes considers Yvonne forever lost and his quest at its end.

But Seurel, ever loyal to the romantic Meaulnes's quest for the lost place, seeks to learn more about Yvonne and indeed discovers that she is unwed and still awaiting Meaulnes's return. Seurel travels to the town of Vieux-Nançay, meets Yvonne there, and then arranges a party on the banks of the Cher in order that Meaulnes and his well-beloved may be reunited. Seurel directs Meaulnes to Yvonne, and it seems that at long last the wedding will take place. What Seurel does not know is that Meaulnes, because Valentine has been his mistress, feels honour-bound to reunite her with Frantz. So genuine is this noble intent that, on the morning after the wedding, Meaulnes abandons his new bride and sets off to find Valentine. During the year of Meaulnes's absence, Yvonne dies giving birth to his child. Seurel ministers to Yvonne, then to the child, whom he virtually adopts as his own. Meaulnes returns after he has succeeded in reuniting Valentine with Frantz to receive his daughter from the hands of his loyal friend. Here the novel ends, with Meaulnes holding in his arms his daughter by the dead Yvonne.

No summary can begin to capture the appeal of Fournier's narrative, which John Fowles has praised as a novel in which 'the hero refuses to let go of his boyhood glimpse of a mysterious, archaic revelation, and pursues the eager quest into adulthood and the landscape of the mind'.[50] But a summary may suggest the point in Giannoni's view that *Le Grand Meaulnes* derives from *Tess* and *Jude* in several of its most important episodes. Yvonne's disappointment on the morning after her wedding recalls Tess's disappointment on the evening of hers. A more interesting connection may exist between Augustin Meaulnes and Angel Clare. Meaulnes's flight, allegedly to reunite Frantz and Valentine, may well be a flight from the sexual reality he has experienced on the first night of his marriage. His is a love, like Angel Clare's that thrives best at a distance from its object. It seems altogether plausible that Clare's motive in abandoning Tess is not just moral outrage, but sexual timidity brought on when Tess confesses that she has borne a child. In Angel Clare, Fournier perhaps found exhibited something in himself – a need to love an idealized woman but not to close with her.

Both Meaulnes and Angel, in Fournier's view, probably seem tragic in their belief in the impossibility of repetition. Meaulnes can no more find his way back to the happy children and the lovely Yvonne at Les Sablonnières than Angel can re-create the innocent maid dressed in white he had first met at the May festival at Marlott, then came to know and love in the idyllic atmosphere of Talbothays. And Seurel's attempt to mend affairs, like Angel's attempt to reunite with Tess upon his return from Brazil, a sadder but wiser man, must also fail. As Giannoni points out, once Tess confesses, the world changes in her and Angel's eyes. Their return to Talbothays shortly after their decision to separate finds an ugly leer on the face of the lovely, smiling nature they had once perceived there. Similarly, when Meaulnes returns to Les Sablonnières under Seurel's guidance, he finds its old charm has vanished: the happy children of his first visit have been replaced by peasant children who delight in mistreating their donkey; the pleasure ship that once adorned the lake has been sold; the manor itself is partly pulled down; the once well-stocked stables now hold only the decrepid old horse Belisaire, soon to be put down. For Meaulnes, as for Clare, the past is irretrievable because the passage of time is a process of decay. The recovery of time past in the manner of Proust, the trust in the creative power of the human mind of Powys, the faith in the liberating power of human passion in Lawrence are simply not present in *Le Grand Meaulnes*. The promise represented in Meaulnes's child by Yvonne, like the promise in Angel Clare's apparent future with Tess's sister Liza-Lu, may be seen as a compensation. But Meaulnes's and Clare's dreams of a perfect love, are, like Yvonne and Tess themselves, dead and gone for ever. Philosophically, in his belief in the irretrievability of things past, Alain-Fournier is one of Hardy's most loyal disciples.

If Fournier found in *Tess* and *Jude* an exhibition of the sad truth that love dies on contact, he also found Hardy – and here it is important to recall that he read Hardy in English – a poetic realist of the rural school who helped him break with Symbolist values. Hardy's ability to poeticize the actual, to create a magical aura out of precise notations from life, was most congenial to Fournier in his need to incorporate his memories of rural life into a mature art that revealed the significance of those past realities. As Giannoni says 'Through the mediation of the Symbolists, [Fournier] had had the revelation of art and of literature. But, in the person of Hardy, he found a precious guide who helped him to see clearly into himself.'[51]

Since discussion of Hardy's appeal to two French novelists of the early twentieth century, even two of the stature of Proust and Fournier, may seem less than representative, it is worth looking briefly, by way of conclusion, into several studies of Hardy that appeared in France between 1901 and 1928. Firmin Roz's article in 1906 in *La Revue des deux mondes* has already been mentioned, but I would like to inspect it more closely here. Also, with Proust's and Fournier's admiration for Hardy in mind, I will describe several other important French assessments of him: F. A. Hedgcock's *Thomas Hardy: penseur et artiste* (1911); Ramon Fernandez's 'Hardy et le realisme', which appeared in the Thomas Hardy special issue of *La Revue nouvelle* in 1928; and particularly Pierre d'Exideuil's *Le Couple humain dans l'oeuvre de Thomas Hardy* (1928).

Roz's 'Thomas Hardy', which appeared at the very time Proust and Fournier were reading certain of the Wessex Novels, is a forthright attempt to locate Hardy's greatness as a novelist: first and foremost in his treatment of love; then in his satire, his depiction of rustic characters, his pessimism, and his poeticized realism. According to Roz, one thing truly distinguished Hardy from other nineteenth-century English novelists and placed him among the great European writers of the century: his depiction of passion as the dominant force in human life. English novelists, noted Roz, were usually as restrained in their treatment of human passion as French novelists were unrestrained. In Hardy, however, as not in Scott, Thackeray, Dickens or Eliot, passion is always present ('la passion est toujours en jeu'). And the law of passion in Hardy is that it creates suffering. This, said Roz, is the basis for Hardy's philosophy of character and for his tragic view of things. In Hardy's sternly ironic view, passion invites self-destruction: passion is ephemeral but is believed eternal, and it is unavoidable. Men and women are fated to love and therefore fated to suffer. Where, wondered Roz, can one find anything more thoroughly tragic: 'Passion is the inexhaustible theme of the novels of Thomas Hardy.' Hardy's attack on society derives from this perception that men and women's enslavement to passion is exacerbated by the repressive morality of English society. Hardy's greatest characters are in one way or another a response to the central and overwhelming place of passion in human life. Farmer Boldwood, Clym Yeobright, and Jude Fawley are its victims. Troy and Fitzpiers are its predatory agents. Henry Knight and Angel Clare are inadequate before its demands on them through the women they love and then destroy out of their emotional inadequacy. Hardy's heroines are its irresistible presence in human life. Hardy's strongest, wisest and best characters – Oak, Venn, Winterborne – are fortunate in being able to control their passions. Hardy's rustics, like his 'better' characters, are enslaved by love's demands; for in the Wessex Novels passion has no regard for the artificial barriers of class. Hardy's celebrated pessimism grows from his perception that life's greatest demand, that one person love another, is also the source of life's greatest misery. His celebrated descriptions of the English landscape unroll in the light of his sense that man's fate is to love and to lose in love. As a realist, Hardy is without peer in England; his peers are Flaubert, Daudet, Maupassant, Tolstoy and Dostoevsky. The great power behind Hardy's art is his humanity, and the depth of his humanity is proportionate to the depth of his conviction that men and women are born to love and to suffer as a result of loving.[52]

Roz is still of interest for his synthesis, his wide-ranging citations from the Wessex Novels, and his utter confidence, which anticipates Proust's in *The Captive*, that Hardy belongs in the company of the greatest French and Russian novelists of the nineteenth century. Roz's central perception – that Hardy is the greatest

English novelist of human love – was developed at length by F. A. Hedgcock in his *Thomas Hardy: penseur et artiste*. The work of an Englishman who had studied in France, wrote in French, and used the method of Taine and Sainte-Beuve, Hedgcock's study is adorned with two portraits of Hardy by Blanche, a photograph of Hardy at about thirty, a detailed bibliography of Hardy's writings, a list of French translations of Hardy's novels, and a letter on Hardy and Schopenhauer from Edmund Gosse. Probably through Gosse's intercession, Hedgcock had visited Hardy at Max Gate in 1910 while still at work on his book. Earlier, in 1905, he had sent Hardy a questionaire for information to aid him in his study. When the finished work reached Hardy in 1911, however, Hardy wrote in his copy as follows: 'Biographical details . . . mostly wrong.' Then he set it aside. Eleven years later, when Oxford University Press proposed to Hardy an English tranlation of *Penseur et artiste*, Hardy objected violently on the grounds of its inaccuracy. What Hardy objected to – frequently for dubious reasons – was Hedgcock's probing analysis of his life in its relation to his art. In a letter to Hardy in the 1920s, however, Hedgcock ably explained that, far from merely prying into Hardy's private affairs, he had engaged in a serious study, 'criticism *à la* Taine, into which ancestry and environment all enter as determining factors'.[53]

Hedgcock's description of his book is an accurate one, for his is the most thoroughly researched of all the early accounts of of Hardy, comparable in quality and conception to early English studies such as Lionel Johnson's *Art of Thomas Hardy* (1894) and Lascelles Abercrombie's *Thomas Hardy: A Critical Study* (1912). Hedgcock offers a view of Hardy founded on careful investigation of Hardy's life and times, and a searching study of Hardy's early poems, particularly their importance as an expression of his religious doubt. This interest in Hardy's personal and intellectual life colours Hedgcock's analysis of all the novels, as well as his separate chapters on Hardy's fatalism, pessimism, philosophy of nature, and style. Interwoven throughout are two arguments: that Hardy is the great exhibitor of men and women in love ('la reaction d'un sexe sur l'autre'); that Hardy's fiction is nurtured by a strong element of self-portraiture and is therefore an exhibition of both personal and philosophic views. Noting the scope and technical virtuousity of *The Dynasts*, and praising in particular Hardy's kinship with Schopenhauer, Hedgcock concludes that Hardy belongs beside great modern pessimists such as Schopenhauer, Leopardi, de Vigny and Renan. Hardy, in Hedgcock's view, gives the philosophy of despair the finest expression it has received in English literature. Hedgcock anticipates Virginia Woolf in describing Hardy as the greatest English tragedian of the nineteenth century. Like Proust, Roz, and Fournier's teacher Melinand, Hedgcock ranks Hardy with the greatest European writers and thinkers of the modern world.

What Firmin Roz and F. A. Hedgcock were saying about Hardy as *the* English novelist of love gave him an appeal to which Proust and Fournier could, and did, creatively respond. This particular appeal was confirmed and further defined in 1928, the year of Hardy's death, when the expected spate of writings on Hardy appeared: articles (apart from obituaries) by Gérard de Catalogne, Abel Chavelley, Proust's friends Léon Daudet and Jacques-Émile Blanche, Henri Davray, Edmund Jalous, and J. J. Mayous; a book on Hardy's treatment of rural themes in his novels (Gérard de Catalogne's *Le Message de Thomas Hardy*); a special Thomas Hardy issue of *La Revue nouvelle* (mentioned above), with contributions from both French and English writers; a book on sexuality in Hardy (d'Exideuil's *Le Couple humain*).[54] Most noteworthy in this outpouring is the praise of Hardy as the creator of a 'new' reality, an achievement mentioned by Murry, Schlumberger, Hellens, du Bos and, of course, Proust in *La Revue nouvelle*, but analysed most effectively by Ramon Fernandez and Pierre d'Exideuil, the former with reference to Hardy's treatment of nature, the latter with reference to Hardy's depiction of men and women in love.

In 'Hardy et le realisme', Fernandez describes Hardy as a poetic naturalist ('un Zola poètique') who resembles the naturalists but has profoundly modified naturalistic technique. Comparing the treatment of external nature by Zola in *La Terre* and Hardy in *The Return of the Native*, Fernandez notes that, where Zola was content to evoke the fact, or the law, of nature's process, Hardy's evocations are always 'explicative'. That is, in the opening pages of *The Return*, for example, Hardy offers notations of facts with precise analyses of their significations. In Hardy, natural realities are penetrated with ideas, and his art is an art of thought ('une vision pensée'); and this is possible because Hardy is as intimately acquainted with his own vision as with the spectacle he evokes. Hardy's analyses and descriptions are therefore at once creative of knowledge and creative of life, while the analyses and descriptions of the ordinary naturalistic novelist are merely the poetic use of a science and a life which does not belong to him. Fernandez calls this feature of Hardy's fiction his 'objectivism', his genius for infusing with thought the world of objects so as to at once be faithful to the common sense of that world's reality and to make intelligible a quite uncommon sense of the beauty of its inner workings.

Where Fernandez describes Hardy's 'objectivism' with regard to external nature, d'Exideuil describes something similar in Hardy's treatment of the human heart. Like Fernandez, d'Exideuil recognizes Hardy's affinities with the French naturalists: the importance of environment to character; the use of the language of science; the interest in pathological cases. And, like Fernandez, d'Exideuil calls Hardy a visionary naturalist, one who invests his notations of actuality with an 'interpretation' and 'application', with 'an impressive force and with the poetic element never absent from a moving revelation of truth'. Hardy possesses

> a Romantic gift of conferring an anthropomorphic existence upon cosmic elements, of bestowing upon events the imprint of an implacable and almost eschatological direction. In him there is something of the visionary who perceives the process of becoming in the world, of the mystic who holds an unknowable, transcendental secret, the very antipodes of the vulgar materialist.[55]

Linking Hardy especially with Swinburne among nineteenth-century English writers, d'Exideuil notes that in Hardy the love of men and women is expressive of a universal will to union and procreation that works ceaselessly and indifferently. Hardy's great triumph is that he does not sacrifice the individuality of his many lovers – Tess, Jude, Eustacia, for example – to the depiction of the inexorable law of love working through them. They are puppets, but finally more than puppets, because deeply, lovingly and memorably brought to life in his pages. This representation of the human pair as unique and at the same time typical 'constitutes one of the loftiest characteristics of Hardy's work'. This is another way of saying, perhaps, that Hardy's love of the thought and truth of art was more than equalled by his love of toiling, suffering humanity.

When one thinks of Hardy's treatment throughout his career by

English reviewers and editors, it is clear that the French differed from their English brethren in at least one way – they sympathized with, even embraced, Hardy's heterodoxy, both religious and emotional. Even Hardy's most sympathetic and able English readers had disappointed him in this. One recalls Leslie Stephen's reservations about the treatment of love in *Far from the Madding Crowd* and *The Return of the Native*, or Edmund Gosse's astonishing hostility in a review of *Jude the Obscure* – views, both of them, oddly consistent with the sense among other commentators, which still persists, that Hardy's is a seriously flawed greatness.

5

'The Immortal Puzzle': Hardy and John Fowles

> *The shadow of Thomas Hardy, the heart of whose 'country' I can see in the distance from my work room window, I cannot avoid. . . . I don't mind the shadow. It seems best to use it. . . .*
>
> (Fowles, 1969)

John Fowles has been as great an admirer of Alain-Fournier as of Thomas Hardy, and for much the same reason. In an interview in 1974, when asked about the importance of *Le Grand Meaulnes* to his fiction, Fowles replied: 'I was brought up really in a French tradition in literature.'[1] Fowles was quite possibly recalling his work at Bedford School, where French was his favourite subject, as well as his studies at New College, Oxford, where he read French, achieving his BA in 1950. In yet another interview (in 1964), he stated that his knowledge of French literature 'makes me feel by acquired instinct more interested in what I say than how I say it; it makes me impatient with the feeble insularity of so much English writing. France is, among other things, what we were always too hypocritical or too puritanical or too class-ridden or too empire-minded to be.'[2] The French element in Fowles's education probably affected his attitude toward Hardy, for in 1969, while at work on *The French Lieutenant's Woman*, he acknowledged Hardy's influence (in the remark quoted in the epigraph) and observed that Hardy's later novels stand out among nineteenth-century English novels for their candour: they exhibit 'how [men and women] made love, what they said to each other in their most intimate moments, what they felt then'.[3] In 1977, the year of *Daniel Martin*, Fowles praised Hardy's *Well-Beloved* much as he had praised Alain-Fournier's *Le Grand Meaulnes* earlier – as an example of an artist's need to mature, put off his dream of eternal youth and at the same time 'keep a profound part of himself not just open to his past, but *of* his past'.⁴ Fowles's fascination with Alain-Fournier's masterpiece explains in part his deep interest in Hardy's *Well-Beloved:* in each he found exhibited a profoundly nostalgic hero (Augustin Meaulnes and Jocelyn Pierston, respectively) unable to let go of a youthful vision of joy and perfection and pursuing that vision into adulthood.

Hardy had struggled to exhibit, in guarded terms to be sure, the sexual origin of this pursuit of a primal truth and beauty, and, as has been noted, Hardy had run afoul of the English reviewing establishment. Fowles has valued Hardy particularly as an English precursor who tried to exhibit, in veiled personal terms, the working of the sexuality of an artist in relation to his art. For Fowles, therefore, as for Proust, Hardy's life has held special interest – particularly the romance in Hardy's life as described by Lois Deacon in 1966 and Robert Gittings in 1975. One finds Fowles asking, as Proust had asked, 'what kind of a man was Hardy, a lover of society, a fancier of women?' Hardy has appealed to Fowles for yet other reasons. Both are nature writers, writers for whom the landscape is an important aspect of characterization and mood. Both are Dorset novelists, Hardy by birth and Fowles by adoption. But Fowles is most deeply interested in what Hardy, in his 1895 Preface to *The Woodlanders*, called 'the immortal puzzle – given the man and woman, how to find a basis for their sexual relation'. And, like Hardy in *The Well-Beloved*, Fowles is interested in the sexual relation in its connection with the psychology of the creative process, especially the creative process governed by nostalgia, by a desire to recover time past.

Hardy's influence on Fowles is first visible in *The French Lieutenant's Woman* (1969), his third novel, and it has continued: in Fowles's review of J. Hillis Miller's *Thomas Hardy: Distance and Desire* (1970); in 'Hardy and the Hag', Fowles's essay on Hardy's *Well-Beloved* published in the same year as *Daniel Martin* (with which it has striking connections); and in *Daniel Martin* itself, published in 1977. In *Daniel Martin*, the main concern of this chapter, the growth of the writer-hero Daniel toward emotional and artistic maturity, which is a matter of Daniel's learning that loyalty to one woman can produce a stable sense of self, parallels Daniel's movement away from the expediencies of commercial film-writing and toward the serious human concerns of novel-writing. That is, Daniel's philandering (with the American sisters Jane and Nell; with the expatriate Pole Andrea; with a promiscuous

British actress known as 'the British Open'; with the cockney sisters Miriam and Marjory; with an unnamed woman during a visit to America; with the talented Scot Jenny McNeil) is made to parallel his debasement of his literary talent before the allurements of Hollywood film-writing. Daniel's eventual return to Jane, his first passionate love, is the counterpart of his return to a long-buried, 'true' aspect of himself and his art. His turn back to Jane is also his turn away from film-writing to the writing of an autobiographical novel and its demand for intense self-knowledge. Dan's decision to turn from film-writing to novel-writing – his most important decision in the novel – quite possibly 'derives' from Fowles's awareness of a similar decision by Thomas Hardy at a critical moment in his life. For Hardy had indeed made such a choice, in part through the writing and rewriting of *The Well-Beloved* in the 1890s, between the (for him) 'false' art of novel-writing and the 'true' one of writing poetry. But this is to anticipate. More will be said later about *Daniel Martin* and *The Well-Beloved*, after brief examination of Fowles's uses of Hardy in his writings between 1969 and 1977.

In *The French Lieutenant's Woman* the struggle of Fowles's Victorian hero toward self-discovery is also a campaign against the repressive sexual morality of his age. Charles Smithson, a gentleman by birth, learns through his passionate encounter with Sarah Woodruff (the French Lieutenant's Woman) that truth-to-feeling is superior to the code of the English gentleman. Smithson, like Daniel Martin later, seeks his authentic self through a woman's love; and Smithson's quest, like Martin's, is lent a distinctively Hardyan flavour. A number of the novel's chapters take their epigraphs from poems by Hardy. Charles and his fiancée Ernestina's first sight of Sarah Woodruff on the stormy Cobb at Lyme Regis (ch. 1) has as its prelude nine lines from Hardy's poem 'The Riddle', a haunting account of a lonely woman gazing seaward, impervious both to the motion of the waters and the urgings of her love. Lines from Hardy's 'At a Seaside Town in 1869' and 'On a Midsummer Eve' provide epigraphs for chapters 17 and 18, respectively, chapters in which Charles, while in the presence of Ernestina, ponders his growing obsession with the mysterious woman on the Cobb (a similar reflection occurs in 'At a Seaside Town') and returns, against his better judgement, to the Undercliff, where he had encountered Sarah earlier and now meets her again. This critical third encounter places Charles in Sarah's power, for here she presents him with 'two excellent *Micraster* tests', an act that makes him her debtor, both as a palaeontologist and perhaps as a man. For it is now that they touch for the first time ('She wore no gloves, and their fingers touched. He examined the two tests; but he thought only of the touch of those cold fingers.') The mood for this decisive encounter is set by an epigraph from the second stanza of Hardy's 'On a Midsummer Eve':

> I went, and knelt, and scooped my hand
> As if to drink, into the brook,
> And a faint figure seemed to stand
> Above me, with the bygone look.

The instability of human love, perhaps the greatest single theme of Hardy's poems, is Fowles's touchstone at this time of Smithson's approaching abandonment of Ernestina for Sarah.

A morbidly funny couplet from Hardy's poem 'Transformations' ('Portion of a yew / Is a man my grandsire knew') opens chapter 23, in which Charles returns to Winsyatt, a Smithson family estate belonging to a bachelor uncle who virtually reared Charles and who intends (at least at this point in the story) to settle his magnificent estate on his nephew. The situation nine chapters later, in which Ernestina, jolted by the news that Charles has probably lost Winsyatt (and she a title) because his uncle has married, repents her anger and lack of sympathy for Charles, is counterpointed by an epigraph from Hardy – lines 21–4 of Hardy's 'The Musical Box', a poem sometimes taken to depict Hardy's growing estrangement from his wife Emma during their days at Sturminster Newton in the 1870s. Smithson's deepening alienation from Ernestina (chapter 31 finds him in Sarah's passionate embrace in a barn near the Undercliff) is given historical and human authenticity by his glance in the epigraph at Hardy's poetic reflection on a troubled moment in his first marriage.

Is Smithson, via allusions such as these, becoming a 'Hardy figure' of a kind? The answer is yes, though so blunt an answer would be deeply suspect if, in chapters 34 and 35, Thomas Hardy were not suddenly omnipresent, both in epigraphs from his poems and in an extended account of a romantic phase of his personal history. Fowles's epigraph for chapter 34, in which Charles (fresh from Sarah's embrace that same morning) informs Ernestina that he must travel to London to inform her father of his reduced circumstances, is a ferocious alliterative line from Hardy's 'During Wind and Rain' ('And the rotten rose is ript from the wall'). Charles is on the brink of social ruin (he's about to throw over a lady of station for a 'whore') and of emotional deliverance (he is about to honour his deepest feelings). It is precisely now, at this turning-point in his hero's career, that Fowles turns more explicitly and extensively to Hardy than at any other point in the novel. The epigraph for chapter 35 is from Hardy's 'Her Immortality' ('In you resides my single power/Of sweet continuance here'); and it is glossed here by Fowles as descriptive of Hardy's love for Tryphena Sparks, the maternal first cousin Hardy allegedly had rejected when he decided to marry Emma Gifford in the 1870s.[5] It is here, amidst a lengthy digression on the repressive sexual ethos of Victorian England, that Fowles announces the pressure of Hardy – as a man and an artist – on his novel. Quite abruptly, Fowles digresses to plunge the reader of the story of Charles Smithson's growing passion for Sarah Woodruff in the fictional year of 1867 into the story of Thomas Hardy's thwarted love for Tryphena Sparks in the historical year 1867. One notes the similarity between this passage and our epigraph from 'Notes from an Unfinished Novel':

> I have now come under the shadow, the very relevant shadow, of the great novelist who towers over this part of England of which I write. When we remember that Hardy was the first to break the Victorian middle-class seal over the supposed Pandora's box of sex, not the least interesting (and certainly the most paradoxical) thing about him is his fanatical protection of the seal of his own and his immediate ancestors' sex life. Of course that was, and would still remain his inalienable right. But few literary secrets – and this one was not unearthed until the 1950s – have remained so well kept. It, and the reality of Victorian rural England I have tried to suggest in this chapter, answer Edmund Gosse's famous reproof: 'What has Providence done to Mr. Hardy that he should rise up in the arable land of Wessex and shake his fist at his Creator'? He might reasonably have inquired why the Atreids should have shaken their bronze fists skyward at Mycenae.
>
> This is not the place to penetrate far into the shadows beside Egdon Heath. What is definitely known is that in 1867 Hardy,

then twenty-seven years old, returned to Dorset from his architectural studies in London and fell profoundly in love with his sixteen-year-old cousin Tryphena. They became engaged. Five years later, and incomprehensibly, the engagement was broken. Though not absolutely proven, it now seems clear that one engagement was broken by the revelation to Hardy of a very sinister skeleton in the family cupboard: Tryphena was not his cousin, but his illegitimate half-sister's illegitimate daughter. Countless poems of Hardy's hint at it: 'At the Wicket Gate', 'She Did Not Turn', 'Her Immortality' and many others; and that there were several recent illegitimacies on the maternal side in his family *is* proven. Hardy himself was born 'five months from the altar'. The pious have sometimes maintained that he broke his engagement for class reasons – he was too much the rising young master to put up with a simple Dorset girl. It is true he did marry above himself in 1874 – to the disastrously insensitive [Emma] Lavinia Gifford. But Tryphena was an exceptional young woman; she became the headmistress of a Plymouth school at the age of twenty, having passed out fifth from her teachers' training college in London. It is difficult not to accept that some terrible family secret was what really forced them to separate. It was a fortunate secret, of course, in one way, since never was an English genius so devoted and indebted to one muse and one muse only. It gives us all his greatest love elegies. It gave us Sue Bridehead and Tess, who are pure Tryphena in spirit; and *Jude the Obscure* is even tacitly dedicated to her in Hardy's own preface – 'The scheme was laid down in 1890 . . . some of the circumstances being suggested by the death of a woman. . . .' Tryphena, by then married to another man, had died in that year.

This tension, then – between lust and renunciation, undying recollection and undying repression, lyrical surrender and tragic duty, between the sordid facts and their noble use – energizes and explains one of the age's greatest writers; and beyond him, structures the whole age itself. It is this I have digressed to remind you of.[6]

Fowles's view of Hardy and Tryphena is borrowed largely from Lois Deacon and Terry Coleman's *Providence and Mr Hardy* (1966), a highly controversial biography which posited not just a courtship and betrothal in 1867–8, but the birth to Tryphena of a son (Randal) by Hardy. Fowles prudently omits this doubtful (and now discredited) detail, but holds to the view that incest, or potential incest ('some terrible family secret') kept Hardy from his true love and inspired some of his finest work. Further, Fowles sees Hardy's adherence to 'renunciation' and 'tragic duty' as illustrative of Smithson's dilemma and of the Victorian Age's 'greatest mystery'.

If Fowles's digression on Hardy is somewhat lengthy, it is perhaps because, as two critics have argued, Fowles is pointing to a source for his novel in Hardy's *A Pair of Blue Eyes* (1873), various aspects of which influenced 'the plot . . . [,] the characterizations [and] character relationships, the significant image patterns, and even the existentialist theme of Fowles's novel'.[7] It seems entirely plausible that *A Pair of Blue Eyes*, and certain other of the Wessex Novels, have left their marks on *The French Lieutenant's Woman*. It is inviting, for example, to seek an origin for Fowles's seductive Sarah in Hardy's Bathsheba Everdene, Eustacia Vye or even Arabella Donn; or for Fowles's reluctant Charles in Hardy's Henry Knight, Clym Yeobright or Angel Clare; or for the wronged and respectable Ernestina in Hardy's Thomasin Yeobright or Grace Melbury. But more significant than even Fowles's acknowledged debts to Hardy are two other things: his detailed interest in Hardy's life as a means by which to 'explain' Hardy's novels and poems; and his radical departure from Hardy in insisting in this novel (as later in *Daniel Martin*) on the reality of self-willed and self-wrought change and freedom. Charles and Sarah are seen as capable of defying their society and creating their own lives and values. This same, profoundly un-Hardyan, belief in a person's power to thwart the dictates of heredity and environment characterizes Fowles's view of the novel as a personal instrument through which the writer can alter, reform or transcend the self. At the same time as Fowles is in debt to Hardy, he is establishing his independence of him. Like Proust, Powys and Lawrence, Fowles accepts Hardy's influence and yet rejects Hardy's tragic sense of things.

The importance that Fowles saw in the relation between Hardy's life and his art is strongly evident in a review he wrote of Joseph Hillis Miller's *Thomas Hardy: Distance and Desire* (1970), a study in which Miller attempts to locate Hardy's peculiar uses of language in his temperamental detachment from persons and events. In an otherwise friendly review, Fowles expressed deep disappointment because Miller had not traced Hardy's 'creative and autobiographical tracks':

> The Tryphena *affaire* is given short shrift. . . . In . . . [one] passage . . . [Professor Miller] dismisses autobiographical data as irrelevant to the understanding of a writer, and here . . . is where the practising novelist in his reviewer begins to take exception. Hardy's writing has been very thoroughly dismantled by the end of this book. . . . We learn a lot about how Hardy 'worked' as a creative 'machine'. But I found increasingly that all this expertise only raised the hare that had been earlier denounced as a red herring. *Why* was Hardy like this? What *did* happen in his real life in that dark and fertile decade between 1865 and 1875? Why did he break with Tryphena? Why did his first marriage sour so disastrously fast? What real-life factors structured his literary pessimism? To say that 'the facts of Hardy's life . . . are not physical facts' . . . is too easy a way out. . . . Hardy set out to demonstrate what countless non-literary factors . . . had conditioned him to be – and see. There was something to be proved to the world. . . .[8]

As this suggests, for John Fowles a biographical approach to Hardy's work does not just reveal Hardy's mind and manner; it is a necessary part of any attempt to understand the form and content of his writing. As Fowles remarks at one point in *The French Lieutenant's Woman*, 'If we want to know the real Mill or the real Hardy, we can learn more from the deletions and alterations of their biographies than from the published versions, from the petty detritus of the concealment operation' (ch. 49). The probable reason for Fowles's intense interest in Hardy's life in 1970, as examination of *Daniel Martin* will show, is that in 1970 Fowles was learning things about himself as a writer from what he was reading about Thomas Hardy as a man and a writer. And it seems clear that Robert Gittings's *Young Thomas Hardy* (1975) helped Fowles articulate the connection between life and art in Hardy's, and in his own, novels.[9]

As can now be seen, in the history of Hardy biography Gittings's *Young Thomas Hardy* (like his *Thomas Hardy's Later Years*) stands out because, among other things, it extends the 'new' view of Hardy's life in relation to his work that emerged in the 1960s with Lois Deacon's unveiling of the Tryphena Sparks episode of

Hardy's life. Gittings, while correcting some of the conjectural aspects of Deacon's work, also expanded it, making it clear, for example, that Hardy's thwarted love for Tryphena was but one love, and that neither the first nor the last, in a series of interrupted loves that occurred throughout his life and that he projected most revealingly in *The Well-Beloved*. Gittings, more than any previous biographer, made visible the unmistakable imprint of Hardy's sexual temperament on his novels, particularly *The Well-Beloved*. Evidence for the origin of such an imprint is precisely what Fowles was demanding of Miller in his 1970 review of *Distance and Desire*, but not just in the interest of a biographical criticism. Fowles's demand that Miller view Hardy's art as an allegory of his life is the demand, as he states, of a 'practising novelist' – of one who is himself engaged in transmuting 'real-life factors' into the terms of prose fiction. And so, in 1977, two years after the publication of the first volume of Gittings's biography of Hardy, Fowles is found publishing not just the autobiographical novel *Daniel Martin*, with its several striking resemblances to Hardy's *Well-Beloved* (as interpreted by Gittings) and its explicit references to Hardy, but also a highly personal critical essay on the autobiographical element in *The Well-Beloved*.

Fowles titled this essay 'Hardy and the Hag', and the Hag, as Fowles explains, is the mother-ideal of unconscious memory that he believes Hardy pursued in woman after woman, through novel after novel, during much of his life – but most explicitly and revealingly in *The Well-Beloved*. The Hardy of this essay is the 'new' Hardy of Gittings's *Young Thomas Hardy*, published two years before. *The Well-Beloved* is in Fowles's view (as in Gittings's) Hardy's most complete revelation of this element in his artistic personality. Gittings had called *The Well-Beloved* 'a sketch of Hardy's own temperament in very realistic detail', a 'personal allegory carried to near-absurd depths'. Fowles echoes Gittings by describing the novel as 'the closest conducted tour we shall ever have of the psychic process behind Hardy's written product'. He continues, 'No biography will ever take us so deep. . . . Here is . . . the case of a god whose supposedly living Adams and Eves now seem to be a tatter of *trompe-d'oeil*, a creak of cogs and levers – and who can only abscond in horror from the realization that he himself is the arch-automaton.'[10] Hardy is an 'arch-automaton' because he was, according to Fowles (and to Gittings), compelled to seek in woman after woman and book after book the forever-lost mother-ideal first known to him in infancy. To explain this more fully, and in terms more clearly connected with his own artistic motives and practices, Fowles drew at this point on a professional opinion – in the form of a similar analysis of himself carried out five years earlier in the pages of *American Imago* by Dr Gilbert J. Rose, a professor of clinical psychology at the Yale University Medical School.[11] As Fowles points out, Dr Rose psychoanalysed him by proxy through *The French Lieutenant's Woman*. Fowles is quite happy with the analysis, perhaps because he finds it descriptive not just of himself, but also of Thomas Hardy in *The Well-Beloved*. In brief, Fowles tacitly accepts Dr Rose's view that *The French Lieutenant's Woman* is the symbolic expression of his (Fowles's) unconscious need 'to restore the lost unity with the mother', then identifies himself with Hardy by suggesting that the same drive in Hardy produced the portrait of the artist in *The Well-Beloved*. Fowles's remarks are worth quoting at length because they clarify his view of creativity, cast some retrospective light on Powys, Proust and Alain-Fournier, and anticipate the psychology of the hero of *Daniel Martin*.

> I had the interesting experience, a few years ago, of being psychoanalysed by proxy – through one of my novels, *The French Lieutenant's Woman*. Professor Gilbert J. Rose . . . wrote a good paper on the book, but I was rather more interested in his general theory of what produces the artistically creative mind, since it largely confirmed – and greatly clarified – intuitive conclusions of my own.
>
> In simple terms his proposition was that some children retain a particularly rich memory of the passage from extreme infancy, when the identity of the baby is merged with that of the mother, to the arrival of the first awareness of separate identity and the simultaneous first dawn of what will become the adult sense of reality; that is, they are deeply marked by the passage from an unified magical world to a discrete 'realist' one. What seemingly stamps itself indelibly on this kind of infant psyche is a pleasure in the fluid, polymorphic nature of the sensuous impressions, visual, tactile, auditory and the rest, that he receives; and so profoundly that he cannot, even when the detail of this intensely auto-erotic experience has retreated into the unconscious, refrain from tampering with reality – from trying to recover in other words, the early oneness with the mother that granted this

ability to make the world mysteriously and deliciously change meaning and appearance. He was once a magician with a wand; and given the right other predisposing and environmental factors, he will one day devote his life to trying to regain the unity and the power by recreating adult versions of the experience . . . he will be an artist. Moreover, since every child goes through some variation of the same experience, this also explains one major attraction of art for the audience. The artist is simply one who does the journey back for the less conditioned and less technically endowed.

I do not know on how much empirical evidence Professor Rose's theory is based, but I find it plausible and a valuable model. One enigma about all artists, however successful they may be in worldly or critical terms, is the markedly repetitive nature of their endeavour – the inability not to return again and again on the same impossible journey. One must posit here an unconscious drive towards an unattainable. The theory also accounts for the sense of irrecoverable loss (or predestined defeat) so characteristic of many major novelists, and not least of Thomas Hardy in particular. Associated with this is a permanent – and symptomatically childlike – dissatisfaction with reality as it is, the 'adult' world that is the case. Here too one must posit a deep memory of ready entry into alternative worlds – a dominant nostalgia for what Hardy called metempsychosis.

Beyond the specific myth of each novel, the novelist longs to be possessed by the continuous underlying myth he entertains of himself – a state not to be attained by method, logic, self-analysis, intelligent judgement or any other of the qualities that make a good teacher, executive or scientist. I should find it very hard to define what constitutes this being possessed, yet I know when I am and when I am not; that there are markedly different degrees of the state; that it functions as much by exclusion as by awareness; and above all, that it remains childlike in its fertility of lateral inconsequence, its setting of adultly ordered ideas in flux. Indeed, the workbench cost of this possession is revision – the elimination of the childish from the childlike, both in the language and the conception. Like Venus and Cupid, each muse has her accompanying imp. It is also a state that withdraws (like the *Well-Beloved*) as the text nears consummation; and its disappearance, however pleased one is with the final cast, is always deeply distressing . . . one other sense of loss, or reluctant return to normality, that every novelist-child has to contend with.[12]

He and Hardy are alike, Fowles believes, in at least two ways. Both are inclined to use multiple endings in their fiction, as for example in *The Well-Beloved* and *The French Lieutenant's Woman*. This fascination Fowles views as the result of a desire in both to prolong 'the doomed and illicit' but deeply satisfying search for an irrecoverable ideal. Also, Fowles finds Hardy attracted, like himself, to 'the tryst', the 'isolated meeting of a man and woman, preferably by chance, preferably in "pagan" nature and away from the "Christian" restraint of town and house, preferably trapset with various minor circumstances . . . that oblige a greater closeness and eventual bodily contact'.[13] Fowles calls the tryst 'that most Hardyesque of all narrative devices', but any reader of Fowles knows it is a favourite device of his as well. Fowles also calls attention to the critical importance of the women in Hardy's life, particularly of his mother, for the tryst, is, in Fowles's view, 'a scarcely concealed simulacrum of the primary relationship of the child with the vanished mother'.[14] Whether or not one accepts Fowles's Freudian analysis of Hardy's *Well-Beloved*, or Dr Rose's analysis of Fowles's *French Lieutenant's Woman*, is not really to the point here. What is to be noted is that by 1977, the year of *Daniel Martin*'s appearance, John Fowles had absorbed Rose's analysis of him and his novel, and then, even more important, was seeking out similarities between Hardy and himself on the basis of that analysis. It is as if Fowles viewed himself, in his artistic temper at least, as a reincarnation of his Dorset precursor. In this light, Fowles's decision in the mid 1960s to make Lyme Regis (Dorset) his home, and his apparently conscious choice of the year 1867, in Fowles's view a most important year in Hardy's life, on which to centre *The French Lieutenant's Woman*, are highly important, as are the many epigraphs from Hardy's poems and the references to Hardy and Tryphena Sparks in that novel. As shall now be seen, Hardy was an equally important – if not quite so visible – influence on *Daniel Martin*, the autobiographical novel Fowles published in the same year as 'Hardy and the Hag'. From at least 1969 to 1977, John Fowles seems to have been discovering in Hardy, the man and the artist, similarities to himself that would affect the form and content of *Daniel Martin*.

The name 'Martin' and the name 'Hardy', it should be noted

from the outset, sound and are spelled much alike. This is worth mentioning because Daniel Martin (like Powys's Dud No-man) openly associates himself with Thomas Hardy at a turning-point in his (Martin's) career, and because Martin's career as a troubled artist who is also a restless lover of a series of women resembles that of the historical Thomas Hardy, as well as of Jocelyn Pierston, the hero of *The Well-Beloved*, whom Fowles in the essay 'Hardy and the Hag' describes as 'Pierston-Hardy'.[15] Fowles's Daniel, a one-time playwright who has become a successful Hollywood screenwriter in the 1970s, is tormented by the knowledge that he has lost touch with his past and therefore with his 'true' self. This true self has three loci: the grave of Daniel's mother in rural Devon; rural Devon itself, particularly Thorncombe Farm, and Nancy Reed, a childhood sweetheart of the 1940s whose family had occupied Thorncombe for many years; and Jane, an American woman he had met and loved while he was a student at Oxford in the 1950s. It weighs heavily on Dan's conscience that while engaged to Jane's sister, Nell, he had had a love affair with Jane, who at the time was engaged to Anthony Mallory, Dan's closest friend. In spite of their deep and genuine love for one another, Dan and Jane dutifully marry their affianceds, with the result an early divorce for Dan and Nell and a bitterly unhappy, if lasting, marriage for Jane and Anthony.

Daniel Martin opens at two widely separate times and places in Daniel's life: in August 1942, in a wartime harvest field in Devon, England, where the teenaged Dan, son of the village clergyman, aids in the harvest of the grain and watches, in horror, the slaughter of rabbits by the harvesters; and in the 1970s, in a highrise apartment building in Hollywood, California, where Dan, a middle-aged film-writer of international reputation, speaks with Jenny O'Neill, a promising young Scottish actress who is also his mistress, of his need 'metaphorically' to 'go home'.[16] The governing form of the novel is established by this temporal and geographical division in its opening and that opening's announcement of a homecoming. *Daniel Martin* is the story of the return of a native, the story of Daniel's return from Hollywood and the film world to Devon and the world of his rural past; to Jane, his first love; and to his true calling as a writer. That this structure has Hardyan underpinnings is signalled not just by the similarity between Dan's situation and that of Jocelyn Pierston, but also by Fowles's debt in the threshing-scene in the first chapter of *Daniel*

Martin to the more famous threshing-scene in chapter 14 of *Tess of the d'Urbervilles*, where the rodents are slaughtered by the harvesters. Dan's quest is to recover something of the rootedness and community he had known more than thirty years before in Devon, a sense of place as lost to him as a result of his rise in the world as Tess's innocence was lost to her through sexual violation. Like Tess, Dan is seen as a ruined innocent, especially as a result of his initial sexual encounter with Jane. Dan's search is made difficult because between youth and middle age, between the 1940s and the 1970s, he had been guilty of a series of gross infidelities: against Nell (both with her sister Jane before marriage and with other women after); against his friend Anthony (Jane's husband) and against friendship itself, for he had written and staged a spiteful play in which Anthony, Jane and Nell are made *his* betrayers; against the religious piety of his father, an Anglican clergyman, for Dan is an avowed atheist; against the memory of a kindly aunt who cared for him after his mother's death; against his first literary calling, the writing of drama, a calling he had abandoned for the profits and fame of commercial film-writing. Finally, Dan has been unfaithful to something which he can hardly articulate, an impalpable and precious reality he has come to associate with his childhood in Devon. This reality includes a faint memory of his dead mother, who is buried in Devon. It also includes the Reeds of Thorncombe Farm, the Devonshire countryside itself, the Devonshire dialect – all suggestive of what Fowles has elsewhere described as a 'more perfect, happier, magical state'.

Dan's opportunity to 'go home', to recover his lost past and to make amends, comes to him in the unlikely form of a transatlantic telephone call. His conversation with Jenny in Hollywood in the second chapter of the novel is interrupted when Jane and Nell call from Oxford, at Anthony's request, to ask Dan to return to visit his former friend, who is dying of cancer. Dan's meeting with Anthony, now an Oxford philosopher, is his first move toward recovering his lost past and is the beginning of his homecoming; for it is the beginning of his restoration of himself to something like his earlier, better state. Anthony, confessing the failure of his marriage to Jane, admitting as well his duplicity in not telling Dan that he had known of Jane's liaison with Dan at Oxford some twenty years before, extracts from Dan the promise to try to restore Jane to something of her former self. Anthony has, in his own words, 'a kind of . . . hope against hope that you might one day find time to help disinter the person Jane might have been from beneath the person she is now' (*DM*, 'Catastasis'). Dan is left no time to change his mind after agreeing, for Anthony commits suicide moments after Dan leaves the hospital.

In large part Dan will succeed in restoring Jane and himself to a semblance of their former happiness, and this is a point at which Fowles has broken fundamentally with Hardy; for in Hardy there is no homecoming, no recovery of time past, no 'undoing the done'. Dan manages to resurrect Jane's and his own buried self. He does it by returning with her to Thorncombe and by rerooting himself in the soil of his most precious experiences of boyhood. He does it also by rejecting film-writing and committing himself to writing, with Jane's encouragement, an autobiographical novel whose hero is named Simon Wolfe. He does it, finally, by holding to his promise to Anthony to help Jane recover something of her former grace and verve, and he accomplishes this last at no small cost to himself. To turn to Jane is to desert Jenny, whom he still loves, and so the novel closes on a distinctly bitter-sweet, though not a tragic, note. It at once recalls and rejects the close of Hardy's *Well-Beloved*, the novel so much on Fowles's mind in the year he published *Daniel Martin*. Hardy's Pierston gives up his pursuit of youthful lovers to return to an older former lover, the aging Marcia Bencomb. But, where Pierston's return to Marcia spells the death of his art, Dan's return to Jane (like Proust's Marcel's return to Combray) is, it seems, the rebirth of his. Dan, like Pierston, is an artist whose creative inspiration is sustained by a relentless pursuit of women. But Dan is unlike Pierston in two important ways: he is capable of physical intimacy with the women he pursues, and, perhaps for this reason, he succeeds in recovering, or at least in finding a substitute for, his lost paradise.

What has been said thus far should suggest that Thomas Hardy cast as long a shadow across *Daniel Martin* as across *The French Lieutenant's Woman*. The rural scenes in *Daniel Martin*, both in the opening and in the later Devon chapters ('Phillidia', 'Thorncombe', 'In the Orchard of the Blessed' and 'Rain'), strongly recall Hardy's *Tess of the d'Urbervilles*. And Fowles invites this connection not just by echoing chapter 14 of *Tess* in his own first chapter, but also by referring to Hardy's greatest heroine on the eve of his second Devon episode. The novel's indictment of the stuffy, humourless, hidebound aspects of Oxford intellectual life recalls Hardy's indictment of Christminster in *Jude the Obscure*. Also, *Daniel Martin*, like several of Hardy's novels, *The Well-Beloved* among them, is the story of a homecoming, as has been noted. Daniel shares something not just with Jocelyn Pierston of *The Well-Beloved*, but with Clym Yeobright of *The Return of the Native* and Grace Melbury of *The Woodlanders*. The lives of all are shaped by their departure from and attempt to return to their rural beginnings. Fowles's own return in the 1960s to live permanently in his adopted West Country home of the 1940s[17] is probably the basis for Daniel's return to Devon and recalls also Hardy's own return to his native Dorset in 1867 and again (this time for good) in the 1880s. Like John Cowper Powys, Fowles was attracted to Hardy's depiction of the dilemma of the uprooted because he had himself experienced it. Daniel Martin, less schematically but no less definitely, is like Jocelyn Pierston (and Thomas Hardy) a man in pursuit of an ideal in its supposed female incarnations. This is the mother-fixated Hardy of Gittings's *Young Thomas Hardy*, not unlike (in Fowles's judgement in 'Hardy and the Hag') the mother-fixated John Fowles diagnosed by Dr Rose of Yale. Daniel Martin, like the historical Thomas Hardy, is torn by a guilty sense that he has betrayed his true artistic calling: Hardy had sacrificed poetic composition to the money-making alternative of serial fiction; Daniel has sacrificed play-writing to the profitable alternative of screenwriting. Hardy's Pierston, a sculptor, also fears the temptation of the market for popular art. He deplores, for example, his friend Somers's turn from a 'peculiar and personal taste in subjects' to the execution – the highly lucrative execution – of 'many pleasing aspects of nature addressed to the furnishing householder through the middle critic' (*The Well-Beloved*, pt III, ch. 4). Finally, Daniel Martin, like Jocelyn Pierston (and Thomas Hardy, in Fowles's view), has abandoned a true love in order to marry another: Dan's Nancy Reed is Pierston's Avice Caro the first (and perhaps Hardy's Tryphena); Jane is Pierston's Marcia (perhaps Hardy's Emma). To mention the name Caro is to recall that even that Hardyan name, the surname of the three Avices of Pierston's native Isle of Slingers, floats through Fowles's novel – it is the nickname of Caroline, Dan's daughter by Nell; and Caroline (as appealingly youthful as the three Avies) is for Dan another fleeting incarnation of the well-beloved, for on at least one occasion Dan is disturbed to find himself entertaining incestuous thoughts about her.

Lest it be thought that these connections between Fowles and

Hardy are purely imaginary or merely coincidental, the product of what Dr Johnson might have called the ingenuity, if not the dogmatism, of learning, it must be pointed out that in *Daniel Martin*, as in *The French Lieutenant's Woman*, Thomas Hardy makes a personal appearance. More accurately, Eric Kennington's statue of Hardy on Colliton Walk in present-day Dorchester makes an appearance. In the manner of John Cowyer Powys in *Maiden Castle* (see above, pp. 101 ff.), Fowles invokes Kennington's Hardy twice in his novel: first, and rather casually, during Dan and Jane's westward journey from Oxford to Thorncombe after the burial of Anthony, a journey that marks the beginning of their reconciliation; then again at a critical moment of self-realization for Dan just one day after he and Jane had passed the 'mournful' bronze Hardy in Dorchester.

Central to Dan's development in the novel, to his recovery of a 'self' he had lost, is his discovery that his resurgent love for Jane is endangered by his 'life-long need for emotional relationships with the female, with mother substitutes, or younger women carefully if unconsciously chosen to avoid that accusation' (*DM*, 'In the Silence of Other Voices'). In a passage that echoes Fowles's summary of Dr Rose's analysis in 'Hardy and the Hag', Daniel measures his own moral and psychological growth by his increasing understanding of the 'mother–son charge' that he has carried into all his liaisons with women:

> Dan was very slowly realizing something: that he was looking or seeking for her [Jane's] old self as if it were a reality he was deliberately hiding from him; which was not only . . . to discuss the much greater reality of all that had happened since, but betrayed a retardation in himself, a quasi-Freudian searching for the eternally lost, his vanished mother. . . . Something in him must always look for that, even in much younger women – one could invert the whole process and say that he was looking for Jenny in Jane still. All his close relationships with women, even his completely asexual ones . . . were variations on the model; and broke down precisely because they could not support what his unconscious demanded of them. It was fundamentally absurd, a repetition compulsion. . . .   (*DM*, 'Barbarians')

In 'Hardy and the Hag', while silently acknowledging the existence of a similar compulsion in himself in writing *The French Lieutenant's*

Woman, Fowles urges a similar 'searching for the eternally lost . . . mother' in the author of *The Well-Beloved*.

Daniel recovers his ties with his past only upon returning to Thorncombe, the Devon farm on which he had worked as a boy (the harvest scene that opens the novel is set there) and which he has now purchased as a retreat from his professional duties in London and Hollywood. As he drives from Oxford west to Thorncombe with Jane and her son Paul, he stops near Shaftesbury to examine some ancient earthworks. Some flints he finds in a ploughed field there remind Jane of Hardy's Tess and her ordeal at Flintcomb-Ash: 'It would have done . . . perfectly for a Tess turnip-hoeing or stone-picking', she remarks. Shortly after, once more on the road west to Devon, Dan drives through Dorchester and in front of Kennington's statue of Tess's creator: 'Soon we were going past Hardy's statue, mournful and traffic-disapproving as ever' (*DM*, 'Westward'). If the fields near Shaftesbury in Dorset remind Jane of Tess's misery at Flintcomb, Thorncombe in Devon may be seen as Dan's Talbothays, as much his place of renewal as Talbothays had been Tess's. But one notes that Fowles has effected a reversal: Tess had moved from Talbothays to Flintcomb-Ash and on from there to even greater spiritual miseries; Dan moves from Hollywood and London (his spiritual Flintcomb) toward Thorncombe, reconcilation with his past, a new beginning with Jane, and a renewed commitment to art. Dan's movement is toward renewal as surely as Tess's is toward obliteration and death. Fowles imitates Hardy only up to a point; then he swerves decisively from the tragic view of things presented by his precursor.

In the sequence of chapters titled 'Phillidia', 'Thorncombe', 'In the Orchard of the Blessed', and 'Rain' – chapters that have been called the finest in the novel – Fowles exhibits the restoration of Daniel Martin to something like his authentic self. After his many infidelities and almost total divorce from the ways of his Devon past, Daniel is restored. He recalls and relives in memory his boyhood love for Nancy Reed, the youngest daughter of the yeoman farmer who had owned Thorncombe; he recovers his affection for the farm itself and for its present caretakers, the Devon-born Ben and Phoebe; he commits himself to reconstructing his long-interrupted love for Jane by inviting her to accompany him on a journey through Syria and Egypt; he decides that film-writing is a betrayal of his talent and dedicates himself to writing a novel, an autobiographical novel whose hero is named Simon Wolfe.

It is worth remarking once again on the suggestiveness of the names in the novel. The name 'Wolfe' is an anagram for 'Fowle', just as the name 'Martin' is an echo of 'Hardy'. John Fowles is writing of Daniel Martin writing about Simon Wolfe, of a version of himself who, in collusion with a great precursor, is shaping yet another version of himself. One recalls again the resemblance between Dan's struggle to set aside film-writing for novel-writing and Hardy's vacillation in the 1890s between the writing of fiction and the writing of poetry. The struggle ended for Hardy with his turn to poetry after revising *The Pursuit of the Well-Beloved* into *The Well-Beloved: A Sketch of a Temperament*, in 1897. For Dan, the struggle ends with his abandonment of screenwriting for the writing of autobiographical fiction.[18] Fowles may well have had this similarity in mind as he wrote, for Dan's critical decision to write a self-probing novel is explained with a final reference to Thomas Hardy:

> He [Dan] felt an interweaving of strands, both of and far beyond the last twelve hours, an obscure amalgam of rain, landscapes, pasts, fertilities, femalenesses, all of which could perhaps have been derived from that one wet gravestone, his unknown mother's he had stared at so briefly that morning; *and which would certainly have been so derived by the verdigrised old sage in bronze whom Dan had passed, with no more than an amused glance, in Dorchester that previous afternoon?* (DM, 'Rain'; italics added)

'But I didn't derive it so myself, in the implacable first person of the moment', Fowles's first-person narrator hastens to explain. Daniel's retrospective and detached third-person voice, not his confiding first-person voice, has announced this Hardyan insight, this moment of artistic and sexual self-consciousness, during Daniel's visit to the grave of his mother. He does so because he sees, more clearly than ever before, that his restless yearning, his movement from woman to woman, is 'a searching for the eternally lost, his vanished mother'. And Hardy ('the old sage in bronze . . . in Dorchester'), Daniel's third-person voice confidently explains, would make the same derivation, presumably because Hardy too had been a novelist whose narratives were an expression of his search for the vanished mother. Fowles seems to have modelled the psychology of his autobiographical hero, at least in part, on the psychology of Thomas Hardy – the Thomas Hardy portrayed by Gittings in *Young Thomas Hardy* and by Hardy himself in *The Well-Beloved*.

To argue that *Daniel Martin* owes a good deal to Hardy, particularly to Hardy's *Well-Beloved*, is not to say that it is unoriginal or merely imitative. One might suggest in fact that its interest begins where its dependence on Hardy ends. In its international setting (England, America, Egypt, Syria), in its concern with international politics, in its complex narrative method (the interwoven narratives of Dan and Jenny; the sudden shifts, sometimes in the same sentence, between first and third-person narration), and especially in its final optimism about Daniel's ability to return, restore and make amends, *Daniel Martin* is a distinct departure from Hardy and his local settings, third-person narrators, and gloomy insistence that there is no going home again, no restoring things past, no making amends for old errors or offences. Fowles is as wedded, one might say, to a belief in the regenerative nature of things as Hardy was to a belief in deteriorism. Fowles would have it seem that Daniel can recover time past, can turn from film-writing to the nobler craft of fiction, can make a new life with and for Jane, fulfilling thereby Anthony's dying plea that he raise her from the living dead. And this great change in Dan – for until sent on his mission of redemption by Anthony he had been sceptical about human and all other powers of regeneration – occurs in Edenic Thorncombe, where Dan 'came to the most important decision of his life': to reject 'cultural fashion . . . elitist guilt . . . existential nausea . . . and, above all, . . . the imagined that does not say, not only in, but behind the images, the real' (*DM*, 'In the Orchard of the Blessed'). Fowles also rejects, in effect, Hardyan melancholy and Hardyan pessimism. At the same time, it seems clear he put himself to school in *The Well-Beloved* and the life of its author. Fowles is not a mere imitator. His hero can consummate his love, and this is another great difference between Daniel Martin and Jocelyn Pierston. The tender scene between Dan and Jane in a rural hostel in the wilds of Syria is a moving account of the glories and the limits of love between the middle-aged. And so Fowles's hero does not give in to despair as Pierston does. Pierston's return to an aging Marcia marks the end of his pursuit of the well-beloved and the end of his art. Daniel's return to Jane and the prospect of domestic harmony marks the beginning of his. In this humanistic faith, Fowles is more like Proust than like Hardy, and more like Proust than like his favoured Alain-Fournier.

For these reasons, perhaps, Fowles chose to end his story not with Daniel's retreat from or triumphant mastery of his art, but with his encounter with a self-portrait by another old master, the Rembrandt of 'the famous late Rembrandt self-portrait' that hangs in a London gallery. In that self-portrait, as not in Hardy's self-portrait in *The Well-Beloved*, Daniel finds something like direction and consolation:

> The sad, proud old man stared eternally out of his canvas, out of the entire knowledge of his own genius and of the inadequacy of genius before human reality. Dan stared back.... Dan felt dwarfed, in his century, his personal being, his own art. The great picture seemed to denounce, almost to repel. Yet it lived, was timeless, it spoke very directly, said all he had never managed to say and would never manage to say.... Standing there before the Rembrandt, he experienced a kind of vertigo: the distances he had to return.... He could only see one consolation in those remorseless and aloof Dutch eyes. It is not finally a matter of skill, of knowledge, of intellect; of good luck or bad; but of choosing and learning to feel. Dan began at last to detect it behind the surface of the painting; behind the sternness lay the declaration of the one true marriage of the mind mankind is allowed, the ultimate of humanism. No true compassion without will, no true will without compassion. (*DM*, 'Future Past')

This strategically placed glance at Rembrandt, in its emphasis on the artist's self-knowledge, on free will and the possibility of remedy, seems a dismissal of the Thomas Hardy who casts so long a shadow over Fowles's narrative and an act of homage to a rival master. Even Hardy's favourite virtue, 'lovingkindness', is seen as impossible in the absence of free will ('No true compassion without will'). Fowles's attitude toward Hardy is mixed – sympathetic yet cautious – for Fowles is a powerfully original writer even when he is most derivative.

This strength and originality emanate in part from Fowles's fear lest he be trapped in the very way he found Hardy trapped in *The Well-Beloved* – by an attempt to destroy the 'tyranny' of the 'younger self' over the 'supposedly "mature" and middle-aged artist'. A novelist rejects this tyranny, Fowles insists, at the expense of his 'ability to write novels'.[19] Examination of two of Fowles's remarks on Hardy, the first made in 1969 (quoted in part above), the second in 1977, suggests the growth in him of just such a fear of exorcising 'a younger self' at the expense of nothing less than his ability to write. Here is Fowles in that statement of 1969 we have already noted:

> The shadow of Thomas Hardy, the heart of whose 'country' I can see in the distance from my workroom window, I cannot avoid. Since he and Peacock are my two favourite male novelists of the nineteenth century I don't mind the shadow. It seems best to use it; and by a curious coincidence, which I didn't realize when I placed my own story in that year, 1867 was the crucial year in Hardy's own mysterious personal life. It is somehow encouraging that while my fictitious characters weave their own story in their 1867, only thirty miles away in the real 1867 the pale young architect was entering his own fatal life-incident.

Now here is Fowles again, eight years later, in the year of *Daniel Martin*. Again he is gazing out of his workroom window in Lyme Regis unto the land of Hardy to the east:

> Hardy's nightmare [at being tyrannized by a 'younger self' that he could no longer incorporate in his fiction] is painfully familiar to most contemporary novelists. The question of whether fiction is at the end of its tether is now universally in the air. It comes to us, far more consciously, as a nausea at the fictionality of fiction . . . or as a dread of once more entering an always ultimately defeating labyrinth. No further explanation is needed of the marked drop in fertility that has beset novelists during the last fifty years. The more you are aware of a hopeless obsession, the less you are driven by it. This is why *The Well-Beloved* is infinitely the most important of all of Hardy's books for a practising novelist or intending writer of fiction to establish an attitude towards. The others, his far greater novels in ordinary terms, are now Victorian monuments, safe prey for the literary surveyors. *The Well-Beloved* still waits, potent, like a coiled adder on the Portland Cliffs that brood distantly on where I sit, across Lyme Bay.[20]

One must wonder why Fowles, between 1969 and 1977, changed so drastically his metaphor for the influence of Hardy on him: from that of a 'shadow', an image faintly threatening but also sheltering, to that of a 'coiled adder', an image sinister and even lethal in its implication. Is it because *The Well-Beloved*, as fiction 'at the end of its tether', is fiction dangerous, even fatally dangerous, for a practising novelist to imitate uncritically? This is altogether plausible, for Fowles's autobiographical hero's turn at the end of *Daniel Martin* to the heartening Rembrandt self-portrait *and* to his own self-portrait-in-progress is implicitly a turn-away from the element of self-defeat in *The Well-Beloved*. It signals a vital new beginning in a humanism growing out of belief in an artist's ability to descend within himself and find there ever-fresh terms of expression and appeal. For reasons of temperament, education and experience, Fowles refused to follow Hardy in the latter's pessimism. But he is no less in Hardy's debt for this, for Fowles has been led by Hardy into writing in the autobiographical *Daniel Martin* his most ambitious work of fiction to date – his own demonstration of how the 'much younger self still rules the supposedly "mature" and middle-aged artist'.[21]

6
'The Pathetic Side of the World': Hardy and Theodore Dreiser

> *I am almost ready to characterize Hardy . . . as an American whose ancestors failed to migrate at the proper time and who accordingly found himself stranded a couple of centuries later, in the wrong literary climate.*
> (Donald Davidson, 1940)

On 2 June 1920, Thomas Hardy's eightieth birthday, a group of distinguished American writers, among them Sherwood Anderson, Van Wyck Brooks, Robert Frost, E. A. Robinson, Carl Sandburg and Theodore Dreiser, cabled Hardy to wish him well and to express gratitude for his 'living contribution to our literature'. The word 'living' was an appropriate one, for ever since June 1873, when Holt and Williams of New York published *Under the Greenwood Tree* in the Leisure Hours series, Hardy's novels had enjoyed an extraordinary popularity in America – among critics and reviewers, with the general public, and, perhaps most importantly, among American novelists such as William Dean Howells, Sherwood Anderson, Ellen Glasgow, Willa Cather, Hamlin Garland and Theodore Dreiser.[1] Though the main concern here is Hardy's influence on Dreiser, it is helpful to note also some of the responses of other American novelists to the Wessex Novels; for it is clear that Dreiser's admiration for Hardy, like Proust's in France a few years later, was part of a national response.

Howells, the great arbiter of literary taste in America at the time, wrote as follows in 1895:

> I came rather late, but I came with all the ardor of what seems my perennial literary youth, to the love of Thomas Hardy, whom I first knew in his story *A Pair of Blue Eyes*. As usual,

after I had read this book and felt the new charm in it, I wished to read the books of no other author, and to read his books over and over. . . . Hardy is a great poet as well as a great humorist, and if he were not a great artist also his humor would be enough to endear him to me.[2]

In 1901, commenting on Hardy's heroines, Howells wrote,

Mr. Hardy's heroines are good or they are bad, or they are now good and now bad, according to some inner impulse from some agency deeper or more primal than conscience. When they feel the pull of the moral law, they yield it a partial and provisional allegiance. . . . Perhaps we may best define the sort of women this novelist places before us so livingly that we cannot doubt their reality by a process of exclusion in which we need go no farther than to say that they are wholly unlike American women. . . . In the Hardy lower-class heroines we see the primitive Englishwoman before she was touched by Puritanism, and in his middle and upper class heroines the same woman as she has grown into modern civilization unaffected by the tremendous force which has permeated and moulded the nature of the American great-great-grandnieces of that original Englishwoman. I have often wondered what character untouched by Puritanism was like, and I have fancied that in the Hardy heroines I have seen; and if I cannot altogether approve of it, I can own its charm, as I can willingly acknowledge the ugliness and error and soul-sickness which Puritanism produced in building up our intensely personalized American conscience.[3]

In the mid-1890s, Willa Cather, a novelist-to-be working for newspapers in Pittsburgh, Pennsylvania, and Lincoln, Nebraska, reviewed Hardy's *Hearts Insurgent (Jude the Obscure)* for the Lincoln *Courier*. Cather was an admirer of Hardy's fiction, but she despised the story of Jude Fawley and Sue Bridehead:

Then there is that crowning piece of arrant madness and drivelling idiocy, *Hearts Insurgent*. I admire Thomas Hardy; I admire the lofty conception of *Tess of the d'Urbervilles*, the finished execution of *A Pair of Blue Eyes*, the beautiful simplicity of *Far from the Madding Crowd*. But for *Hearts Insurgent* I have no forgiveness. If Mr. Hardy ever had any serious purpose or intention in writing the thing, I suppose he meant to show what idiots a little learning makes of people of the downright plebian stock.[4]

In May 1897, Cather saw Lorimer Stoddard's stage version of *Tess* in Pittsburgh, and her admiration for *Tess* was confirmed. She wrote three long reviews of the play in the six months that followed, for the Pittsburgh *Journal* and *Leader*, and for the Lincoln *Courier*. And it is clear that the future author of *My Ántonia* (1918) was carrying out a careful comparison of the novel and the play. Cather found Stoddard's *Tess* 'a great play' that retained 'wonderfully' the spirit of Thomas Hardy. And Hardy, she declared, was a master in the depiction of English rural life: it is 'the one thing in which [he] excels all the novelists of his time and country'.[5] In yet another review of the play she described it as one of 'the few really great plays of the last quarter of a century', the 'play of the present, the play which best expresses the tendencies of modern art and modern thought'. She found *Tess* so powerful because it worked through 'the only religion that is left us now – the religion of human suffering'.[6] Her enthusiasm is evident in the following: 'I have seen Minnie Maddern Fisk as Tess of the d'Urbervilles four times this week. I could not see her oftener in one week without risking a nervous collapse. Flesh and blood can endure only up to a certain point. Of all the performances now on the American stage, I think this is the only one that will go down in history.'[7]

Testimony such as this suggests the shrewdness in Oscar Cargill's remark that 'the chief merit of Thomas Hardy is that he compelled serious reflection in the most evasive decade in British and American history – the last ten years of Victoria and the end of the Gilded Age'.[8] This was clearly the effect on Theodore Dreiser, who first read Hardy when working as a newspaperman in St Louis and Pittsburgh in 1893–4 and then praised him for the next thirty years; though more about Dreiser later.

In 1925, Sinclair Lewis described Hardy as 'probably the greatest living novelist' and predicted that in the year 2025 Hardy would be seen as 'one of the few geniuses of all prose fiction':

There is in Hardy such a combination of nobility with closeness to earth, of dignity with quick humanity, as can be equalled only in one or two of the Russians. *Jude* and *Tess* and *The Return* of the Native are revelations of somber splendor which yet is never ponderous, which even to the most timorous romantic is forever interesting. . . . The other day a friend asked me in what writer he could best find great and original vision charged with warm humaneness. I suggested Thomas Hardy.[9]

Critics have described in some detail the appeal of Hardy to three other American novelists writing in the first half of the twentieth century: Sherwood Anderson, one of whose stories in *Winesburg, Ohio* (1919) reflects the influence of Hardy's *Jude the Obscure;* Ellen Glasgow, whose *Barren Ground* (1925), probably her best novel, is virtually a Hardy pastiche; and William Faulkner, whose saga of the decline of the rural South has frequently been compared to Hardy's saga of Wessex.

Anderson's encounter with Hardy's late novels occurred after 1907, when, as he recorded in his *Memoirs*, Hardy's *Tess* and *Jude* were being spoken of as vulgar books at certain literary gatherings in Elyria, Ohio. Six years later, in Chicago, he continued to read, and apparently to imitate Hardy's fiction, for he wrote, 'I was the sedulous ape, continually reading novels. . . . I was under the spell of the earlier novels of H. G. Wells, and those of Thomas Hardy, Arnold Bennett, and George Moore.'[10] As Luther S. Luedtke has pointed out, Anderson found much to sympathize with in Hardy; for both 'studied the fragmentation and spiritual hunger of rural backwaters left by the sweep of modern technology and commerce, and both created mythic communities (Wessex and Winesburg) in which to examine the condition of man, woman, and earth in the new age'.[11] More concrete than this is Anderson's 'acknowledgement of his indebtedness to Thomas Hardy' in 'Tandy', one of the earliest written of the tales in *Winesburg, Ohio* and the only survival of a trilogy dating from about 1915 and centring on a heroine named Tandy Hard. 'Tandy', as Luedtke has pointed out, can be read as Anderson's attack on Hardy's pessimism; for it is the story of a religious sceptic named Tom Hard, a man so preoccupied with hatred for religion that he neglects his motherless daughter and is blinded to the manifestations of goodness in the child. Tom Hard's scepticism is countered in the story by the humanism of a drunken stranger, the son of a wealthy Cleveland merchant who has come to Winesburg to cure himself of alcoholism. The tipsy stranger sees in the daughter of Tom Hard what Hard cannot see, 'a new quality in woman' that can be mankind's secular salvation: 'I have a name for it. *I call it Tandy.* I made up the name when I was a true dreamer and before my body became vile. It is *the quality of being strong to be loved.* It is something men need from women and they do not get.' Anderson's stranger recalls the drunkenness but not the despair of Hardy's Jude Fawley when, frustrated in his love for Sue Bridehead, he gives way to suicidal gloom. A projection in Luedtke's view of 'both the desperate Jude and of Sherwood Anderson', Anderson's stranger embodies Anderson's view that the 'relentless fatality of Jude's life [is] a needlessly [hard] one'. The story is a criticism of Thomas Hardy 'for being blind to possibilities of new life beyond the momentary grotesquerie'.[12] Anderson's rejection of Hardy's pessimism strongly resembles Powys's and Lawrence's at about this same time. Like Lawrence and Powys, and later John Fowles, Anderson worked 'toward a way of mending tragedy, gathering the broken parts together and healing the breach between men and women'.[13]

But, if in the story 'Tandy' Anderson rejected Hardyan gloom, there and elsewhere he embraced the Hardyan view 'of women as essentially one with the earth and [like Hardy] accepted her natural sexual tyranny as a cohesive force, corresponding to the fecundity of the land and the flux of the seasons'.[14] And, again like Hardy, 'Anderson viewed the transfer of generative power from land and woman to man-made machines with great foreboding'.[15] This sense of man and woman in relation to the land, which Anderson learned from Hardy and which was reinforced by his reading of D. H. Lawrence, whom he also admired, persisted in *Poor White* (1920), *Many Marriages* (1923) and *Dark Laughter* (1925), and reached a kind of culmination in *Perhaps Women* (1931), in whose Lawrentian introduction Anderson writes of a 'growing conviction that modern man is losing his ability to retain his manhood in the face of the modern way of utilizing the machine and that what hope there is for him lies in woman'.[16] Only 'the mystery and natural rhythms of woman could save men from the fascination, domination, and degradation of the devouring impersonal machines they had created'.[17]

> Anderson read Hardy's novels at the important moment when he first sought to distill in writing his profound feeling and experience. They demonstrated to him that the author should write of the small patch of land he knew best, that his own

haunting provinciality might be a literary virtue, and they dramatized the deeper significances and mystic identities that Anderson had so long wanted to impress in thought, characters, and words. From Hardy as much as from Dreiser (and especially from the controversy over Hardy's unrelenting treatment of sexual relations in *Tess* and *Jude*), Anderson drew courage to break with the genteel tradition and to illustrate the resistance of human passion to mind-made conventions. Both writers imbued sex with mystical significance and identified it as a first force of nature, but of the two Anderson alone held out hope for escape from the machine through liberating the sexual energies themselves.[18]

Much of what Luedtke has said about Hardy's influence on Anderson might be said as well of his influence on Ellen Glasgow (1873–1945). Like Anderson, Glasgow was a regionalist. Like him and other writers of her generation, she was trying to write with candour, though from a woman's point of view, about sexual passion. And like Anderson she was an admirer of Hardy, though even more energetically so. Glasgow visited Hardy at Max Gate in 1914, and again in 1927, and on the latter occasion recorded this impression:

> I never saw so attractive a man of his age as Thomas Hardy, which proves that it is intellect, after all, that counts as one goes over the hill of life. He is far more modern and advanced than most men of twenty-five, and age has not deadened his sensibility in the least. . . . He is profoundly civilized and sympathetic about animals just as he is in his books – and especially in *Jude*.[19]

Hardy's *Tess* had a determinative effect on Glasgow, particularly in *Barren Ground*. No less important is the fact that near the end of her career Glasgow spoke of the whole of her work in regional fiction in much the way Hardy had spoken of the Wessex Novels. Glasgow wished to view herself as having done for the American South what Hardy had done for the English West Country.

In the Preface to *Barren Ground* (volume I of the 1938 Virginia Edition of her novels), Glasgow at several points echoes Hardy in his General Preface to the Wessex Edition of his novels (1912), which Hardy had placed at the head of *Tess of the d'Urbervilles* (volume I of the Wessex Edition).[20] Like Hardy, Ellen Glasgow described her novels as quasi-fictional social history – a chronicle 'of Virginia since the War Between the States' (*BG*, p. ix). Hardy, of course, had set his novels in 'the half-dozen counties . . . reunited under the old name of Wessex' (*TD*, p. 474). Like Hardy, Glasgow wished to make regional legend and history a symbol and part of 'a larger world'. 'I have resolved,' she wrote, 'to portray not Southern "types" alone, but whole human beings, and to touch, or at least feel for, the universal chords beneath regional variations of character' (*BG*, p. x). Hardy had set forth a similar principle: that 'in respect of the elementary passions' regional novels, 'novels that evolve their action on a circumscribed scene', can be 'as inclusive in their exhibition of human nature as novels wherein the scenes cover large extents of country, in which events figure amid towns and cities, even wander over the four quarters of the globe' (*TD*, p. 474). But, if Glasgow embraced Hardy's regionalism, she declared her independence of his philosophy when, like Anderson and others, she insisted that, though indeed 'character is fate' (the phrase, Novalis's, also appears in Hardy's *Mayor of Casterbridge*), men and women are capable of altering, even determining, their fates: 'one may learn to live, one may even learn to live gallantly, without delight' (*BG*, p. xi). This conviction is exhibited in the heroine of *Barren Ground*, just as its converse had been demonstrated in *Tess of the d'Urbervilles*.

Barren Ground is the story of Dorinda Oakley, an American Tess who survives her troubles and even triumphs. Dorinda, like Tess, is seduced and abandoned. Like Tess, she loses her baby. Unlike Tess, however, she returns to her native place, picks up the tangled strands of her life and that of her feckless family, successfully repels the renewed advances of her seducer, and eventually triumphs over him and others by becoming the mistress of the most prosperous farm in the hamlet of Pedlar's Mill.[21] These similarities between the stories are matched by a wealth of shared details, as George O. Marshall Jr has shown. Both Dorinda and Tess are born of a union of social opposites. Angel Clare's sleepwalking is matched by Mrs Oakley's somnambulism. Tess's meeting with a painter of religious texts on gates and barns has its counterpart in Dorinda's meeting with an elderly couple nailing posters with religious texts to trees. Dorinda feels guilt for spending money on a new dress for herself rather than on a new cow for the family, much as Tess is devastated by the loss of

Prince, the Durbeyfield family's sole horse. In both *Tess* and *Barren Ground* the heroine's work on a dairy farm forms an important phase of her experience. The list of similarities can be extended much farther, and in fact far beyond *Tess*. For, as this brief summary should suggest, *Barren Ground* is indebted to other of Hardy's novels. If as a ruined maid Dorinda suggests Tess, then as a woman who becomes mistress of a farm she also suggests Hardy's Bathsheba Everdene of *Far from the Madding Crowd*. And, as a woman who scorns the sexual companionship of a man, even so sympathetic and as kindly a man as Nathan, her husband, Dorinda recalls Hardy's Sue Bridehead and her wish to be free of sexual entanglements. Finally, in so far as she is, after her return to Pedlar's Mill from New York City, a native returning to her rural birthplace, Dorinda recalls Hardy's Grace Melbury and her return to the Hintock Woodlands, or, better, Hardy's Clym Yeobright and his return to Egdon Heath from the boulevards and shops of Paris. And indeed Hardy's furze-covered Egdon and Glasgow's broomsedge-shrouded fields around Pedlar's Mill have much in common, as James Tuttleton has pointed out.

Barren Ground is a Hardy pastiche, a mosaic of Hardyan allusions, characters, ideas and settings – but entirely in the service of a view of human destiny almost wholly antithetical to Hardy's. It is the old story. Like Lawrence, Proust, Powys, Fowles and Anderson, Glasgow felt called upon to imitate Hardy and at the same time to turn away from his pessimistic view of things. For example, the philosophy of both Hardy and Glasgow, as Tuttleton has explained,[22] stems from nineteenth-century 'evolutionary theories that had eventuated in Schopenhauer's philosophy of the Immanent Will . . . which objectifies itself in matter. Both derived from him the notion of the world as idea.' Within this evolving order, Hardy's people find the demands of the passions both overwhelming and unavoidable. An Alec seeks out a Tess, an Arabella a Jude. The playful Bathsheba Everdene sends a valentine to a love-starved man of middle age, with an emotional cataclysm the result. Or, more ironically, men and women uncertain in their sexuality – a Sue Bridehead, Angel Clare or Clym Yeobright – find themselves attached to mates fully prepared to obey the urgings of nature and the Will.

The result of these conflicts between 'the self and impersonal fate' in every case is suffering and death – for Jude, for Tess, for Eustacia.[23] The result of a similar set of circumstances in *Barren*

Ground is Dorinda's qualified triumph: her reclamation of the family land; her deliciously satisfying humiliation of her seducer, Jason Greylock; her acceptance of a loving husband (Nathan) in a marriage she refuses to consummate. Most interesting here is that Glasgow has not simply substituted a happy for a tragic turn of events. Though she insists that Dorinda, unlike Tess, is 'free to grow, to change, to work out her destiny',[24] and though Dorinda does indeed grow, change, and make her own way in the world, she does so at the cost of something precious to her humanity. A hater of men after her mistreatment by Greylock, her desire to punish all men in return makes her the victim of a bitter irony. She becomes a most man-like woman, more like the despotic and selfish creatures she despises than like a normal woman. She learns to outwork the men of Pedlar's Mill; and, though, at the end of her story, she is indeed their superior, she is also hard and tough, lacking in something that Glasgow values highly – compassion and tenderness, something like the 'loving kindness' that Hardy's Tess manages to preserve even through her murder of Alec, her capture and her execution. Dorinda is dehumanized by her passion to reclaim the abandoned fields of the family farm, which becomes the symbol for her obsession to reclaim the innocence she has lost. Dorinda, finally, is the 'barren ground' of the novel's title. In her final cold harshness she recalls Hardy's Elizabeth-Jane of *The Mayor of Casterbridge*, and in her situation poses a highly interesting question: has she lost more than she has gained? Is Dorinda, like Tess, 'heroic and noble, or merely, like . . . Sue Bridehead, pathological'?[25]

As this suggests, like Lawrence before her, Glasgow used to her own end Hardy's use of sexual reversals. Dorinda's strength and aloofness, her triumph over adversity, place her in a position of traditional male prestige and authority (one thinks of Lawrence's Ursula Brangwen). She ends a lonely figure of power, 'finished . . . and thankful to have finished' with love, as she says. But power without sympathy, strength without compassion, is, in Glasgow's view, tyranny and therefore inhumanity. Is Dorinda a monster or a liberated woman? In Sherwood Anderson's (masculine) terms, Dorinda has abandoned the mystery and natural rhythm of her womanhood for a devouring, impersonal, mechanical maleness.[26]

The case for William Faulkner's debt to Hardy has been made so frequently and confidently, and so consistently without actual evidence that Faulkner read Hardy, or talked or thought about him, that one suspects a case of temperamental affinities at work on a similar set of historical circumstances rather than a demonstrable case of literary influence. If, for example, Faulkner's *Absalom, Absalom!* (1936) resembles in certain details of plot and in tragic tone Hardy's *Mayor of Casterbridge*, there is no evidence that Faulkner read or used this novel.[27] Cleanth Brooks raises expectations he does not fulfil (or perhaps is being faithful to the scantiness of evidence) when he begins *William Faulkner: The Yoknapatawpha County* with the remark that readers as quickly associate Faulkner with the American South as they associate Hardy with Wessex, then never mentions Hardy again in his study.[28] And David Jarrett, though wholly justified in 'comparing Faulkner with Hardy in general terms' – the use of rustic humour, the fatalism rooted in cultural decline, the depiction of alien intruders, the 'complexities of plotting' – can only speculate upon the origin of Eula Varner of *The Hamlet* (1940) in Eustacia Vye of *The Return of the Native*.[29] Jarrett's argument rests as much on like-sounding names – Eula Varner, Eustacia Vye; Clym, Flem – as on anything else. There seems to be no basis in available fact for his conclusion that 'Faulkner repeats and adapts *in detail* from Hardy points of character, lines of imagery, narrative methods. . . .'[30]

One might as plausibly name Sherwood Anderson as one source, and that a most important one, of Faulkner's supposed interest in Hardy. As has been seen, Anderson acknowledged his reading and imitation of Hardy between 1907 and 1913, with palpable results in *Winesburg, Ohio*. In 1925, Anderson and Faulkner met in New Orleans, where they talked a great deal about the art of fiction. One result of this meeting was Anderson's persuading Horace Liveright to publish Faulkner's first novel, *Soldier's Pay*, in 1926. *Soldier's Pay* was written apparently with Anderson in mind as a reader. Faulkner's recollection nearly twenty years later of this association with Anderson in New Orleans describes a debt to Anderson's sense of place in his fiction, a sense of place that Anderson in turn may have learned from Thomas Hardy:

> I learned [from Anderson] that, to be a writer, one has first got to be what he is, what he was born; that to be an American and a writer, one does not necessarily have to pay lip-service to any conventional American image such as his [Anderson's] and

Dreiser's own aching Indiana or Ohio or Iowa corn or Sandburg's stockyards or Mark Twain's frog. You had only to remember what you were. 'You have to have somewhere to start from: then you begin to learn', he [Anderson] told me. 'It don't matter where it was, just so you remember it and ain't ashamed of it. Because one place to start from is just as important as any other. You're a country boy; all you know is that little patch up there in Mississippi where you started from. But that's all right too. It's America too; pull it out, as little and unknown as it is, and the whole thing will collapse, like when you prize a brick out of a wall.'[31]

This passage – and one must recall that it is Faulkner's recollection of conversations with Anderson twenty years earlier – echoes Hardy's statement in his General Preface to the Wessex Novels, the statement echoed in turn by Ellen Glasgow in her Preface to the Virginia Edition of her novels in 1938, that in the regional novel lay genuine opportunities for serious fiction. Had Anderson read Hardy's Preface, then recalled it in the particular terms that Faulkner used here? Had Sherwood Anderson and William Faulkner perhaps spoken of Thomas Hardy and his Wessex Novels over drinks on a warm afternoon in New Orleans? Is this one way in which the vision and practice of Hardy came to the attention of the future founder of Yoknapatawpha County, just then launching his career as a novelist? One cannot be certain, though these speculations seem as helpful as some of those mentioned above. Perhaps it is best to suggest that in all likelihood William Faulkner, born after all in 1897, was a second-generation Hardyan, a poetic grandson rather than a poetic son, of the author of *The Mayor*, *The Return* and *Jude*.[32]

It is also worth considering some of the implications of the remark by Donald Davidson at the head of this chapter: that Hardy was 'an American whose ancestors failed to migrate at the proper time'. In an essay titled 'Futurism and Archaism in Toynbee and Hardy', Davidson attempts to explain why Hardy might have appealed so strongly to American writers.[33] Attacking Arnold J. Toynbee's assertion (in volume VI of the *Study of History*) that 'social evolution . . . reveals a theoretical development from the small tribal community, through the nation, to the great world community', Davidson declares Toynbee blind to 'tradition as an abiding continuum of man's social history'. Davidson urges that, by way of contrast, in Hardy's novels, particularly in *The Mayor of Casterbridge*, there is to be found an exhibition of 'the dilemma of modern civilization more sharp . . . and impressive . . . than all of Toynbee's volumes'.[34] This dramatic conflict is, in Davidson's view, the clash between two historical forces, 'business and applied sciences' (represented in *The Mayor* by Donald Farfrae) and 'traditional masculine virtues', such as 'bodily strength, hardihood, valor, fidelity, piety, chivalrousness' (represented by Michael Henchard). The meaning of *The Mayor* for Davidson is *not* the realist one that the traditional virtues must, by dint of historical necessity, give way before science, but rather the tragic one that 'what Henchard is as a valorous human being, with all his human imperfections, is superior to what Farfrae is, as the finally repugnant representative of a logic which in the last analysis is not only anti-traditional but anti-human'.[35] Precisely in this conflict, Davidson argues, American writers can find an anticipation of like conflicts in their own society. In his intuitive understanding of this conflict between the traditional and the modern order may lie Hardy's 'Americanness' and the basis for his 'organic affiliation' with American novelists of the early twentieth century.

Theodore Dreiser's interest in Hardy grew up in this atmosphere of interest in Hardy's novels that Davidson attempts to describe. In this regard, Dreiser's own comments on Hardy are worth noting, for they suggest a highly personal response within the general one. If Hardy's great characters *and* his use of regional materials appealed to Howells, Cather, Glasgow, Anderson and possibly Faulkner, Dreiser responded more specifically to Hardy's characters, particularly his women. But he did this in his own way. Dreiser (like Alain-Fournier) accepted Hardy's tragic pessimism, and admired especially Hardy's affectionate pity for his tragic characters. And, in embracing this tragic pessimism, Dreiser – particularly in *Sister Carrie* and *Jennie Gerhardt* – took it a step further, beyond those human virtues that lighten the gloom of Hardy's tragic stories.

Writing to H. L. Mencken in May 1916 about his reading in the 1890s, Dreiser recalled Hardy's special importance to him:

After Balzac (1894) came first Hardy (1896) and then Sienkiewicz. . . . About this time I did a lot of general reading, Tolstoy, Stevenson, Barrie, Dumas. . . . But Hardy, Tolstoy, and Balzac stand forth in mind all this time. . . . Actually I should put Hardy and Balzac first in that respect though I seriously doubt whether I was influenced for in St. Louis (1892) I was already building plays of a semi-tragic character. My mind just naturally worked that way.[36]

Perhaps Dreiser had read *Tess* when it appeared in *Harper's Bazaar* between July and December 1891, or in the Holt Leisure Hours version, published in January 1892. And he may well have read *Jude* (under the title *Hearts Insurgent*) in *Harper's New Monthly* (December 1894 – to November 1895), for in 1895, while trying to make a living as a newspaperman in New York, Dreiser studied the fiction in *Harper's*, as well as in the *Century* and the *Atlantic Monthly*.[37] In 1896, as editor of *Ev'ry Month*, ostensibly a fashion magazine, Dreiser published stories by Bret Harte and Stephen Crane, evincing a strong interest in contemporary fiction. What is more, as a 'confirmed theatregoer' and student of the stage since his St Louis days, Dreiser in all likelihood saw Minnie Maddern Fisk in Lorimer Stoddard's *Tess*, which opened in New York on 2 March 1897 and ran for eighty-eight performances.[38] It seems most probable that when he came to write *Sister Carrie*, just three years later, Hardy's (and Stoddard's) treatment of the story of a ruined maid would have been fresh in his mind.

In a letter to Howells in May 1902, Dreiser grouped Hardy with Howells and Tolstoy as writers who answered some 'need of fellowship when I can no longer feign to believe that life has either a purpose or a plan':

> Thomas Hardy has provided some of this spiritual fellowship for me. Count Tolstoy yet some more. Of you three however I should not be able to choose, the spirit in each seeming to be the same, and the large, tender kindliness of each covering all of the ills of life and voicing the wonder and yearning of this fitful dream, in what, to me, seems a perfect way. I may be wrong in my estimate of life, but the mental attitude of you three seems best – the richest, most appealing flowering-out of sympathy, tenderness, uncertainty, that I have as yet encountered.
>
> I have some times wondered that your expressed opinion of Hardy is what it is – he who reaches out to you, as you do to him – the same sympathetic solicitude for life, sorrow for suffering – care for the least and the greatest even to the fall of a sparrow,

which is so marked a feature of both of your natures. I had rather hoped to find an acknowledgement of the soul of the Englishman, equal to that of the Russian – a chain of spiritual sympathy binding you together.[39]

Hardy's *Tess* and *Mayor of Casterbridge* have a place in *Sister Carrie*, as shall be seen. In the meantime, Dreiser's admiration for Hardy continued unabated, stimulated undoubtedly by his friendship with that most exuberant of Hardy worshippers, John Cowper Powys, whom Dreiser met in Chicago in December 1912. In 1925, looking back over his reading of the nineteenth-century novelists, Dreiser found Hardy unique for the poignancy of his tragic vision:

> Ever since I began to look over books in a bookstore in America, it seems to me I have encountered Hardy in one or another of his splendid pictures of Wessex life, along with Stevenson, Dickens, Ouida, Hugo, and Thackeray. And except for Hugo and Thackeray I am by no means satisfied that he was in the best company. Mentally and emotionally and as a painter of the human scene he seems to me to outrank most of his contemporaries. I rank him with but one other, really – Feodor Dostoievsky. *The Brothers Karamazov* and *Crime and Punishment* are as individual as *A Pair of Blue Eyes*, *The Woodlanders*, and *Jude the Obscure*, but no more so. And they are far from being as poignant. In many respects, unless we return to Euripides and Sophocles he is quite alone – a great Greek wandering in a modern and hence an alien world.[40]

At least one appeal Hardy had for Dreiser was his mingling of tragedy with sympathy in his exhibition of the 'fitful dream' of human life. When Dreiser wrote in 1925 of Hardy's superiority 'mentally and emotionally and as a painter of the human scene', he was undoubtedly referring to what in the 1902 letter to Howells he had described as Hardy's 'sympathetic solicitude for life, sorrow for suffering – care for the least and the greatest even to the fall of a sparrow'. The eloquence in these phrases seems almost forced; it bespeaks Dreiser's wish to convey a profound admiration for Hardy and his humane outlook. It explains why, in the remarks of 1925, he could find novels so great as Dostoevsky's *The Brother's Karamazov* and *Crime and Punishment* 'as individual as *A Pair of Blue*

Eyes, The Woodlanders, and *Jude the Obscure*', but 'far from being as poignant'. It is, then, the poignancy in Hardy, a poignancy rooted in Hardy's sympathy for suffering humanity, that Dreiser most admired and, one can argue, sought to emulate in both *Sister Carrie* (1901) and *Jennie Gerhardt* (1911). Without denying the influence of Balzac in this, or of Dreiser's memory of the misfortunes in his own family,[41] it seems clear that he learned from Hardy an attitude toward suffering, particularly the suffering of a wronged woman. The plight of the victimized or misunderstood woman was of course a part of the literary climate in America in the 1890s. Stephen Crane's *Maggie: A Girl of the Streets* had first appeared in 1893, then again in an expurgated version in 1896. Hamlin Garland's *Rose of Dutcher's Coolly* had first appeared in 1895, affected somewhat by the scandal attending Hardy's *Jude the Obscure*, then again in a less offensive version in 1899.[42] *Sister Carrie* was to face similar hostility – from a publisher's wife more than from the reviewers – a hostility severe enough to discourage the thin-skinned Dreiser from completing another novel until *Jennie Gerhardt* in 1911. One cannot help but recall Hardy's similar reaction only a few years earlier when *Jude* had received a similar drubbing by the reviewers, one of the most outspoken of whom was Jeanette Gilder of the *New York World*.[43]

So widely was Hardy known in America, that the authors of *Maggie*, *Rose* and *Carrie* were widely regarded as sailing under the flag of the author of *Tess* and *Jude*. A reviewer of *Sister Carrie* in the Cleveland *Plain Dealer* (16 June 1907) described Carrie as 'the most notable woman character in fiction since Hardy's Tess':

> She is notable, too, for the same qualities which make the best of Hardy's women so amazingly convincing. She is a mere everyday human being, about whom there is no glamor of romance, whose sins seem but the errors natural to an average woman placed as she is placed, whose virtues are but normal virtues, whose development appeals irresistibly to the reader as the working out of the natural law of environment. . . .
>
> The stories of Mr. Hardy and Mr. Dreiser are strangely alike in their unwavering study of the development of feminine character under conditions most unfavorable. For both Tess and Carrie there is much more of sympathy than of condemnation. Neither was bad. Relentless force of circumstance shaped the destiny of each.[44]

This remark was to prove to be an inspired one, for in the 1907 version of the novel (the B. W. Dodge and Company impression, the second from the original plates of 1900) there were *no* specific references to *Tess*. Indeed, a case can be made for Carrie's having been made much unlike Tess: Tess is as extraordinary – in her beauty, virtue, and sensitivity – as Carrie is ordinary; Tess suffers, declines and dies, whereas Carrie triumphs; Tess is shaped by circumstances, Carrie to a significant degree shapes her circumstances. The intuition of kinship expressed by the reviewer for the *Plain Dealer* was correct, however. For (though he could not have known it) in the manuscript version of *Carrie*, now available as the Pennsylvania Edition of *Sister Carrie*, it is clear that not just Hardy's *Tess* but also his *Mayor of Casterbridge* played an important role in Dreiser's conception of Carrie, and Hurstwood.[45] The particular episode referred to, originally a part of chapter 49 of the manuscript, was removed by Dreiser, probably at the urging of his friend and collaborator Arthur Henry, and of Dreiser's wife Sarah. It consists of a long conversation about Carrie's reading of Hardy and Balzac between Carrie, now well on her way to fame and wealth as the actress Carrie Madenda, and Robert Ames, a successful scientist and inventor whom Carrie has met through her fashionable friend Mrs Vance. Ames, at an earlier meeting with Carrie, had advised that she read, among other novels, those of Balzac and Hardy. Carrie has followed Ames's advice, and the result is a conversation in which it is clear that Dreiser thought of his heroine in connection with Hardy's Tess. Even more interesting, it seems possible that he conceived of Hurstwood – who at the moment of this conversation is dying in abject poverty – as akin to Michael Henchard of *The Mayor of Casterbridge*, a connection that immediately aligns Carrie, particularly in her desertion of Hurstwood, not only with the victimized Tess but also with the resourceful Elizabeth-Jane Henchard of *The Mayor*. One cannot help but think of the conversation between Proust's Marcel and Albertine about Hardy's novels in *Remembrance of Things Past* while reading these words of Carrie, Ames and Mrs Vance on *Tess* and *The Mayor:*

> 'I've been reading the books you suggested.' . . .
> 'What were they?' . . .
> '*Saracinesca*,' she answered. '*The Great Man from the Provinces. The Mayor of Casterbridge.*'

'Oh, yes', he interrupted. 'How do you like Balzac?'

'Oh, he's delightful to me. I liked *The Mayor of Casterbridge*, though, as well as any', she answered.

'I should imagine you would', he said, submitting one of those keen observations which was the result of his comprehension of her nature.

'Why?' she asked.

'Well,' he said, 'you are rather gloomy in your disposition, and all of Hardy's novels have that in them.'

'I?' asked Carrie.

'Not exactly gloomy', he added. 'There's another word – melancholia, sad. I should judge you were rather lonely in your disposition.'

For answer Carrie only looked.

'Let's see,' put in Mrs Vance, 'didn't Hardy write *Tess of the d'Urbervilles*, or something like that?'

'Yes', said Ames.

'Well, I couldn't see so much in that. It's too sad.'

Carrie turned her eyes on Ames for a reply.

'No one who didn't feel the pathetic side of life would', he retorted.

'There!' thought Carrie triumphantly.

'Oh, I don't know', replied Mrs Vance, rather shocked at the blunt reply. 'I think I feel something of it.'

'Not so very much', laughed Ames.

This served to ward off interference for awhile.

(*SC*, pp. 481–2)[46]

Ames directs the conversation next to the novels of Balzac, which appeal to Carrie less than those of Hardy (though she will be reading *Père Goriot* in the closing scene of the novel). Ames goes on to explain to Carrie the secret of happiness: make knowledge, not material gain, one's goal in life; cultivate one's talents and enjoy the exercise of these talents rather than the pursuit of public acclaim. He then reminds her that he had advised her during their first meeting to act in serious drama; and she is deeply, even sexually, moved by this advice because he connects it, as he explains, with her 'large, sympathetic eyes and pathetic mouth' (*SC*, p. 483). Carrie's turn, in heart and mind, to the confident, well-educated Ames and her rejection of the weak-willed, declining Hurstwood, her enjoyment of social intercourse and physical comfort at the Waldorf at the very moment Hurstwood is starving and near to taking his own wretched life in a 15-cent-a-day tenement, recalls not Hardy's *Tess* but his conclusion to *The Mayor*. There Elizabeth-Jane, daughter of the ruined and declining Michael Henchard, seeks out her dying father in the company of Donald Farfrae, who has replaced Henchard as mayor and leading merchant of Casterbridge, had defeated him in the competition for the hand of Lucetta, and has also married Elizabeth-Jane. Though there is no reason to doubt that Carrie's sexual ruin and her ability to feel 'the pathetic side of life' makes her a sister to Tess, Dreiser's use of Tess is actually more ambitious in *Jennie Gerhardt*, which he began writing soon after the publication of *Sister Carrie*, then set aside for a decade. In *Carrie*, his debt is as much to Hardy's *Mayor* as to his *Tess*, as a number of striking parallels suggest.

Both Michael Henchard and George Hurstwood are prosperous men of business who descend into an abyss of economic, social, and personal ruin. In a state of drunken brutality, Henchard sells his wife and daughter for 5 guineas to a passing sailor, repents immediately, then – unable to find those he had sold and make amends to them – takes a vow of total abstinence from strong drink and in a period of some twenty years rises to the lofty position of mayor and leading merchant of the town of Casterbridge. But he cannot escape the hand of the past. His wife Susan and daughter Elizabeth-Jane (actually Susan's daughter by the sailor, the first having died) return to seek him out. Though he generously agrees to remarry Susan and to support them, he is still not free of the consequences of his crime. A witness to his act of twenty years before exposes him to the Casterbridge public. Henchard's social ruin has begun, and it is hastened when another ghost of his past appears in Casterbridge, this one a former paramour (Lucetta La Soeur), who has returned to claim her due. At the same time, Henchard's business takes a downward turn as a result of his rash speculations on the grain market. Earlier, on an impulse, Henchard had taken into partnership a young Scotsman, Donald Farfrae. In his knowledge of advanced methods of farming, in his personal charm and philosophy, as well as in his winning ways with Lucetta and then Elizabeth-Jane, who now has become Henchard's last emotional resource, Farfrae plays a role like that of Bob Ames in *Sister Carrie*.

Hurstwood, of course, does not sell a wife and child, though he does abandon his family to flee with Carrie. Hurstwood's crime is theft, not wife sale, but the result in the mind of Hurstwood – as in the mind of Henchard – is the same: both believe there is no undoing the act. The safe-door that swings shut just when Hurstwood might have decided to return the money seems, like the sailor who with his newly purchased wife and daughter disappears as if swallowed up by the earth, to act at the ironic behest of forces beyond the comprehension or control of either man. Henchard's temper, like Hurstwood's lust, is an unchangeable, incurable defect of character; and in both *Carrie* and *The Mayor* character – whether weak or strong – largely determines fate. Henchard's and Hurstwood's lack of self-control draws them under, just as surely as Carrie's and Elizabeth-Jane's; and Ames's and Farfrae's tenacity and self-control enable them to prosper in the struggle for existence. This is where Carrie differs fundamentally from Tess – in a capacity for survival and success rooted in a powerful instinct for self-preservation. Tess is, after all, as handicapped by her capacity for self-sacrifice and self-incrimination as by her misfortune in meeting a mail cart, then Alec d'Urberville, and then Angel Clare.

In both *Sister Carrie* and *The Mayor of Casterbridge*, the structure is governed by the decline of a tragic male counterpointed by the ascent and 'victory' of a once-victimized woman. When Henchard is losing out to Farfrae in politics, business and love, Elizabeth-Jane – in spite of Henchard's neglect of her – is improving herself, growing in resolution, and winning the affection of Farfrae. Similarly, in *Sister Carrie*, Hurstwood's financial decline is contrasted with Carrie's financial and professional ascent. After gaining a bit part in a chorus line, Carrie is selected for promotion because of her skill, wit and beauty (and her frown), and soon becomes a celebrity. Perhaps the most striking similarity between Hardy's way of depicting the decline of Henchard and Dreiser's of depicting the decline of Hurstwood is their use of clothing and dwelling-places as symbols of deterioration. Hurstwood's clothing grows shabbier and shabbier, and in one instance he decides to conserve it by wearing his oldest clothes when at home, much to Carrie's disgust. Henchard, at one memorable point, sheds the black broadcloth he has worn as mayor and merchant and puts on the rough labourer's garb he had worn when he committed his crime twenty years before. Even more graphic is Henchard's descent from one of the largest and finest houses of Casterbridge into a cottage, then to rented rooms, and finally to a hut on Egdon Heath, where Elizabeth-Jane and Farfrae find him after his death. Hurstwood's social and psychological collapse is measured not just by the steady decline of his funds and clothing, but also by his movement from a modest apartment into cheaper and yet cheaper quarters, until he reaches his nadir – the 15-cent-a-night room with its bed and gas jet.

If Hurstwood resembles Henchard and Ames Farfrae, Carrie – whose origin had been an ongoing issue in criticism of the novel[47] – resembles Elizabeth-Jane. Like Elizabeth-Jane, Carrie rises from relative poverty to affluence. Where Elizabeth-Jane had woven fishing-nets, Carrie had worked in a shoe factory in Chicago. Though Elizabeth-Jane does not, like Carrie, become a kept woman, she is, along with her mother, 'repurchased' by Henchard (he gives Susan the symbolic sum of 5 guineas upon reunion), just as the original Elizabeth-Jane had been sold by him. Elizabeth-Jane is, in other words, wholly dependent on Henchard's whimsy for her economic and social well-being. And, like Carrie, Elizabeth-Jane must be content to wait on the goodwill of the men in her life. Carrie's habit of rocking and of looking out the windows of the various rooms in which she lives recalls Elizabeth-Jane's habit of watching Casterbridge life from the window of the rooms she takes after Henchard rejects her because she is not his natural daughter. Callous treatment by a man makes her at once more perceptive and more unfeeling. Carrie's shrewd discernment of Drouet's weaknesses, as well as her unfeeling abandonment of Hurstwood (her departing note to him is a masterpiece of understated hatred), has its equally painful counterpart, and partial origin perhaps, in Elizabeth-Jane's dismissal of Henchard upon learning that he had kept from her the fact that her natural father was alive. When Henchard (carrying the pathetic gift of a caged finch) attempts to make amends by attending Elizabeth-Jane and Farfrae's wedding-celebration, held in the splendid house formerly occupied by Henchard, Elizabeth-Jane turns him away. And, though she later regrets this hardheartedness, she sees, quite calmly, that she cannot improve him or alter the situation. Henchard's visit to Elizabeth-Jane resembles Hurstwood's backstage visit to Carrie, and Elizabeth-Jane's hardness of heart, like Carrie's, derives from her understanding that the misery of the world is not often remediable. In its human form – especially in the characters of the men in their lives – this misery is something that must be endured and, when possible, amended.

If Carrie 'liked *The Mayor of Casterbridge* . . . as well as any' of the novels she had read at Ames's recommendation, it is probably because, unlike the heroine of *Tess* and like the heroine of *The Mayor*, Carrie triumphs. Elizabeth-Jane's withdrawal from Henchard resembles Carrie's own withdrawal from the man she had once loved and depended upon. Here, however, a major difference emerges; for, if the sympathy in *Carrie* is mainly with the heroine, the sympathy in *The Mayor* is with its flawed and fated and abandoned hero. Elizabeth-Jane's hard-won triumph, however admirable, is made to seem less humanly attractive than Henchard's failure. Henchard, not Elizabeth-Jane, and certainly not Donald Farfrae, is the emotional and aesthetic centre of *The Mayor*. The reader's sympathy is made to flow toward Henchard. In contrast, the ability of Elizabeth-Jane and Farfrae to adjust, endure, and act humanely is made to seem by comparison a paltry and even inhuman thing, particularly when seen beside Henchard's futile effort to redeem his defective self. This recalls Donald Davidson's argument, noted above, that *The Mayor* exhibits a clash between the forces of business and science and the 'traditional masculine virtues'. But Dreiser turns away from Hardy's sympathy with human defect and, more like the historian Toynbee of Davidson's description, exhibits the inevitable march of progress: Hurstwood dead, his family on their way to a vacation in Europe, Carrie uncertain what the future holds, Drouet going his jolly way. And Dreiser's sympathy seems to lie with the living and their march into the future. Hardy's sympathy lies with Henchard and all he represents – the past and the agricultural-natural order – over against the knowledge and undoubted humaneness of Farfrae, who, interestingly enough, had been on his way to America when Henchard intercepted him. Though Dreiser seems to favour the forces of progress, their value to him is not certain. Carrie is left groping because she does not know whether Ames (her Farfrae) will ever draw near: 'She was already the old, mournful Carrie – the desireful Carrie, – unsatisfied' (*SC*, p. 487). And this is so because *she* is ever in pursuit of, ever yearning for, something beyond her grasp: 'Carrie! Oh Carrie! ever whole in that thou art ever hopeful, know that the light is but now in these his eyes. Tomorrow it shall be melted and dissolved. Tomorrow it shall be on and further on, still leading, still alluring, until thought is not with you and heartaches are no more' (ibid.).

Perhaps because he left Carrie in this state of uncertainty, Dreiser (as H. L. Mencken was quick to note) rewrote *Carrie* in *Jennie Gerhardt*, which he began in 1901. As Donald Pizer has pointed out, Dreiser shaped the story of Jennie in large part by fusing the experiences of his sister Mary, 'seduced at sixteen by a prominent and middle-aged Terre Haute lawyer', with the experiences of Hardy's Tess:

> Mame's career appealed to Dreiser as the basis for a novel because it could be adapted to demonstrate . . . that a woman's instinctive nature created its own moral truth whatever the conventional social and moral attitude toward her actions. Dreiser had reshaped Emma's [another sister's] experiences to represent [in *Sister Carrie*] one aspect of his large theme – that of the woman as seeking artist; he could remold Mame's to express another – that of the woman as the spirit of generosity. In Dreiser's recasting of Emma's life [in *Sister Carrie*] Balzac had played a major role by suggesting how a biographical narrative could be transformed into fiction; for Mame, Hardy's *Tess of the d'Urbervilles* served much the same purpose.[48]

H. L. Mencken's instant recognition of the influence of *Tess* on *Jennie* (in his November 1911 review of the novel) was echoed by a reviewer for the Chicago *Record-Herald*, who described *Jennie* as 'in some respects an American *Tess of the d'Urbervilles*, though . . . calmer, less tragic – and absolutely true to life'.[49]

This last remark poses an interesting question about *Jennie* and *Tess* – which is not whether or in what ways Hardy's *Tess* influenced *Jennie* – but of just what 'an American *Tess of the d'Urbervilles*' might consist. It is clear that Hardy, along with Balzac, was Dreiser's mentor in his first two novels. But Dreiser was no slavish imitator of Hardy – no more than Proust or Lawrence was to be, just a few years later. Dreiser is an artist in his own right and his borrowings from Hardy always serve the ends of his own mystery-tinged realistic art, one of whose ends in *Carrie* and *Jennie* was to exhibit the insignificance of much that passes as valuable in human affairs – love, wealth, prestige, beauty. In his use of Hardy's *Mayor* in *Sister Carrie*, Dreiser went beyond Hardy in his pessimism and bleakness of outlook. Hardy's Henchard, though dealt his share of suffering, is endowed with value in Hardy's tragic conception of him. His memory is consecrated by his survivors' regrets, and most poignantly and particularly by the poetic beauty in Abel Whittle's last words on him.[50] Hardy's novel steadily insists that what has displaced Henchard – namely, Donald Farfrae and the new order he represents – is inferior in human terms to Henchard. Henchard is a dead lion, Farfrae a living dog. Dreiser's Hurstwood, in contrast, is portrayed as a coward of a kind. He is endowed with few appealing traits; he is shallow, a philanderer and liar, a person of charm and style but of little substance. This is most tellingly revealed through Carrie's growing perception of his weaknesses, particularly his lack of resolve and final willingness to become her dependant. Hurstwood is unmanned; Henchard never loses, in fact somehow inexplicably grows in, virtue. Though the reader is led to sympathize with Hurstwood in his decline and want, his passing is not presented as the loss of something of permanent value, as is the case with Henchard. Henchard sins, tries to atone, is thwarted in this attempt by his character and circumstances, attempts yet a second time to atone, fails yet a second time, then withdraws in his pride and strength to die. Hurstwood sins, flees, attempts to begin again, fails in that attempt, then simply gives in. Hurstwood represents nothing beyond himself. No Abel Whittle offers *his* eulogy.

There is in Dreiser's treatment of his characters a coldness that makes Hardy – scarcely a sentimentalist – seem warm by comparison. This is especially apparent if one compares Hardy's treatment of Elizabeth-Jane with Dreiser's treatment of Carrie. Elizabeth-Jane, by the end of the novel the wife of the town's mayor and leading businessman, reaps the rewards of her stoic patience. Suffering has brought her wisdom, wisdom patience, and patience prosperity and respectability. But Carrie, uncertain of Ames, indifferent toward Hurstwood, scornful of Drouet (in his attempt to rekindle old fires), seems by comparison a creature deficient in feeling. As in the case of Ellen Glasgow's Dorinda Oakley, suffering has made her hard rather than wise, and her hardness – her ability to strike out on her own with little regard for Hurstwood – has brought her success. She feels no obligation to seek out Hurstwood and share her prosperity and comfort with him. She is caught up entirely in the aura of her success, as is Hardy's Elizabeth-Jane. But, where Hardy softens his heroine's soul and in several ways redeems his hero, Dreiser leaves Carrie her hard, aloof, ambitious self, and leaves Hurstwood in the gutter. When the reviewer for the Chicago *Record-Herald* called *Jennie* 'an American *Tess*, . . . calmer, less tragic – and absolutely true to life', he was – especially in that last phrase – perhaps putting a finger on something Dreiserian, perhaps even 'American', in Dreiser's reshaping of elements of Hardy's *Tess:* a hardness and cruelty that Dreiser as an American brought with him to his shaping of character. Hardy heroizes Henchard by associating him with the values of a vanishing traditional order. Dreiser, as both the shaper and the product of an emerging society, makes no comparable association with something of the past. But, then, neither is he able to place value on a Carrie as representative of a new order, for that too is uncertain. Perhaps, contrary to what Donald Davidson has said, Hardy would not have fared well in the American literary climate, had his ancestors thought to migrate.

One key to Dreiser's departure from Hardy and perhaps to an 'Americanness' behind his shaping of Jennie as well as Carrie is that, even more completely than Hardy, he banishes evil from the world of his fiction. For example, Alec d'Urberville, Tess's seducer, is portrayed as a heedless, selfish man out to take his pleasure wherever he may find it. Though Hardy tries to deepen this motive by attributing to him certain undiscovered spiritual yearnings – as if his appetite for the flesh were but the inverse of a hunger for the spirit – Alec rises scarcely above the level of a villain of melodrama. Jennie Gerhardt has not one seducer, but two – the Hon. George Sylvester Brander, United States Senator from Ohio, and Lester Kane, son of a wealthy manufacturer from Cincinnati. Neither is villainous in the sense d'Urberville is. Brander is always solicitous for Jennie's welfare and would probably have married her had he lived. Kane seems willing to sacrifice an enormous fortune in order to remain with Jennie. He leaves her more at her urging than as a result of his own desire, and he remains devoted to her even after his marriage to Letty, welcoming Jennie's attentions when on his deathbed. In short, both of Dreiser's seducers have more than their share of decency, even though not much is made of it. The result is that Jennie, however much put upon, is never the victim Tess is; and in fact Jennie views herself much less as a reprobate than as a person forced by circumstances to saacrifice her person for her family, a view approved by her mother, though strongly opposed by her father.

Jennie is almost entirely without Tess's self-consuming guilt, just as Hurstwood in *Carrie* is without Henchard's self-defeating sense of wrongdoing. William Dean Howells, in the remarks of 1901 quoted above (pp. 173–4), thought he had found in Hardy heroines 'untouched by Puritanism'. His phrase might be applied even more aptly to Dreiser's heroines, for, though certain of Hardy's women reject puritan morality, they do so precisely because they have been touched by it.

The moral issue is in abeyance in Dreiser's novel, then, to a greater degree than in Hardy's. For example, Hardy uses the baptism of Tess's baby Sorrow as the occasion for a vigorous assault on Christian theology and the Christian clergy. Because Tess's parish priest is reluctant to baptize a bastard, Tess christens the child herself in a painfully moving scene that exhibits Tess's need to make her human needs conform to the demands of her religious beliefs. Carrie has no comparable religious awareness. Dreiser – and in this his use of *Tess* probably gives way to his use of family history – employs the baptism of Jennie's baby Vesta as an occasion for praise of the piety of John Gerhardt and the dignity of his Lutheran belief, just as, later, he is admiring in his description of the beauty of Lester Kane's Roman Catholic funeral mass. Though an avowed enemy of Christianity, and particularly of Roman Catholicism, Dreiser avoids satire because he seeks to exhibit a truth that for him has little to do with the implicit moral judgements of satire: religious rites are not *always* foolish or irrelevant in the context of human suffering; seducers of hapless women are not always unfeeling monsters; victimized women sometimes embrace their state because there is sometimes nothing better for them to do, and in embracing their ruin find an unexpected degree of contentment. Hardy, from his subtitle for *Tess* ('A Pure Woman') to his closing thrust at the sport of the 'President of the Immortals' with Tess, is compelled to make one case for Tess's purity and another against the injustice of her suffering, because he shares with his society the presumption of her contamination at the same time as he fiercely rejects that presumption. Dreiser, in *Jennie* as well as in *Carrie*, seems free of such presumption. More completely than Hardy, he can view his heroine as a product of heredity and circumstances in a world in which ideas of good and evil and everlasting rewards are delusions, and therefore as a heroine remarkable not for her purity or capacity for self-sacrifice, but for her capacity for self-preservation. In this, Jennie recalls George Moore's *Esther Waters* more than Hardy's *Tess*. Like Esther, Jennie rears her bastard child and knows certain pleasures alongside her sorrows; like Esther, Jennie survives the father of her child.

This is not to say that Dreiser, like Moore, avoided tragedy. Dreiser managed to endow Jennie with a degree of tragic stature by multiplying certain of her misfortunes: she is twice seduced; she suffers the loss of nearly all the persons near and dear to her. Tess loses an infant and later her father. Jennie loses her first lover, then Brander, and then her teenaged daughter, her mother, her father, and finally Lester. The death of Vesta occurs after Lester has left her for Letty, a time when Jennie is most dependent on her daughter for companionship and affection. Her loss of her mother deprives her of her only ally within her immediate family. The death of her father is the loss of the man her conduct has most offended, the man to whom she most wished to make amends. Dreiser's depiction of her patience before the criticism and petty interferences of the old man, her seeking him out in his humble quarters to bring him into her luxurious home in Chicago, and of old Gerhardt's gradual softening before Vesta's appeal are the most poignant things in the novel, suggestive of a range of feeling that goes beyond that of *Tess*. Jennie's loss of Lester is, of course, her greatest loss, for she had loved him most. Her loss of Brander is nothing less than the loss of her reputation, the loss that precipitates the special torments of all the deaths that follow. Dreiser understood well how family disgrace can work to taint and deepen family grief, how a child's loss of respect in the eyes of a parent can make that parent's death an exquisite torment for that child. This virtual pounding of Jennie with the terrors of death (not to mention her suffering at the gossip of neighbours) recalls not *Tess* so much as *Jude*, in which Hardy's most unfortunate protagonist is again and again driven to the wall: by Arabella's deceptions, by his rejection at Christminster, by Sue's defections, by the heartless gossip of neighbours, and by the death of his children. Unlike Jude, or Tess, however, Jennie survives her torments. And so, her desolation is unlike that of Tess or Jude, for it is not the desolation of the irreparable, or of a purity forever lost, or of an ideal forever beyond reach. Rather it is that strange desolation that descends on one who has made the best of a bad situation, the desolation, paradoxically, of gain in the face of loss – the desolation not of what might have been but of what will be.

Jennie, one might say then, is 'American' in two senses. Like Ellen Glasgow's Dorinda, like Carrie, Jennie survives adversity – and this is a significant departure from Hardy's Tess, Jude or Henchard. But Jennie has no traditional order on which to lean, and so her future holds no prospect of happiness or deepened understanding. In Carrie's future are more 'blind strivings', more loneliness and mournfulness. Jennie's future is similar: 'But before her was stretching a vista of lonely years down which she was steadily gazing. Now what? She was not old yet. There were those two orphan children to raise. They would marry and leave her after a while, and then what? Days and days in endless repetition, and then – ?'[51]

The answer to that hard question 'and then – ?' is, it seems, 'and then, nothing'; and this is implied in yet another way in which *Jennie* – for all its indebtedness to *Tess* – is, like *Carrie*, a firm departure from *Tess* and perhaps an example of a peculiarly Dreiserian and 'American' view of the human condition. Having stripped Tess of religious consolation or the support of a social order, Hardy could yet endow her with a 'natural' beauty and truth. And he could do this because, though, like Dreiser, an adherent to the view that nature is an unfeeling process in which chance prevails over design, he retained to a significant degree the romantic view that nature is a moral norm and spiritual resource. Tess therefore can be associated sympathetically with the lush, fecund life of the dairy at Talbothays, with the suffering game-birds she comes upon shortly after her own affliction, with nothing less than the regenerative powers of nature itself. Though nature is in one sense for Hardy 'red in tooth and claw', Hardy can grant Tess the power, dignity and strength of nature as creative, enduring force. And so Tess's violation of a merely human law is made to seem a minor offence. Dreiser, of course, also recognized the two faces of nature. On the one hand, Jennie's career illustrates the law that the weak shall succumb to the strong; on the other, Jennie's 'goodness and mercy' ally her instinctively with certain elements of external nature, as in the following sentences:

> When the days were fair she looked out of her kitchen window and longed to go where the meadows were. Nature's fine curves and shadows touched her as a song itself. There were times when she had gone with George and the others, leading them away to where a patch of hickory trees flourished, because there

were open fields, with the shade for comfort and a brook of living water. No artist in the formulating of conceptions, her soul still responded to these things, and every sound and every sigh were welcome to her because of their beauty. When the soft, low call of the wooddoves, those spirits of the summer, came out of the distance, she would incline her head and listen, the whole spiritual quality of it dropping like silver bubbles into her own great heart. Where the sunlight was warm and the shadows flecked with its splendid radiance she delighted to wonder at the pattern of it, to walk where it was most golden, and follow with instinctive appreciation the holy corridors of the trees. Color was not lost upon her. That wonderful radiance which fills the western sky at evening touched and unburdened her heart. 'I wonder', she said once with girlish simplicity, 'how it would feel to float away off there among those clouds.'

(*JG*, ch. 2)[52]

Jenny delights in the beauties of external nature, but this response to great forces outside her never becomes – as it does for Tess – a source of strength and a redeeming force. This is so in part because Jennie's life is lived in the cities, except for her brief sojourn in a lakeside cottage in rural Wisconsin after Lester's return to his family in Cincinnati. But even if Jennie, like Tess, had remained on the land and near the sensations of nature, it is difficult to imagine a supernatural force counting very much to her. Dreiser's nature of trees, flowers and singing birds in shady dells, however deeply felt, is a mere patina when compared with Hardy's sense of nature as a process of death and rebirth of which Tess is an integral part. In spite of his scientific naturalism, Hardy's nature retains a Wordsworthian sense of 'something far more deeply interfused'. Nature in Hardy is not wholly stripped of its mysteries, and this is true both for Hardy's narrator and for his heroine. In *Jennie*, however, the view of nature as a spiritual and aesthetic resource belongs almost exclusively to the novel's narrator. Jennie is said to feel 'there must be something – a higher presence which produced all the beautiful things' (ch. 60), but her actions conform more closely to Lester's view: ' "the one divine, far-off event" of the poet did not appeal to him as having any basis in fact' (ibid.). This dismissal of Tennyson recalls Hardy's more famous dismissal of Wordsworth late in *Tess* when Tess realizes that she has lost her husband, her family their home, and that her only recourse is to become the kept woman of Alec. There is, writes Hardy, for Tess, as 'for not a few million of others . . . ghastly satire in the poet's lines – "Not in utter nakedness/But trailing clouds of glory do we come" ' (*TD*, ch. 52).

Though both Hardy and Dreiser reject nineteenth-century optimism as expressed by two of its greatest poets, they offer strikingly different alternatives. Jennie, at the great crises in her life, at Lester's death, for example, sees herself not in relation to the will of God or nature, but in relation to other persons, persons who may or may not care about her:

> Was not her life a patchwork of conditions made and affected by these things which she saw – wealth and force – which had found her unfit? She had evidently been born to yield, not seek. This panoply of power had been paraded before her since childhood. What could she do now but stare vaguely after it as it marched triumphantly by? Lester had been of it. Him it respected. Of her it knew nothing. (*JG*, ch. 62)

Here and elsewhere for Jennie at moments of crisis, it is not the indifference of nature or the injustice of God that enters her mind; it is the indifference (or the sympathy, as when Vesta dies) of other persons. Jennie's world, unlike Tess's, is entirely human and secular. Tess baptizes her child and seeks its burial in consecrated ground because she believes in the sacraments of the Anglican faith and that faith's promise of eternal happiness for the dead innocent. Later, when out of desperation she turns back to Alec, she does so with a bitterly ironic glance at a Christian Providence that promises more than it delivers. Tess is a participant in that Christian faith, even if an angry and rebellious one. But Jennie, at Lester's funeral mass, for example, is a total stranger to religious ritual and its intimation of a time beyond time. She is deeply moved, and deeply alienated:

> Jennie was overawed and amazed, but no show of form colorful, impression imperial, could take away the sting of death, the sense of infinite loss. To Jennie the candles, the incense, the holy song were beautiful. They touched the deep chord of melancholy in her, and made it vibrate through the depths of her being. She was a house filled with mournful melody and

the presence of death. She cried and cried. She could see, curiously, that Mrs. Kane was sobbing convulsively also. (Ibid.)

Jennie's 'Americanness' may perhaps be seen, then, in her way of experiencing loss, which is different from the way of Tess or Jude. Tess loses her innocence, her child, her good name, and finally her life; but Hardy, for all his grimness, grants her a belated and temporary happiness with Angel, and even the attention of a system of justice, with its roots in the social and religious norms Tess at once embraces and violates. Jude has lost even more, for he is denied the consolation of love, is victimized a second time by his enticer, and is made to seem, finally, something of a warning to the ambitious among the labouring classes. But for the reader watching Jude in his agonies, if not for Jude himself, there is consolation in the anger of Hardy's narrator, a narrator who speaks for a moral idealism rooted in a belief in justice, humanity and liberty. Jennie, though in possession of her life and a comfortable annuity and two orphans to love and rear, cannot address her sense of loss to, cannot measure it by, an idea of the right, the good or the true. And this is not just because she is ignorant or unlettered: it is because such an order is only faintly there, in her world, the 'America' represented in the novel. She is capable of sympathy, sacrifice and patience, but her virtues, precious as they are, do not find a larger resonance in the Chicago or Cincinnati, or even the rural Wisconsin, of the novel. Her farewell to Lester's corpse at the Chicago rail station is drowned out by the activity there (it is Thanksgiving Eve), by the cries for trains to 'Fort Wayne, Columbus, Pittsburgh, Philadelphia', by the sound and sight of a 'long red train' and 'a great black engine', its 'bell . . . ringing, its steam hissing, its smoke-stack throwing aloft a great black plume of smoke that fell back over the cars like a pall. The Fireman, conscious of the heavy load behind, flung open a flaming furnace door to throw in coal. Its light glowed like a golden eye' (ch. 62). The daemon of progress imaged here recalls Tess as she stands beside the steam-powered threshing-machine and its Mephistophelean engineer, or beside the London train that she and Angel meet with a shipment of milk from Talbothays. Tess is always seen as alien to the machine, and also as a human rebuke to its inhuman force and energy. Even though the image of the machine in *Tess* (and in *The Mayor*, where Henchard resists Farfrae's introduction of steam-powered machinery to Casterbridge) can be said to threaten Tess, it is always clear that Tess also threatens the machine – that is, that she (like Henchard) represents a world of human values that we moderns are the less for having lost to the march of progress. In Jennie's world, however, the machine and the system it represents are more nearly the norm. Even in ideal or imaginative terms Jennie is helpless and inferior before it, for it is human, as human as she. But it is much more powerful. It rebukes her weakness and vulnerability, just as it serves the power of the gifted and wealthy like the Kanes. Dreiser does not deny, he may even envy, that power; Hardy is unable to honour it but at the same time acknowledges its inevitable triumph. Because Dreiser does not deny the power of the new, his heroine is peculiarly alone, more completely bereft than a Henchard, a Tess or even a Jude. Jennie can love and give as completely as a Tess, but her acts of love do not find echoes within her society or within the hearts of those she loves.

These are large statements, comparative and general to an extreme degree. But, having made them, it seems appropriate to ask why they might be accurate. Perhaps because, as D. H. Lawrence has said, the conquering and subduing of savage America was accomplished 'at the expense of the instinctive and intuitive sympathy of the human soul'. And so, according to Lawrence, America, though in possession of a 'social creed of benevolence and uniformity', is without a 'sympathetic heart', without an 'instinctive belief which lies at the core of the human heart, that people and the universe itself are *ultimately* kind'. 'The flow from the heart, the warmth of fellow-feeling which has animated Europe and been the best of her humanity, individual, spontaneous, flowing in thousands of little passionate currents often conflicting, this seems unable to persist on American soil.'[53] From the perspective of the 1980s, this seems less a scathing indictment that one acceptable description, and one that suggests why Dreiser's Jennie and Carrie, though women as appealing as Hardy's Tess, seem in human terms to count for so much less.

7
'Canst thou be Virgil?': A Hardy Legacy in the Novel

> *Never in English prose literature was such a seer of beauty as Thomas Hardy.*
>
> (Arnold Bennett)

A number of attitudes have surfaced again and again throughout this survey of Hardy's influence on some novelists of the twentieth century: keen interest in Hardy's pessimism and almost unanimous rejection of it; great concern with Hardy's treatment of men and women in love; surprisingly high regard for certain of Hardy's lesser novels, particularly *The Well-Beloved*; deep respect for his characters, particularly Tess, and an inclination to re-create them; relative indifference to Hardy's faults as a writer; and, finally, recognition that Hardy, out of his tragic view of things, was, in Bennett's phrase, a surpassing 'seer of beauty'. The ultimate source of the first five of these responses to Hardy must lie in this sixth, in Hardy's having, in the view of his successors in English fiction, created a new beauty. Hardy's pessimism, his flawed last novel, and his characters and their passions appealed to later novelists for their beauty, or for their refracting the beauty of his created world. The presence of this beauty overrides, in the eyes of these particular readers, faults of style, plot, or presentation. What Hardy's disciples among later novelists responded to, and sought to imitate and continue, is the peculiar beauty Hardy brought into the world.

Though Lawrence, Proust, Powys and Fowles all rejected Hardy's sense of time, history and consciousness as a deteriorative process, they at the same time found him powerfully appealing. Lawrence was attracted to 'the wonder . . . and . . . beauty of Hardy's novels' deriving from Hardy's 'setting behind the small action of his protagonists the terrific action of unfathomed nature'.

Powys was captivated by Hardy's 'Sophoclean power of transsubstantiating the burden of any victim's suffering all the world over, the very bread by which we live and move'. Proust called *The Well-Beloved* 'a very beautiful thing that unfortunately resembles a very little . . . what I am doing myself'. John Fowles is less interested in the quality of the beauty of Hardy's fiction than in that beauty's origins in the unconscious. Alain-Fournier and Theodore Dreiser embraced the beauty of Hardy's deterioristic view of things. Fournier wrote to Jacques Rivière of 'the divine emotions' he had experienced while reading *Tess*, the movement from 'anguish to anguish, across the boundless sweetnesses of love'. Dreiser acknowledged the appeal of Hardy's 'splendid pictures of Wessex life' and the poignancy in Hardy's rendering of 'the human scene'.

Proust, Powys and Fowles all discovered unusual merit in *The Well-Beloved*, a novel whose central action is an artist's pursuit of Ideal Beauty in its feminine incarnation. Proust – and he seemed sincere in this – found it 'a thousand times better' than the masterpiece on which he himself was at work. Powys, in *Weymouth Sands*, expanded Hardy's portrait of the artist as a seeker after beauty through love into a portrait of humanity as itself in search of beauty through love, and he did this with notable awareness of the so-called deviant forms of human love. The young man seated on a bench on Weymouth Beach reading *The Well-Beloved* is, for Powys, reading the book of humanity, and certainly the book of Powys's own heart. Fowles regarded *The Well-Beloved* as a most important novel for study by an aspiring novelist because it exhibits a very great novelist probing the roots of his genius and its origins in his passion for the beautiful. In *Daniel Martin*, an important novel of the 1970s, Fowles offered his own version of how the artist can keep open and alluring the paths to those lost moments of childhood that nurture his art.

Tess, more than any other of Hardy's characters, captured the imaginations of later novelists. Lawrence's Ursula, Moore's Esther, Alain-Fournier's Yvonne de Galais, Powys's Gerta and Wizzie, Dreiser's Carrie and Jennie, Fowles's Sarah, Glasgow's Dorinda derive in their different ways from Hardy's greatest heroine. Jude Fawley, Michael Henchard and Jocelyn Pierston have had their following among later novelists, but Tess Durbeyfield most inspired rewriting and revision. One reason for Tess's impressive legacy is that Tess – through all her misfortunes – continues to represent convincingly and hauntingly a great spiritual and moral splendour. It seems appropriate to recall here a conversation I had several years ago with a student who had just read *Tess* for the first time. This woman had encountered Scott's Jeanie Deans, Dickens's Esther Summerson, Eliot's Dorothea Brooke, Thackeray's Becky Sharp, and then Hardy's Tess. Her simple and penetrating observation (and she was visibly moved in making it) was that she could not comprehend the precise quality of Tess's love for Angel Clare. She was humbled, she said, by how completely Hardy had convinced her against her wish to be convinced that Tess indeed loved Angel as deeply and tenderly as she did. She was left, she said, with a sudden understanding of the power of the human heart in the face of the worst possible adversities. *Tess*, she said, showed her 'the incredible stubbornness of real human love'. This observation by a 'naïve' reader of *Tess* confirmed my own sense that in the character of Tess goodness, tenderness and passion so interpenetrate that the splendour of her person and personality are one and therefore are not diminished by her defeat at the hands of human tormentors, her circumstances, and 'the President of the Immortals'. Tess has been reconceived so frequently, and so memorably, since 1891 because Lawrence, Moore, Alain-Fournier, Powys, Dreiser, Fowles and others found themselves, as artists, compelled to participate in the making of an image of human beauty that Hardy had discovered, and undertaken, but had not exhausted. To read *Tess* is to 'dr[ink] deep of the beauty of the earth', in the words of Virginia Woolf. Even Henry James found that the novel *Tess*, though 'chock-full of faults and falsities[,] yet has a singular beauty and charm'.

More than any other single admirer of Hardy among later novelists, Arnold Bennett was moved to remark at length on the beauty peculiar to Hardy's fiction. Bennett expressed the opinion, in 1904, that Hardy had created 'a new kind of novel, distinct from the realistic novel of Richardson and the romantic novel of Scott: it contains a new beauty, a new thrill for the amateurs of beauty; it does not "derive" '. Twenty years later, Bennett still held this view:

> [Hardy's] literary life now reaches over more than half a century, and during those fifty years he has published nothing that does not show great creative and emotional power, and nothing that is not beautiful. Further, his inventive resource in the conduct

of a story has never been surpassed, and at its best his style attains the most poignant beauty. . . . I have used strong language about Thomas Hardy, but I could not say less.[1]

Bennett's estimate is all the more impressive when it is realized that behind it lay more than a quarter-century of reading in Hardy, and not all of it by any means approving or admiring. Bennett complained elsewhere about Hardy's ponderous methods of narration and his too-obvious humour, about his verbosity when compared with Chekhov, his blunders in *Tess*, and his excessive gloominess in *Jude*. Bennett had even scolded John Middleton Murry for his attack (in Hardy's behalf) on George Moore. While rejecting as absurd Moore's final verdict on Hardy, Bennett reminded Murry that in *Confessions of a Young Man* Moore had 'put down some criticisms of Hardy which are unanswerable'.[2] Though Bennett was no mere hero-worshipper, his remarks still seem quaint, too impressionistic to be useful. Though he specifies his reasons for claiming Hardy the maker of a new beauty – 'creative and emotional power', 'inventive resource in the conduct of a story', poignant beauty in his style at its best – one probably comes away agreeing and yet not knowing exactly what it is Bennett finds 'beautiful' in Hardy. Each reader of Hardy is likely to discover his own sense of the beautiful in the Wessex Novels, and some will find little or none at all. An answer to the question about the quality of the beauty Hardy has created is suggested perhaps by Proust's Marcel, when he speaks to Albertine about the repetitive symmetry he finds in Hardy's novels, the 'stone-mason's geometry' of *A Pair of Blue Eyes*, *Jude* and *The Well-Beloved* which amounts to Hardy's artistic signature. 'The great men of letters', he instructs his mistress, 'have never created more than a single work, or rather have never done more that refract through various media an identical beauty which they bring into the world'. Bennett's 'seer of beauty' is Proust's refractor of beauty, and the origin of that beauty lies in the mystery of all origins. But the nature of that beauty is not beyond description, and Hardy himself attempted to describe it.

As interesting as the question of the origin of Hardy's perception of a new beauty is Hardy's clear awareness of himself as a maker of a new beauty. There can be no doubt – as suggested by remarks in *The Life*, in *The Return of the Native* and in *Tess* – that Hardy viewed himself as the creator of a new pleasure to the human mind and spirit. In April 1878, shortly after publishing *The Return of the Native*, Hardy wrote as follows:

> The method of Boldini, the painter of 'The Morning Walk' in the French Gallery two or three years ago (a young lady beside an ugly blank wall on an ugly highway) – of Hobbema, in his view of a road with formal lopped trees and flat tame scenery – is that of infusing emotion into the baldest external objects either by the presence of a human figure among them, or by mark of some human connection with them.
>
> This accords with my feeling about, say, Heidelberg and Baden *versus* Scheveningen – as I wrote at the beginning of *The Return of the Native* – that the beauty of association is entirely superior to the beauty of aspect, and a beloved relative's old battered tankard to the finest Greek Vase. Paradoxically put, it is to see the beauty in ugliness.   (*Life*, pp. 120–1)

Here one finds Hardy, shortly after publishing his first great tragic novel, rejecting a 'beauty of aspect' for an 'entirely superior' beauty, a 'beauty of association'. The artist infuses with emotion the land (and its objects) by placing on it 'human figures' or some 'mark of human connection'. In short, it is the presence of the human that determines the quality of this beauty. Even more startling, a surpassing formal work of art such as 'the finest Greek vase' is inferior to a domestic object such as an 'old battered tankard' if that tankard bears the marks of use by a 'beloved relative'. The vase is, in its way, beautiful; but not so beautiful, for Hardy, as the tankard. And this is so because for him beauty is defined mainly in affective rather than in aesthetic terms; and this, in turn, is so because for him, quite simply, humanity is more important than art, even though art is obviously of enormous importance.[3] It follows from this that in *The Return* Hardy should have sought to create a beauty associable with the troubled human spirit of his times. His opening in *The Return* is worth quoting at length because in it he attempts to describe more fully than anywhere else in his writings both this new beauty and its origin in the artist's instruction – not by other artists – but by nature itself:

> [Egdon Heath] was a spot which returned upon the memory of those who loved it with an aspect of peculiar and kindly

congruity. Smiling champaigns of flowers and fruit hardly do this, for they are permanently harmonious only with an existence of better reputation as to its issues than the present. Twilight combined with the scenery of Egdon Heath to evolve a thing majestic without severity, impressive without showiness, emphatic in its admonitions, grand in its simplicity. The qualifications which frequently invest the façade of a prison with far more dignity than is found in the facade of a palace double its size lent to this heath a sublimity in which spots renowned for beauty of the accepted kind are utterly wanting. Fair prospects wed happily with fair times; but alas, if times be not fair! Men have oftener suffered from the mockery of a place too smiling for their reason than from the oppression of surroundings oversadly tinged. Haggard Egdon appealed to a subtler and scarcer instinct, to a more recently learnt emotion, than that which responds to the sort of beauty called charming and fair.

Indeed, it is a question if the exclusive reign of this orthodox beauty is not approaching its last quarter. The new Vale of Tempe may be a gaunt waste of Thule: human souls may find themselves in closer and closer harmony with external things wearing a sombreness distasteful to our race when it was young. The time seems near, if it has not actually arrived, when the chastened sublimity of a moor, a sea, or a mountain will be all of nature that is absolutely in keeping with the moods of the more thinking among mankind. And ultimately, to the commonest tourist, spots like Iceland may become what the vineyards and the myrtle-gardens of South Europe are to him now; and Heidelberg and Baden be passed unheeded as he hastens from the Alps to the sand-dunes of Scheveningen.

The most thorough-going ascetic could feel that he had a natural right to wander on Egdon: he was deep within the line of legitimate indulgence when he laid himself upon to influences such as these. Colours and beauties so far subdued were, at least, the birthright of all. Only in summer days of highest feather did its mood touch the level of gaiety. Intensity was more usually reached by way of the solemn than by way of the brilliant, and such a sort of intensity was often arrived at during winter darkness, tempests, and mist.   (Bk I, ch. 1)

Hardy is confidently aware here that he does not create 'beauty of the accepted kind'. This conventional beauty, which he describes as 'smiling', 'orthodox' and 'fair', he sees as the product of an optimism about man and his prospects no longer tenable among the 'more thinking' of mankind. Egdon Heath and the story of its inhabitants he is about to tell embody, in contrast, a new beauty ('a subtler and scarcer instinct') which he describes as sad in mood, subdued in colour, mysterious and tragic in nature. By 'tragic' he undoubtedly means 'connected with the working of the inevitable', for the origin of this new beauty is nature speaking to the poet open to her 'legitimate influence', nature teaching the poet the working, and in that working the beauty, of the inevitable.

Some ten years later, while writing *The Woodlanders*, it was precisely the mystery and tragedy of nature that held his attention:

> After looking at the landscape ascribed to Bonington in our drawing-room I feel that Nature is played out as a Beauty, but not as a Mystery. I don't want to see landscapes, *i.e.*, scenic paintings of them, because I don't want to see the original realities – as optical effects, that is. I want to see the deeper reality underlying the scenic, the expression of what are sometimes called abstract imaginings.
>
> The 'simply natural' is interesting no longer. The much decried, mad, late-Turner rendering is now necessary to create my interest. The exact truth as to material fact ceases to be important in art – it is a student's style – the style of a period when the mind is serene and unawakened to the tragical mysteries of life; when it does not bring anything to the object that coalesces with and translates the qualities that are already there – half-hidden, it may be – and the two united are depicted as the All. (*Life*, p. 185)

Hardy's sense of a new, underlying mystery in nature is in part the product of the scientific view of nature he had learned from Darwin, Huxley and Spencer. He learned from these men of science to view nature as a process as well as a prospect or spectacle; his affection for the beauty of nature-as-spectacle he seems to have translated into a regard for the beauty of the mystery behind nature-as-process, the mystery of 'the deeper reality underlying the scenic'. Since this process exacts pain and death, it cannot be beautiful in any traditional sense of the word. Its beauty is a negative beauty, and a new beauty because attached to a new truth about human destiny. 'To find beauty in ugliness is the province of the poet', Hardy observed in a note of August 1888, repeating the phrase he had used ten years earlier to describe his vision in *The Return* (*Life*, p. 213).

September 1888 found Hardy beginning *Tess*, and Angel Clare of *Tess* is Hardy's first protagonist in whom a growth from perception of orthodox to perception of tragic beauty is central. What Hardy exhibits in *Tess*, through its action and the comments of its narrator, is the ugly spectacle of Tess's sexual ruin and social disgrace, her heroic but futile attempts at recovery, her abandonment by the only possible agent of her recovery (Angel Clare), and her execution for the murder of her seducer. What Hardy would have his reader see – from his defiant subtitle on – is that Tess is 'pure' because she is innocent in intention, if not in act. The 'deeper reality' or beauty of Tess, like the 'deeper reality' or beauty of a 'late-Turner' painting, was to be found for Hardy not in 'the exact truth as to material fact', but in 'the tragic mystery of [her] life': the workings of chance that brought her cart into collision with the mail cart, then twice brought her into the presence of the artful Alec, and finally brought her back into the company of the too-late-forgiving Angel. This is, in Tess's case, the working of the inevitable. In the reality of that working lies the beauty Hardy has come to value. Tess herself is portrayed as subject to the working of two realities. She is aware of troublous movements beneath the serene and beautiful spectacle. Hardy labels as 'the ache of modernism' the 'sad imaginings' she on one occasion describes to Angel: the trees have 'inquisitive eyes', she says; and the river says, 'Why do ye trouble me with your looks?' (ch. 19). Tess is here in communication with 'the deeper reality underlying the scenic'. Her movement from the lush and fertile meadows of Talbothays to the barren uplands of Flintcomb objectifies the novel's insistence that there exist two natures, one fair and smiling, one sombre and suggestive of tragical possibilities.

Angel's changing perception of Tess illustrates this duality more dramatically than anything else in the novel. He first loves Tess because she is a maiden fair, good and pure, the embodiment of innocence in the traditional sense. He then learns that she is impure and in horror rejects her. He finally comes to recognize the beauty of her 'ugliness' – that is, the purity of intention that, shining through the impurity of her violation, is the glow of a new kind of beauty:

During this time of absence [in Brazil] he had mentally aged a dozen years. What arrested him now as of value in life was less its beauty than its pathos. Having long discredited the old systems of mysticism, he now began to discredit the old appraisements of morality. He thought they wanted readjusting. Who was the moral man? Still more pertinently, who was the moral woman? The beauty or ugliness of a character lay not only in its achievements, but in its aims and impulses; its true history lay, not among things done, but among things willed. . . .

Viewing [Tess] in these lights, a regret for his hasty judgment began to oppress him. Did he reject her eternally, or did he not? He could no longer say that he would always reject her, and not to say that was in spirit to accept her now. (ch. 49)

Angel is asking himself 'why he had not judged Tess constructively rather than biographically, by the will rather than by the deed' (ch. 53). Simply put, Angel has learned to look beneath the surface of things. He resembles the narrator of *The Return* seeking a new kind of beauty; he resembles the novelist and poet of *The Life*, seeking beauty in ugliness, learning to see life's 'tragical mysteries'. Hardy found a phrase for this phenomenon in *Tess* when, late in the novel, describing Tess's hopeless outrage upon being approached by Alec (now a convert to Christianity) to marry him and thereby make things right, he places the couple near 'the spot called "Cross-in-Hand" ': 'Of all spots on the bleached and desolate upland this was the most forlorn. It was so far removed from the charm which is sought in landscape by artists and view-lovers as to reach a new kind of beauty, a negative beauty of tragic tone' (ch. 45). Perhaps this 'negative beauty' is one thing Arnold Bennett had in mind when he spoke in 1904 of a 'new beauty' Hardy had produced in the Wessex Novels. The point here is that Hardy was himself caught up in defining a new sense of beauty compatible with his tragic sense of human destiny; the novelists drawn to imitate him recognized him as a great and original artist because he was the discoverer of a new beauty.

This raises a question about the working of literary influence, for it suggests that Hardy's disciples among later novelists were attracted to him less as a competitor than as a discoverer and embodier of something they wished to rediscover and re-embody – namely, a new beauty. One of the implausible aspects of Harold

Bloom's theory of literary influence is the central assumption that the ephebe or belated author is consumed by the need to wrest his language and vision from the grip of a precursor. The later writer may swerve from his precursor so as to execute a 'corrective movement' (*clinamen*). He may retain the terms of the parent work but 'mean them in another sense' (*tessera*). He may move towards 'discontinuity with the precursor' (*kenosis*). He may move toward 'what he believes to be a power in the parent poem that does not belong to the parent proper, but to a range of being just beyond that precursor' (*daemonization*). He may purge himself of part of his artistic endowment by 'so stationing [his work] in relation to the parent-poem as to make that poem undergo [a truncation] too' (*askesis*). Or, finally, he may hold his work open to his precursor, with 'the uncanny effect . . . that the new poem's achievement makes it seem to us, not as though the precursor were writing it, but as though the later poet himself had written the precursor's characteristic work' (*apophrades*). These strategies of revision may occur separately, or in various combinations, according to Bloom. They represent, on analogy with Freud's terms for the various defences the human psyche erects against the predations of the unconscious, the different strategies a belated artist adopts *against* his literary precursors. And revisionary struggle and competition is, according to Bloom, an unavoidable aspect of post-Enlightenment art. There is, apparently, nothing new under the literary sun. The modern writer is doomed not to writing, but to rewriting, not to vision, but to re-vision.[4]

The value of Bloom's theory is obvious enough. His categories provide a conceptual framework with which to examine one writer's way of using another. John Fowles, in *Daniel Martin*, seems to retain the terms of Hardy's *Well-Beloved*, but to mean them 'in another sense' (as in Bloom's *tessera*). Theodore Dreiser's move in *Carrie* and *Jennie* beyond the tragedy of Hardy's *Tess* and *The Mayor* resembles Bloom's *daemonization*, the creation of a counter-sublime. Something similar can be said of Lawrence's move beyond the tragic vision of *Tess* and *Jude* in *The Rainbow* and *Women in Love*. But what Bloom does not account for, at least in the several cases under study here, is the ever-present air of cooperation, the sense of shared enterprise, the possibility that the poetic offspring dearly wishes to be – on his own terms of course – what the poetic parent has been.

Bloom's rather rigid use of a Freudian model introduces an

inescapable tension, even an overt hostility, into the process of influence he seeks to describe. Perhaps because he almost entirely ignores historical evidence – for instance, the often affectionate or admiring remarks of a later artist *about* an earlier one, the explicit references to an earlier writer *in* the works of a later one – Bloom's account tends toward the abstract, the ahistorical, even the fantastic. But if one considers other possible models for the working of influence – for example, T. S. Eliot's idea of tradition, or the poet Dante's depiction of the pilgrim Dante's journey with Virgil in the *Divine Comedy* – he finds himself contemplating a fundamentally different relationship between ephebe and precursor, and one helpful in generalizing about the relationships between Hardy and his 'disciples' among modern novelists.

Tradition in Eliot's sense of the word presupposes an attainable fellowship, community and harmony. Bloom's family romance resembles a family quarrel. In Eliot's communal metaphor for the working of influence, tension, anxiety and competition give way to order and a sense of belonging. This difference arises in part from the fact that for Bloom, by the terms of his family metaphor, influence cannot be avoided. It is inherited and therefore determinative. For Eliot, tradition and the influence implicit in its working 'cannot be inherited'; it is to be obtained only 'by great labour'.[5] The implications of this difference are vast. Bloom's later writer is under a compulsion to carry out the demands of his revisionary fate. Eliot's ephebe is relatively free to labour to acquire or to ignore the historical sense. Of course, without it he cannot, in Eliot's view, be a poet "beyond his twenty-fifth year", and, once having acquired a sense of both the pastness and the presence of the past, he is indeed under a compulsion 'to write not merely with his own generation in his bones, but with a feeling that the whole of the literature of Europe from Homer and within it the whole of the literature of his own country has a simultaneous existence and composes a simultaneous order'.[6] In spite of this, however, the writer within Eliot's literary community is not like a child labouring anxiously in the shadow of a great parent he fears he can never equal or exceed. Eliot's writer is bound by communal, not family, ties, by affection and not affection *and* blood. As citizen he is free in a way that as child he could not possibly be.

Similarly, Eliot's artist recognizes a communal rather than a personal glory and ideal. Bloom's revisionary strategies all serve the ephebe's attempt to achieve a personal transcendence. Eliot's 'new work of art' becomes a personal sublime only when it becomes an integral part of an 'ideal order' made up of 'the existing monuments' of literary art.[7] Bloom's ephebe is a supplanter and displacer, Eliot's a joiner and co-operator; Bloom's new poet is engaged in conquest, Eliot's in 'surrender of himself as he is at the moment to something which is more valuable'.[8]

In Dante's *Comedy*, the family metaphor for influence gives way not to the metaphor of community, but to the metaphor of friendship and love. Virgil represents to Dante the tradition of great epic poetry reaching back to Homer. Dante has chosen to position his poem and himself as the poem's hero in intimate relation to that tradition. To Dante, Virgil is his supreme and beloved master:

> 'Canst thou be Virgil? thou that fount of splendour
> Whence poured so wide a stream of lordly speech?'
> Said I, and bowed my awe-struck head in wonder;
>
> 'Oh honour and light of poets all and each,
> Now let my great love stead me – the bent brow
> And long hours pondering all thy book can teach!
>
> Thou art my master, and my author thou,
> From thee alone I learned the singing strain,
> The noble style, that does me honour now.
>
> See there the beast that turned me back again –
> Save me from her, great sage – I fear her so,
> She shakes my blood through every pulse and vein.'[9]

To Dante, Virgil is guide, protector and friend, a paradigm of human wisdom who will lead him out of the wilderness of sin to the very threshold of Paradise. Virgil is not, of course, Dante's salvation; but he is one of the inescapable terms of that salvation. Dante's medieval Catholic 'revision' of Virgil is tremendous and far-reaching, but Virgil is scrupulously and lovingly given his due. And this is nowhere so clear as in the thirtieth canto of *Purgatory*, where Virgil vanishes at the approach of Beatrice and Dante utters what are to this reader some of the most poignant words of the entire poem:

> I turned to leftward – full of confidence
> As any little boy who ever came
> Running to mother with his fears and pains –
>
> To say to Virgil: 'There is scarce a dram
> That does not hammer and throb in all my blood;
> I know the embers of the ancient flame.'
>
> But Virgil – O he had left us, and we stood
> Orphaned of him; Virgil, dear father, most
> Kind Virgil I gave me to for my soul's good;
>
> And not for all that our first mother lost
> Could I forbid the smutching tears to steep
> My cheeks, once washed with dew from all their dust.[10]

This is not the anxiety but the piety of influence, a piety of influence soon to give way to the everlasting joy of the influence of Beatrice and through her of the divine inflowing.

Neither Eliot's idea of tradition nor Dante's image of a beloved Virgil provides an exact model for the relation between Hardy and his seven 'disciples', but then neither does Bloom's use of the family romance. Bloom's categories are only partially descriptive. They are helpful in the cases of Lawrence, Fowles and Dreiser, as has been seen. On the other hand, Lawrence and Powys were explicitly aware of Hardy as part of an English tradition in the novel into which they sought to incorporate themselves. Also, Powys, Fowles, Proust and Dreiser – somewhat in the manner of Dante – chose to bring images of Hardy and his novels and those novels' incarnations of the beauty of the inevitable into the very fabric of their own novels. Their manner in this resembles Dante's, and their motive – affection, respect, even piety – is much the same. They turn to Hardy not for his supreme wisdom or noble style, as Dante did to Virgil, but for his tragic sense of beauty, which, almost predictably, most of them set aside, as Dante had to set Virgil aside, because finally and sadly nothing less than the loving abandonment of the parent is the price of the child's growth and transcendence.

Notes

CHAPTER 1 Introductory: Hardy, George Moore and Others

1. Thomas Hardy, *Complete Poems*, ed. James Gibson (London, 1978) p. 954. See G. K. Chesterton, *The Victorian Age in Literature* (London, 1913) p. 143; also Michael Millgate, *Thomas Hardy: A Biography* (New York, 1982) pp. 571–2.
2. See 'On Thomas Hardy', in *Generally Speaking* (New York, 1929) pp. 285–91, where Chesterton expresses sympathy for Hardy's philosophy ('as an error') and praises Hardy's 'splendidly unconscious simplicity', the 'really powerful' pictorial element of his style, and the 'humility' and 'humanity' of his personality.
3. George Moore, *Confessions of a Young Man* (1888), ed. Susan Dick (Montreal and London, 1972) pp. 156–8, 172, 211. See Bailey, *The Poetry of Thomas Hardy: A Handbook and Commentary* (Chapel Hill, NC, 1971) p. 648.
4. Moore's attack on Hardy first appeared in 'George Moore and John Freeman', *Dial* (New York), 75 (1923) 341–62; it was reprinted in *Conversations in Ebury Street* (New York, 1924) pp. 111–20. See pp. 111–16 for the remarks quoted here.
5. Murry's reply to Moore appeared under the title *Wrap me up in my Aubusson Carpet* (New York, 1924). Hardy's letter to Moore is quoted in Bailey, *The Poetry of Thomas Hardy*, p. 649.
6. *Thomas Hardy's Notebooks, and Some Letters from Julia Augusta Martin*, ed. Evelyn Hardy (London, 1955) p. 104.
7. Murry, *Wrap me up in my Aubusson Carpet*, pp. 7–8.
8. See Malcolm Brown, *George Moore: A Reconsideration* (Seattle, 1955) pp. ix–x.
9. See Graham Hough, 'George Moore and the Novel', in *George Moore's Mind and Art*, ed. Graham Owens (Edinburgh, 1970) pp. 166–75.
10. See Harold Bloom, *The Anxiety of Influence: A Theory of Poetry* (New York, 1973) esp. pp. 5–16, 19–45.
11. See Joseph M. Hone, *The Life of George Moore* (New York, 1936) pp. 194–5.
12. Moore, *Conversations in Ebury Street*, pp. 114–15.
13. Ibid., p. 113.
14. From Geraint Goodwin, *Conversations with George Moore* (New York, 1930) p. 151.
15. George Moore, *Esther Waters* (1894), ch. 48. All quotations from this

novel (cited as *EW*) are from the Houghton Mifflin Riverside Edition, ed. Lionel Stevenson (Boston, Mass., 1963). Subsequent references appear in the text.

16. See Anthony Farrow, *George Moore* (Boston, Mass., 1978) p. 68; also Lionel Stevenson, Introduction to the Riverside Edition of *Esther Waters*, pp. xiii–iv.
17. Moore, *Conversations in Ebury Street*, p. 117.
18. Repr. in *Thomas Hardy: The Critical Heritage*, ed. R. G. Cox (London, 1970) p. 31.
19. *The Letters of Henry James*, ed. Percy Lubbock, 2 vols (New York, 1920) I, 190. See Dan H. Laurence, 'Henry James and Stevenson Discuss "Vile" Tess', *Colby College Quarterly*, 3 (1953) 164–8.
20. Quoted ibid., p. 167.
21. Quoted ibid.
22. F. R. Leavis, *The Great Tradition* (New York, 1967) pp. 22–3.
23. See K. W. Salter, 'Lawrence, Hardy, and "The Great Tradition" ', *English*, 22 (1973) 60–5. As Salter argues, Lawrence's 'central judgement of the nature of Hardy's work cannot be easily set aside, and indeed ought not to be by those who place Lawrence in the great tradition while excluding Hardy' (p. 61).
24. Quoted in H. M. Block, 'James Joyce and Thomas Hardy', *Modern Language Quarterly*, 19 (1958) 337.
25. Ibid., p. 339.
26. Ibid., p. 338.
27. Quoted ibid., p. 340.
28. Ibid., p. 340.
29. Ibid., p. 341.
30. Virginia Woolf, ' "Jane Eyre" and "Wuthering Heights" ' (1916), in *The Common Reader*, First Series (New York, 1925) p. 222.
31. Ibid., pp. 222–3.
32. Ibid., p. 223–4.
33. Virginia Woolf, 'The Novels of Thomas Hardy' (1928), in *The Common Reader*, Second Series (London, 1932) pp. 246–57.
34. Ibid., p. 248.
35. In *After Strange Gods* (London, 1934) p. 54, where Eliot remarks that Hardy 'was indifferent even to the prescripts of good writing: he wrote sometimes overpoweringly well, but always very carelessly; at times his style touches sublimity without ever having passed through the stage of being good'. For a spirited reply to Eliot, see Katherine Anne Porter, 'Notes on a Criticism of Thomas Hardy', *Southern Review* (Thomas Hardy Centennial Edition), 6 (1940) 150–61.
36. For Gissing, see Pierre Coustillas, 'Some Unpublished Letters from Gissing to Hardy', *English Literature in Transition*, 9 (1966) 197–209; for Howells, see *My Literary Passions* (New York, 1895) p. 182; for Cather, see *The World of the Parish: Willa Cather's Articles and Reviews, 1893–1902*, ed. W. M. Curtin (Lincoln, Nebr., 1970) I, 266–7; for Dreiser, see William White, 'Dreiser on Hardy, Henley and Whitman: An Unpublished Letter', *English Language Notes*, 6 (1968) 122; for Bennett, 'My Literary Heresies', *T. P.'s Weekly*, 4 (23 Sep 1904) 392,

quoted in *Thomas Hardy: An Annotated Bibliography*, comp. and ed. Helmut E. Gerber and W. Eugene Davis (De Kalb, Ill., 1973) p. 105; for Proust, see George D. Painter, *Marcel Proust: A Biography*, 2 vols [1959] New York, 1978) II, 154–5, also pp. 110–33 below.
37 For Lawrence, see *Phoenix: The Posthumous Papers of D. H. Lawrence (1936)*, ed. Edward D. McDonald, 2 vols (New York, 1972) I, 410, 419; for Lewis, see *Thomas Hardy: Notes on his Life and Work*, ed. Henry Seidel Canby (New York, 1925) p. 14.
38 For Cary, see *Art and Reality* (Cambridge, 1958) pp. 168–9. For Fowles, see 'Notes on the Unfinished Novel', in *Afterwords: Novelists on their Novels*, ed. Thomas McCormack (New York, 1969) p. 146.
39 See Glen Cavaliero, *The Rural Tradition in the English Novel, 1900–1939* (London, 1977) esp. ch. 1. For Romain Rolland, see W. F. Starr, 'Romain Rolland and Thomas Hardy', *Modern Language Quarterly*, 17 (1956) 99–103. See also Johannes Riis, 'Naipaul's Woodlanders', *Journal of Commonwealth Literature*, 14 (1979) 109–15.

CHAPTER 2   *'Now it Remains'*: Hardy and D. H. Lawrence

1 Jessie Chambers, *D. H. Lawrence: A Personal Record* (1935), ed. J. D. Chambers (London, 1965) p. 110. Jessie Chambers recalled that 'Hardy's name had been a familiar one in our house since childhood days.' See also Harry T. Moore, *The Life of D. H. Lawrence* (New York, 1952) p. 35; and Émile Delavenay, *D. H. Lawrence: The Man and his Work, the Formative Years, 1885–1919* (London, 1972) p. 43.
2 See J. R. Ebbatson, 'Thomas Hardy and Lady Chatterley', *Ariel: A Review of International English Literature*, 8 (1977) 85–6. Ebbatson identifies one of the four volumes as *Two on a Tower*.
3 See Rose Marie Burwell, 'Schopenhauer, Hardy, and Lawrence: Toward a New Understanding of *Sons and Lovers*', *Western Humanities Review*, 28 (1974) 109–10.
4 See Raney Stanford, 'Thomas Hardy and Lawrence's *The White Peacock*', *Modern Fiction Studies*, 5 (1959) 19–28.
5 See Ross C. Murfin, *Swinburne, Hardy, Lawrence, and the Burden of Unbelief* (Chicago, 1978) p. 187. Murfin continues, one of the weaknesses of *The White Peacock* is that 'it never really transcends its most basic purpose, that is, to be a Hardy novel that shows Hardy was wrong' (p. 188). Before Lawrence could write his own fiction 'he must first write a novel showing why Hardy's novels went wrong, thus convincing himself of the need of that which he fears may be utterly redundant and thus unnecessary – more novels by D. H. Lawrence' (p. 192).
6 In *Phoenix*, II, 304–7.
7 D. H. Lawrence, *Study of Thomas Hardy* (1914), in *Phoenix*, I, 410. All quotations from the *Study* (cited thus) are from this edition. Subsequent references appear in the text.
8 I am much indebted in this summary to Keith Cushman, *D. H. Lawrence at Work: The Emergence of the Prussian Officer Stories* (Charlott-

esville, Va, 1978) pp. 224–34; also to Mark Kinkead-Weekes, 'The Marble and the Statue: The Exploratory Imagination of D. H. Lawrence', in *Imagined Worlds: Essays of Some English Novels and Novelists in Honour of John Butt*, ed. Maynard Mack and Ian Gregor (London, 1968) pp. 371–418.

9. Mark Spilka, *The Love Ethic of D. H. Lawrence* (London, 1966) p. 43; see also John Paterson, 'Lawrence's Vital Source: Nature and Character in Thomas Hardy', in *Nature and the Victorian Imagination*, ed. U. C. Knoepflmacher and G. B. Tennyson (Berkeley, Calif., 1977) pp. 455–69.

10. *Collected Letters of D. H. Lawrence*, ed. Harry T. Moore, 2 vols (New York, 1962) I, 488, 526. See also Lawrence's *Studies in Classic American Literature* ([1923] New York, 1966) pp. 91, 111, 112.

11. See note 2, above.

12. Quoted by Ebbatson, in *Ariel*, 8, pp. 86–7.

13. *Collected Letters of D. H. Lawrence*, I, 204.

14. Bloom, *The Anxiety of Influence*, esp. pp. 5–16.

15. Ian Gregor's remark appears in *The Great Web: The Form of Hardy's Major Fiction* (London, 1974) p. 233. See Richard D. Beards, 'D. H. Lawrence and the *Study of Thomas Hardy*, his Victorian Predecessor', *D. H. Lawrence Review*, 2 (1969) 210–29; also Richard Swigg, *Lawrence, Hardy, and American Literature* (London, 1972).

16. Delavenay (in *The Formative Years*, p. 324) notes that Lawrence analysed Hardy's characters 'from the angle of the distribution in each of male and female principles'.

17. See ibid., p. 308, for an account of Lawrence's reading of Otto Weininger's *Sex and Character*, published in England in 1906, in which Weininger advances a theory of 'the co-existence of male and female traits in every individual'.

18. D. H. Lawrence, *The Rainbow* (1915) ch. 13. All quotations from this novel (cited as *R*) are from the Penguin edition (New York, 1980). Subsequent references appear in the text.

19. D. H. Lawrence, *Women in Love* (1920) ch. 29. All quotations from this novel (cited as *WL*) are from the Penguin edition (New York, 1981). Subsequent references appear in the text.

20. Cf. Hardy's remark of 1895 in the *Life* (p. 272): 'Of course the book [*Jude*] is all contrasts – or was meant to be in its original conception . . . – e.g., Sue and her heathen gods set against Jude's reading the Greek Testament; Christminster academical, Christminster in the slums; Jude the saint, Jude the sinner; Sue the Pagan, Sue the saint; marriage, no marriage; etc., etc.'

CHAPTER 3 *'An Undying Underground Stream'*: Hardy and John Cowper Powys

1. John Cowper Powys, *Autobiography* (London, 1934) p. 56. All quotations from the *Autobiography* (cited as *Auto*) are from this edition. Subsequent references appear in the text. The epigraph to this chapter

is from Powys's essay 'Thomas Hardy', in *Enjoyment of Literature* (New York, 1938) p. 446.
2. John Cowper Powys, *Odes and Other Poems* (London, 1896) pp. 11–12.
3. Llewelyn Powys's recollection of Hardy's visit also conveys John Cowper Powys's high excitement at making Hardy's acquaintance:

> I well remember my brother's return from his first visit to Max Gate. It was during the summer holidays and the rest of us children were crowded together in a wooden hut which my youngest brother had built for himself in one of the shrubberies. This brother had invited us all to tea and his saucepan was just beginning to boil under the laurel bushes when John appeared, full of exciting talk about his expedition. I recollect how he drew for us a caricature of Hardy on one of the white deal boards that formed the walls of this 'Bushes' home, a striking picture that the passagings of snail, ant, and woodlouse were never able quite to obliterate. Especially did the sketch emphasize the novelist's hooked nose and goblin eyebrows.

See 'Some Memories of Thomas Hardy' (1938), in *Monographs on the Life, Times, and Works of Thomas Hardy*, 64, ed. J. Stevens Cox (St Peter Port, 1969) p. 390.
4. *John Cowper Powys: Letters to Nicholas Ross*, ed. Llewelyn Powys (London, 1971) p. 119. See also the letters to Ross of January and November 1943 (pp. 49–55). Also the letter to Louis Wilkinson of October 1959, in which Powys wrote, 'I am a terrific hero-worshipper and genius-worshipper and I have never felt ashamed to boast of my various encounters with Hardy or with Walter de la Mare. I feel very strongly that we all have a right to be proud of touching History or Poetry or Literature as embodied in any person. In that sense I am proud to be a Boswellian' – *Letters of John Cowper Powys to Louis Wilkinson, 1935–1956* (London, 1958) p. 383.
5. The other two great men were Augustus John and Charles Chaplin (*Letters of John Cowper Powys to Louis Wilkinson*, p. 338).
6. Powys is referring to his brothers Llewelyn and Theodore and his sister Philippa. See R. C. Churchill, *The Powys Brothers* (London, 1962); also Kenneth Hopkins, *The Powys Brothers: A Biographical Appreciation* (London, 1974).
7. John Cowper Powys, *Visions and Revisions* ([1915] New York, 1955) pp. xviii–xix. Barnes, so far as is known, was never Hardy's schoolmaster, though it is said that Hardy, while an architect's assistant in the office of John Hicks of Dorchester in the 1850s and 1860s, occasionally consulted Barnes on questions of Greek and Latin grammar. Barnes's school was next door to Hicks's office at 39, South Street (see *Life*, pp. 27–8).
8. Powys, *Visions and Revisions*, p. 161.
9. John Cowper Powys, *Wood and Stone* (London, 1915) pp. x–xi. All quotations from the novel (cited as *W&S*) are from this edition. Subsequent references appear in the text.

10 Cf. *The Woodlanders*, ch. 1: Little Hintock 'was one of those sequestered spots outside the gates of the world where may usually be found more meditation than action; . . . yet where from time to time dramas of a grandeur and unity truly Sophoclean are enacted in the real, by virtue of the concentrated passions and closely-knit interdependence of the lives therein'.
11 John Cowper Powys, *Rodmoor: A Romance* (New York, 1916) ch. 8. Subsequent references to the novel are to this edition and appear in the text. The letters from Powys to Hardy can be seen in the Dorset County Museum, Dorchester.
12 Powys's letter is in the Dorset County Museum: 'Perhaps you will recollect, you were kind enough to pay us a visit, years ago, at Montacute.'
13 Llewelyn Powys, 'Glimpses of Thomas Hardy', *Dial*, 72 (1922) 286–90.
14 Llewelyn Powys, *Thirteen Worthies* (New York, 1923). See also the letter from Llewelyn Powys to Hardy dated 22 April 1923, in the Dorset County Museum.
15 John Cowper and Llewelyn Powys, *Confessions of Two Brothers* (New York, 1916) pp. 76–7.
16 John Cowper Powys, *Ducdame* (New York, 1928).
17 John Cowper Powys, *Wolf Solent* ([1929] New York, 1964) ch. 15. All quotations from this novel (cited as *WfS*) are from the 1964 edition. Subsequent references appear in the text.
18 In the Preface to *Jude* Hardy had described his novel as an account of 'a deadly war waged between flesh and spirit'.
19 Among Powys's novels of the 1930s, Hardy's influence may seem least important in *A Glastonbury Romance* (1932), an epic account, in Powys's words in the Preface, of the effect of the Grail legend 'upon a particular spot [Glastonbury] . . . together with its crowd of inhabitants of every age and every type of character'. In fact, however, Hardy's *Dynasts* (1903–8), his epic poem of the Napoleonic wars, is an important model whose machinery of the celestial Spirits Powys imitates in his conception of the overseeing Powers in his gigantic romance. As Powys at one point writes, 'the invisible Watchers of that Glastonbury Divine Comedy recall the spirits of *The Dynasts*'. The magnitude of Hardy's greatest poem is present in other ways as well: in the huge cast of characters; in the concern with a national ideal embodied in a central heroic figure (Powys's Johnnie Geard, Hardy's Nelson and Napoleon); in the dimensions of the romance's central triadic conflict between capitalism, communism and Christianity. In one significant way, Powys's 'invisible Watchers' differ from Hardy's Spirits: the power of Powys's Watchers is subordinate to that of the human minds they look down on, for the Watchers are, after all, the creations of those human minds they sometimes baffle. Powys posits, more confidently than Hardy, a force for good; and, unlike Hardy and his idea of an evolutionary meliorism, Powys places that force in the human heart rather than at the centre of a natural process.
20 John Cowper Powys, *Weymouth Sands* ([1963] London, 1980) ch. 11. All quotations from this novel are from the 1980 edition. Subsequent

references appear in the text. For a striking account of the autobiographical aspects of *The Well-Beloved*, see Robert Gittings, *Young Thomas Hardy* (Boston, Mass., 1975) esp. ch. 20; also Gittings's *Thomas Hardy's Later Years* (Boston, Mass., 1978) esp. chs. 6 and 7.
21. The phrase is Edmund Gosse's in a letter to Thomas Hardy in March 1897: 'The Tragedy of a Nympholept – that is what your [*Well-Beloved*] is. And so delicate, and sculptural, and uplifted' (Dorset County Museum).
22. John Cowper Powys, *A Glastonbury Romance* ([1932] London, 1957) pp. x–xi, xv.
23. See Malcolm Elway, 'Prefatory Note' to *Maiden Castle* (London, 1966) pp. 7–10; also Peter J. Casagrande, *Unity in Hardy's Novels: 'Repetitive Symmetries'* (London, 1982) pp. 183ff.
24. John Cowper Powys, *Maiden Castle* ([1937] London, 1966) pt I, ch. 1; pt II, ch. 5; pt III, ch.9. All quotations from this novel (cited as *MC*) are from the 1966 edition. Subsequent references appear in the text.
25. Quirm is thinking of the well-worn features of a griffin above the door of High Place Hall, Lucetta's residence in *The Mayor*. The same figure now adorns the arch of the door of the library of the Dorset County Museum.
26. Henchard takes a similar walk in *The Mayor* shortly after discovering that Elizabeth-Jane is not his natural daughter.
27. The last four words echo Hardy's poem 'Afterwards', in which he describes his own keen sense of Dorset's loveliness, with the refrain 'He was a man who used to notice such things'. Cf. *MC*, pt III, ch. 9, where Dud in his indifference to Wizzie's style of dress is described as 'one who never noticed such things'.
28. Cf. Hardy's remarks (*Life*, pp. 112, 114); 'Laughter always means blindness – either from defect, choice, or accident'; and, again, 'Art lies in making [Nature's defects] the basis of hitherto unperceived beauty'.
29. After *Maiden Castle* Powys turned from English to Welsh materials in novels such as *Owen Glendower* (1940) and *Porius* (1951). For a helpful account of Powys's later career as a novelist, see Glen Cavaliero, *John Cowper Powys: Novelist* (Oxford, 1973).

CHAPTER 4 Three 'Nostalgicians': Hardy, Marcel Proust and Alain-Fournier

1. See Walter A. Strauss, *Proust and Literature: The Novelist as Critic* (Cambridge, Mass., 1957) esp. ch. 1; L. A. Bisson, 'Proust and Hardy: Incidence or Coincidence', in *Studies in French Language, Literature, and History Presented to R. L. Graeme Ritchie* (Cambridge, Mass., 1949) pp. 24–34; and Painter, *Proust: A Biography*, II, esp. pp. 118–28.
2. Léon Boucher, 'Le Roman pastoral en Angleterre', *Revue des deux mondes*, 12 (1875) 838–66. Here and elsewhere, translations from the French are my own, unless otherwise indicated.
3. By 1928 (the year of Hardy's death), nine of the fourteen Wessex novels had been translated into French: in 1882 *The Trumpet-Major (Le*

Trompette-Major, tr. Yorick Bernard-Derosne); in 1891 *Far from the Madding Crowd* (*Barbara*, tr. Mathilde Zeys); in 1901 *Tess* (*Tess d'Urberville*, tr. Madeleine Rolland) and *Jude* (*Jude l'Obscur*, tr. Firmin Roz); in 1909 *The Well-Beloved* (*La Bien-aimée*, tr. Eve Paul-Marguerite); in 1910 *Under the Greenwood Tree* (*Sous la verte feuillé*, tr. Arthur Franks); in 1913 *A Pair of Blue Eyes* (*Deux yeux bleus*, tr. Eve Paul-Marguerite); in 1922 *The Mayor of Casterbridge* (*Le Maire de Casterbridge*, tr. Philippe Neel); in 1923 *The Return of the Native* (*Le Retour au pays natal*, tr. Eve Paul-Marguerite). *The Woodlanders* (*Les Forestiers*, tr. Antoinette Six) appeared in 1932.

4. Henri Davray, 'Lettres Anglais', *Mercure de France*, 46 (1903) 264–5.
5. Firmin Roz, 'Thomas Hardy', *Revue des deux mondes*, 34 (1906) 176–207.
6. In 1906, Jacques-Émile Blanche recommended *Jude the Obscure* to Proust. Blanche had painted Hardy's portrait in London in the summer of 1906. He returned to Paris full of praise for Hardy's work. See Blanche's *Mes Modèles* (Paris, 1928) p. 80; also Bisson, in *Studies in French Language, Literature and History*, p. 26.
7. *Correspondance de Marcel Proust*, ed. Philip Kolb, VI (Paris, 1980) 286. Proust seems to have read Hardy entirely in translation. See Bisson, in *Studies in French Language, Literature, and History*, p. 26.
8. *Cahiers Marcel Proust: le carnet de 1908*, ed. Philip Kolb (Paris, 1976) esp. pp. 18, 39, 41. Proust read *A Pair of Blue Eyes* in *Les Dèbats*, where it appeared between October and December 1910.
9. *Marcel Proust: choix de lettres*, ed. Philip Kolb (Paris, 1965) pp. 170–1. The letter continues, 'It is curious that among all the most different kinds of writers, from George Eliot to Hardy, from Stevenson to Emerson, there is no literature that has power over me comparable to that which English and American literature has. German, Italian, often even French literature leaves me indifferent.'
10. *Cahiers Marcel Proust: le carnet de 1908*, p. 114.
11. Robert Gittings, in *Young Thomas Hardy* and *Thomas Hardy's Later Years*, is the first of Hardy's biographers to view *The Well-Beloved* as extended fictional self-portraiture.
12. Painter, *Proust: A Biography*, II, 154. Painter points out (pp. 155–7) that at the moment Proust was reading *The Well-Beloved* he perceived a like set of circumstances within his own circle of friends. The death of Mme Arman Caillavet (Mme Verdurin of *Remembrance*) brought him into contact with her daughter (Gilberte of *Remembrance*), with whom he had once been in love, as well as Mme Caillavet's granddaughter Simone (Mlle de Saint-Loup). For a brief time, grandmother, daughter-in-law and granddaughter were in his thoughts, just as in Hardy's novel Avice the first, Avice the second and Avice the third are in Pierston's.
13. See, for example, P.-E. Robert, *Marcel Proust: lecteur des Anglo-Saxons* (Paris, 1976) pp. 121–40.
14. The remarks that follow are indebted to Painter, *Proust: A Biography*, II, 1–179; also P. A. Spalding, *A Reader's Handbook to Proust*, rev. R. H. Cortie (London, 1975).
15. Painter, *Marcel Proust*, II, 146.

16 Marcel Proust, *Remembrance of Things Past*, tr. C. K. Scott Moncrieff, rev. T. Kilmartin, III (New York, 1981) 382. All quotations from the novel (cited as *RTP*) are from this edition. Subsequent references appear in the text.
17 The quotations are from Painter, *Proust: A Biography*, II, 154–5.
18 *Collected Letters of Thomas Hardy*, ed. R. L. Purdy and Michael Millgate (Oxford, 1980) II, 99.
19 Strauss, *Proust and Literature*, p. 12. See also Margaret Mein, *A Foretaste of Proust: A Study of Proust and his Precursors* (Farnborough, Hants, 1974) esp. pp. 1–14.
20 Bisson in *Studies in French Language, Literature and History*, p. 27.
21 Ibid., p. 31.
22 Ibid., p. 32.
23 Quoted ibid.
24 Ibid.
25 Robert, *Proust: lecteur des Anglo-Saxons*, pp. 121–40.
26 Bisson in *Studies in French Language, Literature and History*, pp. 26–7.
27 Painter, *Proust: A Biography*, II, 154, 106.
28 Ibid., p. 310. Hardy's remark appeared in 'The Tree of Knowledge', *New Review*, June 1894, p. 681.
29 See Dr Milton M. Miller, *Nostalgia: A Psychoanalytic Study of Marcel Proust* (Boston, Mass., 1956) p. 120. Painter advances the same view.
30 Painter detects a distinct pattern in Proust's sexual life: girls and women from 1886 to 1892, men of the upper classes from 1892 to about 1902, younger men of the working classes from 1907 on. Possible homosexual relationships may have had a place in Hardy's early development: see Millgate, *Hardy: A Biography*, pp. 63–70, 155–6.
31 Miller, *Nostalgia*, pp. 115–18.
32 Ibid., pp. 120–1.
33 The phrase is Hardy's in a letter of March 1897. See *Collected Letters of Thomas Hardy*, II, 155.
34 Miller, *Nostalgia*, pp. 169–70.
35 Miller (ibid., p. 121) comments on this: Hardy tells the story of

> giving up the original incestuous love . . . and separating oneself from the wellsprings of artistic talent. In *The Well-Beloved*, he indicates how physical illness and admitting one's age are connected sometimes with renunciation of this great nostalgic source of erotization. Ambivalence toward the 'jade of an Ideal' is the subject of Hardy's novel. In the end, a platonic marriage and tranquility, with loss of talent or genius, become the sculptor's solution. Proust's hero . . . does just the opposite of Hardy's. Hardy's hero, through repression, achieves a desiccated semblance of normality, renounces art, and becomes happily married, whereas Marcel, at the end, lifts his repressions in order to arrive at artistic fecundity and shuns marriage, deep loves, or friendships in the present, and even life itself except for its representation in his writing.

36 Hardy's awareness of Proust in 1926 is probably traceable to the

publication in 1923 of *Marcel Proust: An English Proust*, ed. C. K. Scott-Moncrieff (London). The first passage Hardy cited is from *À l'ombre des jeunes filles en fleurs*, Plèiade edn (Paris) I, 468. I have been unable to locate the second passage.

37 *Collected Letters of Thomas Hardy*, II, 158–9. In a passage deleted from the *Life* before publication, Hardy's states more clearly his sense of discipleship to Swinburne:

> The amazing consequences of the publication of the book was that certain papers affected to find unmentionable atrocities in its pages. . . . Altogether it was a remarkable instance of what intolerance can do when it loses all cause of truth and honour. But being review-proof by this time, and feeling the person deserving 'two years hard' (as some print put it) to be a lay figure not himself, also remembering the epithet 'swine-born' which Swinburne endured from the press, he [Hardy] was almost if not quite indifferent to these things. . . .
> (Typescript, p. 401, Dorset County Museum)

For an account of Swinburne's influence on Hardy, see Murfin, *Swinburne, Hardy, and Lawrence and the Burden of Unbelief*.

38 *Collected Letters of Thomas Hardy*, II, 155.
39 Jacques Rivière and Alain-Fournier, *Correspondance 1905–1914* (Paris, 1948) I, 110. Cf. Blanche's account of his conversation with Proust in *Mes Modèles*, p. 80. In these remarks on Alain-Fournier's life, I am indebted to Robert Gibson, *The Land without a Name: Alain-Fournier and his World* (London, 1975); also Jean Loize, *Alain-Fournier: sa vie et 'Le Grand Meaulnes'* (Paris, 1968).
40 Gibson, *Land without a Name*, p. 84.
41 Rivière and Alain-Fournier, *Correspondance*, I, 142.
42 See Gibson, *Land without a Name*, chs 5 to 8.
43 Rivière and Alain-Fournier, *Correspondance*, II, 24. The translation to this point is Gibson's (*Land without a Name*, p. 109).
44 The analysis that follows is indebted to Robert Giannoni, 'Alain-Fournier et Thomas Hardy', *Revue de littérature comparée*, 42 (1968) 407–26. *Le Grand Meaulnes* has been translated as *The Wanderer, or the End of Youth* by Lowell Bair, with an afterword by John Fowles (New York, 1971).
45 Giannoni, in *Revue de littérature comparée*, 42, p. 410.
46 Quoted ibid.
47 Quoted ibid., p. 411.
48 Quoted ibid.
49 Ibid., p. 412.
50 See Lorna Sage, 'John Fowles: A Profile', *New Review*, 1 (1974) 32.
51 Giannoni, in *Revue de littérature comparée*, 42, p. 426.
52 The above is a partial summary and paraphrase of Roz's essay, in *Revue des deux mondes*, 34, pp. 176–207.
53 Hardy's much-annotated copy of Hedgcock can be seen at the Dorset County Museum, Dorchester; see Gittings, *Thomas Hardy's Later Years*,

pp. 187–8. See also Peter J. Casagrande, ' "Old Tom and New Tom": Hardy and his Biographers', in *Thomas Hardy Annual No. 1*, ed. Norman Page (London, 1982) pp. 1–32.
54 For the articles by Catalogne and the others, see *Thomas Hardy: Annotated Bibliography of Writings about Him*, ed. Gerber and Davis. James Joyce, John Middleton Murry and Eden Phillpotts were the English contributors to the Hardy issue *La Revue nouvelle*. The other contributors were Charles du Bos, René Boylesve, Pierre d'Exideuil, Ramon Fernandez, G. d'Hangest, Frans Hellens, Edmund Jalous, Jean Schlumberger, Jean-Louis Vaudoyer and Marcel Proust, whose passage on Hardy from *The Captive* was included.
55 I quote from Felix W. Crosse's translation of d'Exideuil, *The Human Pair in the Work of Thomas Hardy* (London, 1930) pp. 79–80.

CHAPTER 5 *'The Immortal Puzzle': Hardy and John Fowles*

1 Lorna Sage, 'John Fowles: A Profile', *New Review*, 1 (1974) 33. In another interview in the same year, Fowles described *The Magus* (1965) as 'in a sense' a 'reworking of *Le Grand Meaulnes*' – James Campbell, 'An Interview with John Fowles', *Contemporary Literature*, 17 (1974) 457. The epigraph for this chapter is from Fowles's 'Notes from an Unfinished Novel', in *The Novel Today: Contemporary Writers on Modern Fiction*, ed. Malcolm Bradbury (Manchester, 1977) p. 146.
2 John Fowles, 'I Write Therefore I Am', *Evergreen Review*, 8 (1964) 17.
3 Fowles, in *The Novel Today*, p. 141.
4 John Fowles, 'Hardy and the Hag', in *Thomas Hardy after Fifty Years*, ed. Lance St John Butler (London, 1977) p. 29.
5 In a footnote to *The French Lieutenant's Woman*, Fowles describes the poem as 'not the greatest, but one of the most revealing poems, in this context, that Hardy ever wrote'.
6 John Fowles, *The French Lieutenant's Woman* ([1969] New York, 1970) ch. 35. References are to the 1970 edition.
7 See A. A. DeVitis and W. J. Palmer, '*A Pair of Blue Eyes* Flash at *The French Lieutenant's Woman*', *Contemporary Literature*, 15 (1974) 91.
8 John Fowles, review of J. Hillis Miller, *Thomas Hardy: Distance and Desire*, in *New York Times Book Review*, 21 June 1970, p. 4.
9 The second volume of Gittings's biography of Hardy, *Thomas Hardy's Later Years*, appeared in 1978.
10 See Gittings, *Young Thomas Hardy*, p. 217; also Fowles, in *Thomas Hardy after Fifty Years*, p. 30. Fowles writes, 'In his recent biography I was taken to task by Dr Robert Gittings for having swallowed whole the Tryphena "myth". Though I would, accepting both the biographical and the autobiographical evidence in *The Well-Beloved* itself, concede at once that the likelihood of there having been only one Tryphena in Hardy's life is non-existent, I remain a total apostate when it comes to dismissing this type of experience as unimportant' (p. 38). Curiously enough, I have found no reference to Fowles in Gittings's *Young Thomas Hardy* or *Thomas Hardy's Later Years*.

11 Dr Gilbert J. Rose, 'The French Lieutenant's Woman: The Unconscious Significance of a Novel to its Author', *American Imago*, 29 (1972) 165–76.
12 Fowles in *Thomas Hardy after Fifty Years*, pp. 31–2.
13 Ibid., pp. 36–7.
14 Ibid., p. 37.
15 Ibid., p. 29.
16 John Fowles, *Daniel Martin* (New York, 1977) 'The Harvest'. All quotations from the novel (cited as *DM*) are to this edition. Subsequent references appear in the text. Since the novel's chapters are not numbered, I identify each by its title.
17 During the Second World War, Fowles with his family retreated to the West Country to escape aerial bombardment. See John Fowles, 'The Tree', in John Fowles and Frank Horvat, *The Tree* (Boston, Mass., 1979) p. 10.
18 An intriguing parallel exists also between Hardy's revision of *The Well-Beloved* and Fowles's revision in 1977 of *The Magus* (1965). In his Foreword to this revision, Fowles wrote,

> [*The Magus*] must always substantially remain a novel of adolescence written by a retarded adolescent. My only plea is that all artists would have to range the full extent of their lives freely. The rest of the world can censor and bury their private past. We cannot, and so have to remain partly green till the day we die . . . a callow green in the hope of becoming a fertile-green. It is a constant complaint in that most revealing of all modern novels about novelists, Thomas Hardy's agonized last fiction, *The Well-Beloved:* how the much younger self still rules the supposedly 'mature' and middle-aged artist. One may reject the tyranny, as Hardy himself did; but the cost is the end of one's ability to write novels. *The Magus* was also (though quite unconsciously) an out-of-hand celebration of the acceptance of the yoke.

See *The Magus: A Revised Version* (New York, 1978) p. 10.
19 Fowles, in *Thomas Hardy after Fifty Years*, p. 33.
20 Ibid., pp. 30–1.
21 Fowles's meditation on fiction-writing continues in his novel *Mantissa* (1982), a book given over entirely to depiction of the encounter between a novelist and his muse in its various feminine incarnations.

CHAPTER 6 'The Pathetic Side of the World': Hardy and Theodore Dreiser

1 From 1873 on, Hardy's novels appeared in America with almost clocklike regularity: *A Pair of Blue Eyes* as well as *Under the Greenwood Tree* in 1873; *Desperate Remedies* and *Far from the Madding Crowd* in 1874; *The Hand of Ethelberta* in 1876; *The Return of the Native* in 1878; *The Trumpet-Major* in 1880; *A Laodicean* in 1881; *Two on a Tower* in 1882; *The Mayor of Casterbridge* in 1886; *The Woodlanders* in 1887; *Tess of the*

d'Urbervilles in 1892; *Jude the Obscure* in 1895; and *The Well-Beloved* in 1897. See Richard L. Purdy, *Thomas Hardy: A Bibliographical Study* (Oxford, 1954); also Carl J. Weber, *Hardy in America: A Study of Thomas Hardy and his American Readers* (Waterville, Maine, 1940).

2 William Dean Howells, *My Literary Passions* (New York, 1915) p. 182. Howells began a personal association with Hardy in 1883, when, as a guest of Edmund Gosse, he met Hardy in London at the Savile Club. Howells joined *Harper's Magazine* in 1886 and wrote a friendly review of Hardy's *Mayor of Casterbridge* in that year. In 1892, Howells invited Hardy to write a story for the *Cosmopolitan*. In 1899 he sent Hamlin Garland to Max Gate with a letter of introduction in which he wrote, 'Personally the only thing I have against him [Garland] is his pretension to a greater love than mine for all that you have written and for you' (Dorset County Museum). See Weber, *Hardy in America*, pp. 57ff.

3 William Dean Howells, *Heroines of Fiction* (New York, 1901) II, 179–80.

4 Willa Cather's review is dated 5 October 1895. *Jude* had appeared under the title *Hearts Insurgent* in *Harper's New Monthly Magazine* from December 1894 to November 1895. One wonders if the similar sentiments in Jeannette Gilder's notorious review of *Jude* in the *New York World* for December 1895 do not owe something to Cather's outburst (see Hardy's *Life*, pp. 279–81). See Cather, *The World of the Parish*, I, 266–7.

5 Review of 30 May 1897. See Cather, *World of the Parish*, pp. 444–5.

6 Review of 16 Nov 1897. See ibid., p. 447.

7 Review of 16 Nov 1897. See ibid., p. 448.

8 Oscar Cargill, *Intellectual America* (New York, 1941) p. 77.

9 Sinclair Lewis, in *Thomas Hardy: Notes on his Life and Work*, p. 14.

10 *Sherwood Anderson's Memoirs: A Critical Edition*, ed. Ray Lewis White (Chapel Hill, NC, 1969) p. 256. Quoted in Luther S. Luedtke, 'Sherwood Anderson, Thomas Hardy, and "Tandy" ', *Modern Fiction Studies*, 20 (1974–5) 532. The remarks that follow are indebted to Luedtke's study.

11 Luedtke, ibid., p. 531.

12 Ibid., p. 534.

13 Richard Swigg, *Lawrence, Hardy, and American Literature* (New York, 1972), p. 53.

14 Luedtke, in *Modern Fiction Studies*, 20, p. 535.

15 Ibid., p. 536.

16 Ibid., p. 537. See Irving Howe, *Sherwood Anderson* (New York, 1951) pp. 179–97, for an account of Anderson's debt to Lawrence.

17 Luedtke, in *Modern Fiction Studies*, p. 537.

18 Ibid., p. 539.

19 *Letters of Ellen Glasgow*, ed. Blair Rouse (New York, 1958) p. 89. Glasgow's personal regard for Hardy was lasting. On 4 October 1939 she wrote, 'Hardy was to me the most sympathetic Englishmen and one of the most sympathetic persons I have ever known. Nothing rang hollow in his nature' (p. 258).

20 Quotations from Ellen Glasgow's *Barren Ground* are from the Virginia

Edition, I (New York, 1938). Subsequent references appear in the text.
21 My discussion of *Barren Ground* is indebted to George O. Marshall, Jr, 'Hardy's *Tess* and Ellen Glasgow's *Barren Ground*', *Texas Studies in Language and Literature*, 1 (1960) 517–21; and to James W. Tuttleton, 'Hardy and Ellen Glasgow: *Barren Ground*', *Mississippi Quarterly*, 32 (1979) 577–90.
22 Tuttleton, ibid., pp. 581ff.
23 Ibid., p. 582.
24 Ellen Glasgow, *A Certain Measure: An Interpretation of Prose Fiction* (New York, 1943); quoted by Tuttleton, in *Mississippi Quarterly*, 32, p. 584.
25 Tuttleton, ibid., p. 590.
26 That this amounted to loss from Glasgow's point of view is suggested by her last novel, *In This Our Life* (1940), in which she carried out – under the influence of Hardy's *Jude the Obscure* – an examination of 'sexual roles . . . [that] extends the basic conceptual investigation of male and female stereotypes'. See Velma Bourgeois Richmond, 'Sexual Reversals in Thomas Hardy and Ellen Glasgow', *Southern Humanities Review*, 13 (1979) 51–62. The quote is from Richmond, ibid., p. 51.
27 See John Paterson, 'Hardy, Faulkner, and the Prosaics of Tragedy', *Centennial Review*, 5 (1961) 156–75. Though a copy of *The Mayor* existed in Faulkner's library, there is apparently no available evidence that he read it. See Joseph Blotner, *William Faulkner's Library: A Catalogue* (Charlottesville, Va, 1964) p. 67.
28 Cleanth Brooks, *William Faulkner: The Yoknapatawpha County* (New Haven, Conn., 1963) p. 1. Much the same can be said of Michael Millgate, who has written books on both Hardy and Faulkner: *Thomas Hardy: His Career as Novelist* (New York, 1971) and *The Achievement of William Faulkner* (New York, 1961). Though Millgate detects resemblance and parallels, it seems clear that – apart from the existence of *The Mayor* (and of *Jude*) in Faulkner's library (Blotner, *Faulkner's Library*, p. 67) – evidence for Faulkner's having read and thought about the Wessex Novels in conjunction with his own fiction simply does not exist. Blotner states in *Faulkner: A Biography* (New York, 1974) that in winter of 1920–1 Faulkner 'read in Hardy and Tolstoy as well as Balzac and other favorites' (I, 299).
29 David Jarrett, 'Eustacia Vye and Eula Varner, Olympians: The Worlds of Thomas Hardy, and William Faulkner', *Novel*, 6 (1973) 164–6.
30 Ibid., p. 173; italics added. For similar speculations, see Peter L. Irvine, 'Faulkner and Hardy', *Arizona Quarterly*, 27 (1970) 357–68: Faulkner's 'twin, then, is not Joyce, Conrad, Shakespeare, or Hawthorne. It is Thomas Hardy.' Also William Miller, 'Hardy, Falls, and Faulkner', *Mississippi Quarterly*, 29 (1976) 435–6: though parallels are not proof of influence, 'Hardy's Mr. Fall, the "weather-prophet" [in *The Mayor*] . . . is almost certainly the original of Faulkner's Will Falls, the 93 year old Civil War veteran who cures the wen on Bayard's face.'

Notes 231

31 William Faulkner, 'Sherwood Anderson: An Appreciation' (1953), in *The Achievement of Sherwood Anderson: Essays on Criticism*, ed. Ray Lewis White (Chapel Hill, NC, 1966) pp. 197–98.
32 I am indebted to my colleague Professor James Carothers for the following in a letter of 24 August 1984:

> Faulkner *could* have known about Hardy from his Oxford, Mississippi, mentor, Phil Stone, . . . who encouraged Faulkner's early readings and writings. . . . Stone gave a copy of Hardy's *A Laodicean* . . . to his friend Katrina Carter on 30 July 1917. . . . Faulkner also signed his Modern Library copy of *Jude* twice. . . . This may indicate Faulkner's special interest in, or fondness for, the book. In sum, I think it's . . . likely that Phil Stone first drew attention to Hardy for the young Faulkner. . . . Anderson may have been reinforcing Stone.

Carothers also notes 'a brief and cryptic allusion' to Hardy in *Knight's Gambit*, pt II (1949).
33 Donald Davidson, *Still Rebels, Still Yankees* (Baton Rouge, La, 1957) pp. 62–83. Davidson also sees in Hardy's humour an affinity with American frontier humour.
34 Ibid., p. 75.
35 Ibid., p. 76.
36 *Letters of Theodore Dreiser*, ed. Robert H. Elias (State Park, Pa, 1959) I, 215. In an interview of 1911, again describing his reading in the 1890s, Dreiser recalled that in Pittsburgh he had discovered Balzac and 'saw for the first time how a book should be written. . . . Balzac lasted me a year or two, then came Hardy, and after him Tolstoi. From them I learned what, in my judgment, really great books are' – *Theodore Dreiser: A Selection of Uncollected Prose*, ed. Donald Pizer (Detroit, 1977) p. 186.
37 See note 1 above; also W. A. Swanberg, *Dreiser* (New York, 1965) pp. 69–77.
38 Swanberg, *Dreiser*, p. 72; also *'Tess' in the Theatre*, ed. Marguerite Roberts (Toronto, 1950) pp. ivff.
39 Quoted in Ellen Moers, *Two Dreisers* (New York, 1969) p. 176. Dreiser's remark on Howells's reservations about Hardy probably derives from Howells's distaste for Hardy's heroines expressed in 1901 in his *Heroines of Fiction* (see pp. 173–4, above). In a letter of February 1902 to William Duffy, Dreiser praised Hardy's poems as 'rousingly beautiful', then added, 'I do think that man is the greatest figure in all English literature. I know of no one to place beside him' – White, in *English Language Notes*, 6, p. 122.
40 Theodore Dreiser, in *Thomas Hardy: Notes on his Life and Work*, p. 15.
41 For Dreiser's sources for *Carrie*, see Moers, *Two Dreisers*, esp. pp. 66–74, 115–18, 130–2, 278–9; Donald Pizer, *Novels of Theodore Dreiser* (Minneapolis, 1976) pp. 3–95; and Thomas P. Riggio, 'Notes on the Origins of *Sister Carrie*', *Library Journal*, 44 (1979) 7–26.
42 See Donald Pizer's Introduction to Garland's *Rose of Dutcher's Coolly*

([1895] Lincoln, Nebr., 1969) esp. pp. xiii–xix, xxix–xxx. Pizer notes (p. xiii) that in 1895 several reviewers of *Rose* 'alluded to the scandal over . . . Hardy's *Jude* . . . and judged *Rose* an additional ill-advised attempt to champion sexual freedom'.

43 Gilder's review appeared on 8 December 1895. See note 4 above.
44 In *Theodore Dreiser: The Critical Reception*, ed. Jack Salzman (New York, 1972) p. 40.
45 Theodore Dreiser, *Sister Carrie* (1900), vol. III of the Pennsylvania Edition, ed. John C. Berkley, Alice M. Winters, and James L. W. West (Philadelphia, 1981). All quotations from this novel (cited as *SC*) are from the Pennsylvania Edition. Subsequent references appear in the text.
46 *Saracinesca* is a novel by Francis Marion Crawford (1854–1909). See *SC*, p. 572.
47 See note 41, above.
48 Pizer, *Novels of Theodore Dreiser*, p. 99. Pizer continues, Dreiser 'was above all moved by Hardy's youthful figures who bring to experience a craving for life and a responsiveness to beauty but who are tragically handicapped' (pp. 99–100).
49 H. L. Mencken, 'A Novel of the First Rank', *Smart Set*, Nov 1911, pp. 153–4; Edwin L. Shuman, Chicago *Record-Herald*, 4 Nov 1911. Both reviews are reprinted in *Theodore Dreiser: The Critical Reception*, ed. Salzman, pp. 63, 64, 69.
50 'Yes, ma'am, he's gone! He was kind-like to mother when she were here below, sending her the best ship-coal, and hardly any ashes from it at all; and taties, and such-like that were very needful to her.' This passage, which continues at length, is remarkable for its use of dialect English to convey grief and wisdom in a simple man (*The Mayor of Casterbridge*, ch. 45).
51 Theodore Dreiser, *Jennie Gerhardt* (New York, 1911) p. 431. All quotations from the novel (cited as *JG*) are from this edition. Subsequent references appear in the text.
52 The conversation between Jennie and Martha that follows this passage bears comparison with the conversation in Hardy's *Tess* (ch. 4) between Tess and her brother Abraham.
53 D. H. Lawrence, review of Edward Dahlberg, *Bottom Dogs*, in *Phoenix*, I, 267–9.

CHAPTER 7   'Canst Thou be Virgil?': A Hardy Legacy in the Novel

1 Arnold Bennett, in *Thomas Hardy: Notes on his Life and Work*, p. 17.
2 *Journals of Arnold Bennett*, ed. Newman Flower (London, 1932) I, 28: III, 216. See also, *The Letters of Arnold Bennett*, ed. James Hepburn (Oxford, 1966) III, 217; and pp. 2–3, above.
3 Speaking of architecture Hardy wrote as follows in 1906: 'The human interest in an edifice ranks before its architectural interest, however great the latter may be.' For 'life, after all, is more than art, and that which appealed to us in the (may be) clumsy outlines of some struc-

ture which had been looked at and entered by a dozen generations of ancestors outweighs the more subtle recognition, if any, of architectural qualities' – 'Memories of Church Restoration', in *Thomas Hardy's Personal Writings*, ed. Harold Orel (Lawrence, Kans, 1966) pp. 207, 215).

4. Bloom, *The Anxiety of Influence*, esp. pp. 14–15. Bloom elaborates upon this basic scheme but does not alter it essentially in two later books: *A Map of Misreading* (New York, 1975) and *Poetry and Repression: Revisionism from Blake to Stevens* (New York, 1976).
5. T. S. Eliot, 'Tradition and the Individual Talent', in *The Sacred Wood: Essays on Poetry and Criticism* ([1920] New York, 1964) p. 49.
6. Ibid.
7. Ibid., pp. 49–50.
8. Ibid., pp. 52–3.
9. Dante, *Hell*, trans. Dorothy Sayers ([1949] London, 1969) 79–90.
10. Dante, *Purgatory*, tr. Dorothy Sayers ([1955] London, 1969) XXX. 43–54.

Select Bibliography

Alain-Fournier [Henri-Alban Fournier], *The Wanderer, or the End of Youth [Le Grand Meaulnes]*, tr. Lowell Bair, with an afterword by John Fowles (New York, 1971).
Alcorn, John, *The Nature Novel from Hardy to Lawrence* (New York, 1977).
Anderson, Sherwood, *Sherwood Anderson's Memoirs: A Critical Selection*, ed. Ray Lewis White (Chapel Hill, NC, 1969).
Bate, Walter Jackson, *The Burden of the Past and the English Poet* (Cambridge, Mass., 1970).
Beards, Richard D., 'D. H. Lawrence and the *Study of Thomas Hardy*, his Victorian Predecessor', *D. H. Lawrence Review*, 2 (1979) 210–29.
Bennett, Arnold, 'My Literary Heresies', *T. P.'s Weekly*, 4 (23 Sept 1904) 392.
Bisson, L. A., 'Proust, Bergson, and George Eliot', *Modern Language Review*, 40 (1945) 104–14.
——,'Proust and Hardy: Incidence or Coincidence', in *Studies in French Language, Literature, and History Presented to R. L. Graeme Ritchie* (Cambridge, Mass., 1949) pp. 24–34.
Blanche, Jacques-Émile, *Mes Modèles* (Paris, 1928).
Block, H. M., 'James Joyce and Thomas Hardy', *Modern Language Quarterly*, 19 (1958) 337–42.
Bloom, Harold, *The Anxiety of Influence: A Theory of Poetry* (New York, 1973).
——, *A Map of Misreading* (New York, 1975).
——, *Poetry and Repression: Revisionism from Blake to Stevens* (New York, 1976).
Blotner, Joseph, *William Faulkner's Library: A Catalogue* (Charlottesville, Va, 1964).
——, *Faulkner: A Biography*, 2 vols (New York, 1974).
Boucher, Lèon, 'Le Roman pastorale en Angleterre', *Revue des deux mondes*, 12 (1875) 838–66.
Brown, Malcolm, *George Moore: A Reconsideration* (Seattle, 1955).
Burwell, Rose Marie, 'Schopenhauer, Hardy, and Lawrence: Toward a New Understanding of *Sons and Lovers*', *Western Humanities Review*, 28 (1974) 105–17.
Cargill, Oscar, *Intellectual America* (New York, 1941).
Cary, Joyce, *Art and Reality* (Cambridge, 1958).
Cather, Willa, *The World of the Parish: Willa Cather's Articles and Reviews, 1893–1902*, ed., W. M. Curtin (Lincoln, Nebr., 1970).

Select Bibliography 235

Cavaliero, Glen, *John Cowper Powys: Novelist* (Oxford, 1973).
——, *The Rural Tradition in the English Novel, 1900–1939* (London, 1977).
Chambers, Jessie, D. H. *Lawrence: A Personal Record* (1935), ed. J. D. Chambers (London, 1965).
Chesterton, G. K., *The Victorian Age in Literature* (London, 1913).
——, *Generally Speaking* (New York, 1929).
Clarke, Anthony H., 'Hardy in Spain and Spain in Hardy', *Hispanic Studies in Honour of Joseph Monson*, ed. Dorothy M. Atkinson and Anthony H. Clarke (Oxford, 1972) pp. 43–64.
Collet, Georges Paul, *George Moore and France* (Geneva, 1957).
Coustillas, Pierre, 'Some Unpublished Letters from Gissing to Hardy', *English Literature in Transition*, 9 (1966) 197–209.
Davidson, Donald, *Still Rebels, Still Yankees* (Baton Rouge, La, 1957).
Davray, Henri, 'Lettres anglais', *Mercure de France*, 46 (1903) 264–5.
Deacon, Lois, and Coleman, Terry, *Providence and Mr Hardy* (London, 1966).
Delavenay, Émile, *D. H. Lawrence: The Man and his Work, the Formative Years, 1885–1919* (London, 1972).
DeVitis, A. A., and Palmer, W. J., 'A Pair of Blue Eyes Flash at The French Lieutenant's Woman', *Contemporary Literature*, 15 (1974) 90–101.
D'Exideuil, Pierre, *Le Couple humain dans l'oeuvre de Thomas Hardy: essai sur la sexualité dans les romans, contes, et poèms du Wessex* (Paris, 1928); tr. Felix W. Crosse as *The Human Pair in the Work of Thomas Hardy* (London, 1930).
Dreiser, Theodore, *Jennie Gerhardt* (New York, 1911).
——, *Letters of Theodore Dreiser*, ed. Robert H. Elias, 3 vols (State Park, Pa, 1959).
——, *Theodore Dreiser: A Selection of Uncollected Prose*, ed. Donald Pizer (Detroit, 1977).
——, *Theodore Dreiser: The Critical Reception*, ed. Jack Salzman (New York, 1972).
——, *Sister Carrie* (1900), vol. III of the Pennsylvania Edition, ed. John C. Berkley, Alice M. Winters and James L. W. West (Philadelphia, 1981).
Ebbatson, J. R., 'Thomas Hardy and Lady Chatterley', *Ariel: A Review of International English Literature*, 8 (1977) 85–95.
Elias, Robert H., *Theodore Dreiser: Apostle of Nature* (1948), emended edn (Ithaca, NY, 1970).
Eliot, T. S., *After Strange Gods* (London, 1934).
——, *The Sacred Wood: Essays on Poetry and Criticism* ([1920], London, 1964).
Farrow, Anthony, *George Moore* (Boston, Mass., 1978).
Faulkner, William, 'Sherwood Anderson: An Appreciation' (1953), in *The Achievement of Sherwood Anderson: Essays in Criticism*, ed. Ray Lewis White (Chapel Hill, NC, 1966) pp. 197–8.
Fowles, John, 'I Write Therefore I Am', *Evergreen Review*, 8 (1964) 16–17, 89–90.
——, *The French Lieutenant's Woman* ([1969] New York, 1970).
——, 'Notes on an Unfinished Novel', in *Afterwords: Novelists on their Novels*, ed. Thomas McCormack (New York 1969).

——, review of J. Hillis Miller, *Thomas Hardy: Distance and Desire*, in the *New York Times Review of Books*, 21 June 1970, p. 4.
——, *Daniel Martin* (New York, 1977).
——, 'Hardy and the Hag', in *Thomas Hardy after Fifty Years*, ed. Lance St John Butler (London, 1977).
——, *The Magus: A Revised Version* (New York, 1978).
——, 'Interview', *Maclean's*, 90 (14 Nov 1977) 4, 6, 8.
——, *Mantissa* (New York, 1982).
Gerson, Carole, 'Canada's Response to Thomas Hardy: A Look at 19th Century Attitudes', *Dalhousie Review*, 55 (1975) 252–62.
Giannoni, Robert, 'Alain-Fournier et Thomas Hardy', *Revue de littérature comparée*, 42 (1968) 407–26.
Gibson, Robert, *The Land without a Name: Alain-Fournier and his World* (London: 1975).
Gittings, Robert, *Young Thomas Hardy* (Boston, Mass., 1975).
——, *Thomas Hardy's Later Years* (Boston, Mass., 1978).
Glasgow, Ellen, *Barren Ground* (1925), vol. I of the Virginia Edition (New York, 1938).
——, *In this our Life* (New York, 1941).
——, *Letters of Ellen Glasgow*, ed. Blair Rouse (New York, 1958).
Goodwin, Geraint, *Conversations with George Moore* (New York, 1930).
Gregor, Ian, *The Great Web: The Form of Hardy's Major Fiction* (London, 1974).
Hardy, Thomas, *Thomas Hardy's Personal Writings*, ed. Harold Orel (Lawrence, Kans, 1966).
——, *Collected Letters of Thomas Hardy*, ed. R. L. Purdy and Michael Millgate (Oxford, 1980) I and II.
——, *Thomas Hardy: An Annotated Bibliography of Writings about Him*, comp. and ed. Helmut E. Gerber and W. Eugene Davis (De Kalb, Ill., 1973).
——, *Thomas Hardy: Notes on his Life and Work*, ed. Henry Seidel Canby (New York, 1925).
——, *Thomas Hardy: The Critical Tradition*, ed. Reginald G. Cox (London, 1970).
Hedgcock, Frank A., *Thomas Hardy: penseur et artiste* (Paris, 1911).
Hindus, Milton, *A Reader's Guide to Marcel Proust* (New York, 1962).
Hone, Joseph M., *The Life of George Moore* (New York, 1936).
Hopkins, Kenneth, *The Powys Brothers* (London, 1967).
Hough, Graham, 'George Moore and the Novel', in *George Moore's Mind and Art*, ed. Graham Owens (Edinburgh, 1970) pp. 166–75.
Howe, Irving, *Sherwood Anderson* (New York, 1951).
Howells, William Dean, *My Literary Passions* (New York, 1895).
——, *Heroines of Fiction*, 2 vols (New York, 1901).
Hutchins, Patricia, 'Thomas Hardy and Some Younger Writers', *Journal of Modern Literature*, 3 (1973) 35–44.
Irvine, Peter L., 'Faulkner and Hardy', *Arizona Quarterly*, 27 (1970) 357–68.
James, Henry, *Henry James: Letters*, ed. Leon Edel, III (Cambridge, 1981).
Jarrett, David, 'Eustacia Vye and Eula Varner, Olympians: The Worlds of Thomas Hardy and William Faulkner', *Novel*, 6 (1973) 163–73.
Kinkead-Weekes, Mark, 'The Marble and the Statue: The Exploratory

Imagination of D. H. Lawrence', in *Imagined Worlds: Essays on Some English Novels and Novelists in Honour of John Butt*, ed. Maynard Mack and Ian Gregor (London, 1968) pp. 371–418.

Lawrence, D. H., *Collected Letters of D. H. Lawrence*, ed. Harry T. Moore, 2 vols (New York, 1962).

——, *Studies in Classic American Literature* ([1923] New York, 1966).

——, *Study of Thomas Hardy*, in *Phoenix: The Posthumous Papers of D. H. Lawrence* (1936), ed. Edward D. McDonald, I (New York, 1968) 398–517.

——, *Phoenix: The Posthumous Papers of D. H. Lawrence* (1936), ed. Edward D. McDonald, 2 vols (New York, 1968, 1972).

——, *The Rainbow* ([1915] New York, 1980).

——, *Women in Love* ([1920] New York, 1981).

Lawrence, Dan H., 'Henry James and Stevenson Discuss "Vile" Tess', *Colby College Quarterly*, 3 (1953) 164–8.

Leavis, F. R., *The Great Tradition* (London, 1948).

Loize, Jean, *Alain-Fournier: sa vie et 'Le Grand Meaulnes'* (Paris, 1968).

Luedtke, Luther, 'Sherwood Anderson, Thomas Hardy, and "Tandy" ', *Modern Fiction Studies*, 20 (1974–5) 531–40.

Marshall, George O., Jr, 'Hardy's *Tess* and Ellen Glasgow's *Barren Ground*', *Texas Studies in Language and Literature*, 1 (1960) 517–21.

Maugham, W. Somerset, *Cakes and Ale* ([1930] New York, 1950).

Mein, Margaret, *A Foretaste of Proust: A Study of Proust and his Precursors* (Farnborough, Hants, 1974).

Miller, Dr Milton M., *Nostalgia: A Psychoanalytic Study of Marcel Proust* (Boston, Mass., 1956).

Miller, William, 'Hardy, Falls, and Faulkner', *Mississippi Quarterly*, 29 (1976) 435–6.

Millgate, Michael, *The Achievement of William Faulkner* (New York, 1961).

——, *Thomas Hardy: His Career as Novelist* (New York, 1971).

——, *Thomas Hardy: A Biography* (New York, 1982).

Moers, Ellen, *Two Dreisers* (New York, 1969).

Moore, George, *Confessions of a Young Man* (1888), ed. Susan Dick (Montreal and London, 1972).

——, *Conversations in Ebury Street* (New York, 1924).

——, *Esther Waters* (1894), Houghton Mifflin Riverside Edition, ed. Lionel Stevenson (Boston, Mass., 1963).

Moore, Harry T., *The Life of D. H. Lawrence* (New York, 1952).

Murfin, Ross C., *Swinburne, Hardy, Lawrence and the Burden of Unbelief* (Chicago, 1976).

Murry, John Middleton, *Wrap me up in my Aubusson Carpet* (New York, 1924).

The Novel Today: Contemporary Writers on Modern Fiction, ed. Malcolm Bradbury (Manchester, 1977).

Painter, George, *Marcel Proust: A Biography*, 2 vols ([1959] New York, 1978).

Paterson, John, 'Lawrence's Vital Source: Nature and Character in Thomas Hardy', in *Nature and the Victorian Imagination*, ed. U. C. Knoepflmacher and G. B. Tennyson (Berkeley, Calif., 1977) pp. 455–69.

———, 'Hardy, Faulkner, and the Prosaics of Tragedy', *Centennial Review*, 5 (1961) 156–75.
Pizer, Donald, *Novels of Theodore Dreiser* (Minneapolis, 1976).
Powys, John Cowper, 'To Thomas Hardy', in *Odes and Other Poems* (London, 1896) pp. 11–12.
———, *Wood and Stone: A Romance* (London, 1915).
———, *Rodmoor: A Romance* (New York, 1916).
———, *Ducdame* (New York, 1925).
———, *Autobiography* (London, 1934).
———, 'Thomas Hardy', in *Enjoyment of Literature* (New York, 1938) pp. 433–50.
———, *Visions and Revisions* ([1915] New York, 1955).
———, *A Glastonbury Romance* ([1932] London, 1957).
———, *Letters of John Cowper Powys to Louis Wilkinson, 1935–1956* (London, 1958).
———, *Maiden Castle* ([1937] London, 1966).
———, *John Cowper Powys: Letters to Nicholas Ross*, ed. Llewelyn Powys (London, 1971).
———, *Weymouth Sands* ([1935] London, 1980).
———, and Powys, Llewelyn, *Confessions of Two Brothers* (New York, 1916).
Powys, Llewelyn, 'A Glimpse of Thomas Hardy', *Dial*, 72 (1922) 286–90.
———, 'Thomas Hardy', in *Thirteen Worthies* (New York, 1923).
———, 'Some Memories of Thomas Hardy' (1938), in *Monographs on the Life, Times, and Works of Thomas Hardy*, 64, ed. J. Stevens Cox (St Peter Port, 1969).
Proust, Marcel, *Marcel Proust: choix de lettres*, ed. Philip Kolb (Paris, 1965).
———, *Cahiers Marcel Proust: le carnet de 1908*, ed. Philip Kolb (Paris, 1976).
———, *Correspondance de Marcel Proust*, ed. Philip Kolb, VI (Paris, 1980).
———, *Remembrance of Things Past* [*À la recherche du temps perdu*], tr. C. K. Scott Moncrieff, rev. Terence Kilmartin, 3 vols (New York, 1981).
Purdy, Richard L., *Thomas Hardy: A Bibliographical Study* (Oxford, 1954).
La Revue nouvelle, nos 38–9 (Jan-Feb 1928), a Thomas Hardy special issue.
Richmond, Velma Bourgeois, 'Sexual Reversals in Thomas Hardy and Ellen Glasgow', *Southern Humanities Review*, 13 (1979) 51–62.
Riggio, Thomas P., 'Notes on the Origin of *Sister Carrie*', *Library Journal*, 44 (1979) 109–15.
Rivière, Jacques, and Alain-Fournier, *Correspondance 1905–1914*, 2 vols (Paris, 1948).
Robert, P.-E., *Marcel Proust: lecteur des Anglo-Saxons* (Paris, 1976).
Rose, Dr Gilbert J., '*The French Lieutenant's Woman*: The Unconscious Significance of a Novel to its Author', *American Imago*, 29 (1972) 165–76.
Roz, Firmin, 'Thomas Hardy', *Revue des deux mondes*, 34 (1906) 176–207.
Sage, Lorna, 'John Fowles: A Profile', *New Review*, 1 (1974) 31–7.
Salter, K. W., 'Lawrence, Hardy, and "The Great Tradition" ', *English*, 22 (1973) 60–5.
Southern Review, 6 (1940), Thomas Hardy Centennial Edition.
Spilka, Mark, *The Love Ethic of D. H. Lawrence* (London, 1955).
Squires, Michael, *The Pastoral Novel: Studies in George Eliot, Thomas Hardy, and D. H. Lawrence* (Charlottesville, Va, 1974).

Stanford, Raney, 'Thomas Hardy and Lawrence's *White Peacock*', *Modern Fiction Studies*, 5 (1959) 19–28.
Starr, W. F., 'Romain Rolland and Thomas Hardy', *Modern Language Quarterly*, 17 (1956) 99–103.
Strauss, Walter A., *Proust and Literature: The Novelist as Critic* (Cambridge, Mass., 1967).
Swanberg, W. A., *Dreiser* (New York, 1965).
Swigg, Richard, *Lawrence, Hardy, and American Literature* New York, 1972).
'Tess' in the Theatre, ed. Marguerite Roberts (Toronto, 1950).
Tuttleton, James W., 'Hardy and Ellen Glasgow: *Barren Ground*', *Mississippi Quarterly*, 32 (1979) 577–90.
Weber, Carl J., *Hardy in America: A Study of Thomas Hardy and his American Readers* (Waterville, Maine, 1946).
Wells, Henry W., *New Poets from Old: A Study in Literary Genetics* (New York, 1940).
White, William, 'Dreiser on Hardy, Henley, and Whitman: An Unpublished Letter', *English Language Notes*, 6 (1968) 122–4.
Woolf, Virginia, *The Common Reader*, First Series (New York, 1925).
——, *The Common Reader*, Second Series (London, 1932).

Index

Abercrombie, Lascelles, 34; *Thomas Hardy: A Critical Study*, 146
Academy (journal), 132
Agostinelli, Alfred, 115
Alain-Fournier (*i.e.* Henri-Alban Fournier): influenced by TH, 112, 130, 133–5, 138–40, 144, 147, 184, 205; background, 134–5; Fowles admires, 134, 150, 170; reads English, 135, 144; on *Tess*, 135–7, 144; in love, 137–8, 140
Le Grand Meaulnes: debt to TH, 31, 122; heroine, 137; autobiographical hero, 139–40; lost purity in, 140–1; summary and themes, 141–4; Fowles on, 143, 150–1
Anderson, Sherwood, 173, 176–8, 181, 182–4; *Memoirs*, 176; 'Tandy', 176–7; *Winesburg, Ohio*, 176, 182
Annunzio, Gabriele d', 135
art: Lawrence on, 44–5
'At a Seaside Town' (TH poem), 152
'At the Wicket Gate' (TH poem), 155
Atlantic Monthly (journal), 185

Bailey, J. O., 2
Balzac, Honoré de, 187–9, 194
Barnes, William, 67–8
Barrie, Sir James Matthew, 23, 112
beauty, 208–12, 216

Bennett, Arnold, 30, 204, 206–7
Billy, Robert de, 112–13, 115, 124
Bisson, L. A., 121–3
Blanche, Jacques Emile, 112, 114–16, 125, 135, 147; portrait of TH, 146
Bloom, Harold, 40–1, 213–16
Boldini, Giovanni, 208
Bonington, R. P., 10
Boucher, Léon, 111
Brontë, Charlotte, 27
Brooks, Cleanth: *William Faulkner: The Yoknapatawpha County*, 182
Brooks, Van Wyck, 173
Burns, Robert, 35
Burroughs, Louie, 32

'Candour in English Fiction' (TH), 26
Cargill, Oscar, 175
Carlyle, Thomas, 41
Cary, Joyce, 31
Catalogne, Gérard de: *Le Message de Thomas Hardy*, 147
Cather, Willa, 30, 173–5, 184
Century (journal), 185
Chambers, Jessie, 32
Channing, Mary, 94–5, 99–100
Chavelley, Abel, 147
Chesterton, G. K., 1, 29
Conrad, Joseph, 3, 25, 37
Cornhill magazine, 29
Crane, Stephen, 185: *Maggie*, 187

Dante Alighieri: *Divine Comedy*,
   214–16
Darwin, Charles, 210
Daudet, Léon, 147
Davidson, Donald, 183–4, 193, 196
Davray, Henri, 111, 147
Deacon, Lois, 151, 157–8
Deacon, Lois and Coleman, Terry:
   Providence and Mr Hardy, 155
Desperate Remedies (TH), 72
Dial (journal), 2, 75
Dickens, Charles, 25, 62, 68
Dodge, B. W. & Co., 188
Dostoevsky, Feodor, 62, 114–15,
   118–19, 186
Dreiser, Sarah (wife of Theodore),
   188
Dreiser, Theodore: admires TH,
   30, 173, 175, 184–5, 205, 216;
   tragic view (pessimism), 130,
   194, 201; and Sherwood
   Anderson, 178; comments on
   TH, 184–7; anti-Christian
   sentiments, 197; on nature,
   199–200
   Jennie Gerhardt: influenced by
      Tess, 23, 31, 187, 190, 194,
      196–202; on nature, 200–1
   Sister Carrie: and *Tess*, 23,
      185–90; debt to TH, 31,
      185–7; and *Mayor of
      Casterbridge*, 186, 188–91,
      193–4; summary and
      themes, 189–95
du Bos, Charles, 147
'During Wind and Rain' (TH
   poem), 154
Dynasts, The (TH), 40, 111, 130, 146

Early Life (TH), 101
Eliot, George, 6, 110–11; *Mill on the
   Floss*, 111
Eliot, T. S., 29, 214–16
'Epitaph to George Moore' (TH), 1
Euripides, 186
Ev'ry Month (journal), 185
Exideuil, Pierre d': *Le Couple
   humain dans l'oeuvre de Thomas
   Hardy*, 144, 147–8

Far from the Madding Crowd (TH):
   George Moore criticises
   gargoyle episode in, 5–6, 21,
   64; Henry James criticises, 23,
   64, 111; published in *Cornhill*,
   29; J. C. Powys reads, 63, 102;
   influence on Powys, 72; Léon
   Boucher praises, 111; French
   translation (*Barbara*), 111;
   hampered sexuality in, 128;
   Leslie Stephen on, 149; and
   Ellen Glasgow's *Barren
   Ground*, 180
Faulkner, William, 175, 181–4;
   Absalom, Absalom!, 182; *The
   Hamlet*, 182; *Soldier's Pay*, 182
Fernandez, Ramon: 'Hardy et le
   réalisme', 144, 147–8
Figaro (newspaper), 115
Fiske, Minnie Maddern, 175, 185
Flaubert, Gustave, 33–4
Fournier, Isabella (sister of Alain-
   Fournier), 134
Fowles, John: on influence of and
   appeal of TH, 31, 154–7,
   171–2, 204, 216; on
   'femaleness', 76; influenced
   by *The Well-Beloved*, 89, 205;
   admires Alain-Fournier, 134,
   150, 170; on *Le Grand
   Meaulnes*, 143, 150–1;
   knowledge of French
   literature, 150; reviews J.
   Hillis Miller on TH, 151,
   156–8; on creativity, 159; lives
   in Lyme Regis, 161, 165; and
   'younger self', 170–1
   Daniel Martin: debt to TH, 31,
      150–2, 156–7, 161–2, 164,
      169–70, 172, 213; summary
      and themes, 162–9, 205;
      Hardy appears in, 166; and
      self-portraiture, 170, 172
   The French Lieutenant's Woman:
      influenced by Hardy,
      150–3, 156–7, 161; summary
      and themes, 152–5;
      psychological analysis of Dr
      Rose, 159, 161; multiple

Index

ending, 160; Hardy appears in, 166; writing, 166–7
'Hardy and the Hag', 151, 158, 161–2, 165–6
'Notes from an Unfinished Novel', 154
France: appreciation of Hardy in, 111–12, 144–9
Freud, Sigmund, 213
Frost, Robert, 173

Garland, Hamlin, 173; *Rose of Dutcher's Coolly*, 187
Georgian Poetry, 1911–1912, 33–5
Giannoni, Robert, 139–40, 143–4
Gibson, Robert, 135
Gilder, Jeannette, 187
Gissing, George, 29
Gittings, Robert, 101, 103, 126, 151, 157–8; *Thomas Hardy's Later Years*, 157; *Young Thomas Hardy*, 157, 165, 169
Glasgow, Ellen, 173, 178–9, 183–4; *Barren Ground*, 23, 176, 178–81, 195, 199
Gosse, Sir Edmund, 23, 146, 149, 154

Hand of Ethelberta (TH), 29
Hardy, Emma (née Gifford; first wife of TH), 67, 153–5
Hardy, Florence Emily (née Dugdale; second wife of TH): *The Life of Thomas Hardy (i.e. by TH)*, 10, 131
Hardy, Jemima (née Hand; TH's mother), 126, 134, 159, 161
Hardy, Mary (TH's sister), 126, 134
Hardy, Thomas: prose style, 19–20, 26–8; reputation among writers, 23–31; nihilism, 33–4; sexuality, 69, 101, 124–5, 128, 151; pessimism, 37–8, 74, 79, 89, 123, 129–30, 169, 176–7, 184, 194, 201, 204; Powys meets, 65–6, 80–1, 89; visits Montacute, 66–7, 102–3; anti-clericalism, 67; appearance and dress, 67, 103; first marriage, 67, 153–5; unities of time and place in, 72–3; correspondence with Powys, 74; statue of, 101, 104–6, 166–8; and Powys's father, 102–4; appreciated in France, 111–12, 144–9; rewriting, 113; bisexual awareness, 125, 181; sheltered childhood and devotion to mother, 125–8, 159, 161; susceptibility to falling in love, 126; as nympholept, 127; on Proust, 130–1; on depiction of love, 132; early career, 134; as 'puritan anarchist', 139; passion and suffering in, 145; humanity, 145; death and tributes, 147; and Tryphena Sparks, 154–8, 161; and trysts, 161; in Fowles' novels, 166–7; on writing poetry or fiction, 168; and tyranny of younger self, 170–1; 80th birthday congratulations, 173; admired in USA, 173–5, 183–4, 187; regionalism, 179; as 'seer of beauty', 204, 207–12, 216
Harper's Bazaar (journal), 185
Harper's New Monthly (journal), 185
Harte, Bret, 185
Hearts Insurgent see *Jude the Obscure*
Hedgcock, F. A.: *Thomas Hardy: penseur et artiste*, 144, 146–7
Hellens, Frans, 147
Henry, Arthur, 188
'Her Immortality' (TH poem), 154
Hind, Lewis, 132
Hobbema, Meindert, 208
'Homage to Thomas Hardy' (1928 obituary tributes), 26
homosexuality, 83; *see also* lesbianism
Howells, William Dean, 29, 173–4, 184–6, 197
Human Shows (TH poems), 79
Huxley, T. H., 210

Ibsen, Henrik, 25

Jalous, Edmund, 147
James, Henry: and George Moore, 3; reservations about TH, 23–4, 27, 29, 64, 111; correspondence with Stevenson, 23–4; praises *Tess*, 206
Jarrett, David, 182
Johnson, Lionel: *Art of Thomas Hardy*, 146
Johnson, Samuel, 166
Joyce, James, 25–6; *Dubliners*, 25; 'Ibsen's New Drama', 25
Jude the Obscure (TH; in USA as *Hearts Insurgent*): Leavis on, 25; V. Woolf praises, 27; influence on Lawrence, 32–3, 38, 45, 54, 56, 60–1, 213; interrelationship with *Tess*, 45–9, 125; influence on Powys's works, 74, 78; French translation, 111–12, 125; Proust reads and refers to, 112–16, 118, 120–5, 130, 207; finality in, 117; sexuality in, 128, 139; attacked by critics, 133, 187; Alain-Fournier reads, 135, 137–40, 144; Gosse criticises, 149; tacit dedication to Tryphena, 155; on Oxford, 164; Willa Cather criticises, 174; influence on Sherwood Anderson, 176–7; and Dreiser's *Jennie Gerhardt*, 198

Keats, John, 64
Kennington, Eric: statue of TH, 101, 104, 106, 166–7
Kipling, Rudyard, 23

Late Lyrics and Earlier (TH), 79
Later Years (TH), 101
Lawrence, D. H.: admires TH, 30, 32, 36–7, 44, 204, 216; on TH's nihilism, 33–5; on 'male' and 'female', 46–51; and Powys, 69; and sexual passion, 69; hatred for conventional, 108; maternal influence on, 116; struggle against indifferent universe, 118; finds TH difficult, 129; and Alain-Fournier, 144; Sherwood Anderson reads, 177; and Ellen Glasgow, 181; on subduing of America, 203
'And Jude the Obscure and his Beloved' (poem), 32
Lady Chatterley's Lover, 37
The Lost Girl, 35
The Rainbow, 31–2, 35–6, 38–9, 44–5, 48–56, 213
Sons and Lovers, 32–3, 36, 76
Studies in Classic American Literature, 42
Study of Thomas Hardy: Leavis overlooks, 25; writing, 33–6; on TH's morality, 37–43, 69; historical approach, 41–2; on art, 44–5; on Lawrence's kinship with TH, 44; on novelist's programme, 45; on *Tess* and *Jude*, 45–8; on male will, 59
The White Peacock, 33, 69
Women in Love, 31, 35–6, 39, 45, 48–56, 59, 106–7, 213
Lawrence, Frieda, 35
Leavis, F. R.: *The Great Tradition*, 24, 27, 29
lesbianism, 95–6, 120, 132; *see also* Sappho
Lewis, Sinclair, 30–1, 175
Lister, Sir Reginald, 112–13
Liveright, Horace, 182
Louris, Georges de, 112
Lowell, Amy, 35
Luedtke, Luther S., 176–8
Lyme Regis (Dorset), 161

McLeod, A. W., 38
Macmillan, Alexander, 73
Marguerite, Eve-Paul, 112
Marshall, George O., Jr, 179

Martin, Lady Augusta, 126, 137
Masefield, John, 34
Mayor of Casterbridge, The (TH):
R. L. Stevenson admires, 23;
V. Woolf on, 28; Powys and,
63, 72; and Powys's *Maiden
Castle*, 63, 89, 94–5, 99–100;
and Ellen Glasgow's *Barren
Ground*, 181; and Faulkner's
Absalom, 182; tradition in,
184; and Dreiser's *Sister Carrie*,
186, 188–91, 193–4; and
Dreiser's *Jennie Gerhardt*, 202
Mayous, J. J., 147
Melinand, Camille, 135, 147
Mencken, H. L., 194
Mercure de France (journal), 111
Miller, J. Hillis: *Thomas Hardy:
Distance and Desire*, 151, 156–8
Miller, Milton M.: *Nostalgia: A
Psychoanalytic Study of Marcel
Proust*, 127
Montacute (Somerset), 66–7, 102–3
Montaigne, Michel de, 74
Moore, George: TH despises, 1;
criticises TH, 1–7, 10, 27, 29,
40, 64, 129, 207; prose style,
18–20; realism, 21; Joyce on,
26
Confessions of a Young Man, 2, 9,
207
Conversations in Ebury Street, 2, 4
A Drama in Muslin, 9
Esther Waters: qualities, 3–4, 40;
influenced by *Tess*, 4, 7–9,
18, 22–3, 31; seduction and
confession scene in, 10–18;
imagery, 21–2; and Dreiser,
198
A Modern Lover, 9
Vain Fortune, 9
Murry, John Middleton, 2–4, 147,
207
'Musical Box, The' (TH poem), 153

Naipaul, V. S., 31
Nation (New York journal), 23, 111
nature: as active force, 6–7, 22;
Moore and, 21–2; Powys on

'inanimate background' of, 67,
71; cruelty in, 82; and chance,
199; Dreiser and, 199–200; and
beauty, 208–10
Nietzsche, Friedrich, 34, 70
nihilism, 33–4
nympholepsy, 89, 92, 103, 117, 127

'On a Midsummer's Eve' (TH
poem), 152–3
Oxford, 139, 164

Painter, George D., 114, 116, 119,
123–4, 127
Pair of Blue Eyes, A (TH): R. L.
Stevenson praises, 23; Proust
reads and refers to, 112, 114,
116, 118–25, 130, 207; finality
in, 117; sexuality in, 125, 128;
influence on Fowles' *French
Lieutenant's Woman*, 156;
Dreiser reads, 173
Pater, Walter: *Denys l'Auxerrois*,
113
Peacock, Thomas Love, 171
pessimism, 37–8, 74, 79, 89, 123,
129–30, 169, 176–7, 184, 194,
201, 204
Pizer, Donald, 194
Plain Dealer (Cleveland
newspaper), 187–8
Poe, Edgar Allan, 66
'Poor Man and the Lady, The' (TH;
unpublished), 73
Pouquet, Jeanne, 137
Powys, Rev. Charles Francis (J. C.
Powys's father), 63, 66, 99,
101–4
Powys, John Cowper: influence of
TH on, 62–4, 66, 68–70,
106–7, 204–5, 216; relations
with father, 63, 99–100,
102–4; meets TH, 65–6, 80–1,
89, 103; and unities of time
and place, 72–3; and sexuality,
73, 83–4, 101, 104, 106;
political themes, 73–4;
correspondence with TH, 74;
lecturing in USA, 74;

parent–child motif in, 75–6; dominated by literature, 76, 93–4; humanism, 108; and mystery, 118; on mind and time, 129; finds TH difficult, 129; and Alain-Fournier, 143; Dreiser meets, 186
Autobiography, 62–4, 67–8, 73, 76, 99, 101–3, 108
Ducdame, 73–8, 82, 93
A Glastonbury Romance, 69–70, 73–5
Maiden Castle: debt to TH, 31, 69–70, 95, 108; autobiographical element, 63; and *Mayor of Casterbridge*, 63, 89, 94–5; unities in, 73; homecoming in, 73; politics in, 73–4, 100; search for father in, 75, 96–100, 108; summary and themes, 95–6, 104–9; lesbianism in, 95–6; competing loyalties in, 104
Odes and Other Poems, 64
Rodmoor, 74–5, 77
'To Thomas Hardy' (poem), 65
Visions and Revisions, 68
Weymouth Sands: and *The Well-Beloved*, 63, 89–90, 92, 205; unities in, 73; family conflict in, 75; love and sex in, 90–2; attacks vivisection, 93
Wolf Solent: debt to TH, 31, 78–9, 85; family conflict in, 75, 81–2, 85; summary and themes, 79–89; poems in, 82–3, 85–6; homosexuality in, 83; physical love in, 85–7, 107
Wood and Stone, 66, 69–75, 82, 108
Powys, Llewelyn, 67, 74–5, 104; *Confessions of Two Brothers* (with J. C. Powys), 75; *Skin for Skin*, 75; *Thirteen Worthies*, 75
Proust, Jeanne Weil (Marcel Proust's mother), 126

Proust, Marcel: praises *The Well-Beloved*, 30, 89, 112, 205, 207; admiration for and references to TH, 111–18, 125, 133, 135, 147, 188, 204, 207; death of parents, 115–16; creative career, 115; homosexual life, 115, 126; literary references in, 121; and subjective love, 125; asthma, 125–6; family background and relations with mother, 126–8; falls in love easily, 126–7; nympholepsy, 127; on mind and time, 129; on redeeming power of art, 130; TH on, 130–1; and Alain-Fournier, 143; and Fowles, 170
Against Sainte-Beuve, 110, 113, 116
The Captive, 114, 117, 131, 145
'The Filial Feelings of a Matricide', 115
Jean Santeuil, 110, 114, 116, 121
Pleasures and Days, 110, 121
Remembrance of Things Past: debt to TH, 31, 112, 114, 121–4; sexual varietism in, 92, 106, 120, 125, 129–30; writing, 110, 116–17; love in, 119–22, 124; and TH's childhood gardens, 126; sea-symbolism in, 127
Proust, Robert (Marcel's brother), 126

Quièvrecourt, Yvonne de, 137–8, 140–1

Rabelais, François, 74
realism, 21
Record-Herald (Chicago newspaper), 194, 196
regionalism, 179, 183
Rembrandt van Rijn, 170, 172
repetitions: as device in Moore, 18–19
Return of the Native, The (TH): Lawrence praises, 36;

influence on Powys's works, 70, 72, 74–8, 96, 100; unities in, 73, 94; parent–child relationship in, 76; cruelty of nature in, 82; and TH's childhood, 126; Fernandez on Zola and, 147; Leslie Stephen on, 149; and Fowles' *Daniel Martin*, 165; and Faulkner's *The Hamlet*, 182; and beauty, 208, 212
Revue des deux mondes, 111–12
Revue nouvelle, La, 26, 144, 147
Richards, Grant, 25–6
Richardson, Samuel, 206
'Riddle, The' (TH poem), 152
Rivière, Jacques, 135, 138–40, 205
Robert, P. E., 123
Robinson, Edwin Arlington, 173
Rolland, Romain, 31
Rose, Gilbert J., 159–61, 165–6
Ross, Nicholas, 67
Roz, Firmin, 111–12, 147; 'Thomas Hardy', 144–5
Ruskin, John, 110

Sainte-Beuve, Charles Augustin, 116, 146
Sandburg, Carl, 173
Sappho, 131–3; *see also* lesbianism
Schlumberger, Jean, 147
Schopenhauer, Arthur, 129, 133, 146–7
Scott, Sir Walter, 62, 206
Shakespeare, William, 36–7, 62, 69
'She Did Not Turn' (TH poem), 155
Shelley, Percy Bysshe, 4, 45, 129, 133
'Singer Asleep, A' (TH poem), 133
snail and thrush image, 82–3
Sophocles, 36–7, 62, 69, 186
Sparks sisters, 104, 126
Sparks, Tryphena, 154–8, 161, 165
Spencer, Herbert, 210
Stendhal (Marie-Henri Beyle), 114, 119
Stephen, Sir Leslie, 29, 149
Stevenson, Robert Louis, 23–4, 27
Stoddard, Lorimer, 175, 185

Strauss, Walter A., 121
Swinburne, Algernon Charles, 4, 46, 129–33, 148; *Poems and Ballads*, 133

Taine, Hippolyte, 146
Tennyson, Alfred, Lord, 200
Tess of the d'Urbervilles (TH): influence on Moore's *Esther Waters*, 3–4, 7–9, 22–3; anti-religious sentiments in, 4; Moore criticises, 4–6, 18–19; seduction and confession scene, 10–20, 136; blood imagery, 21; R. L. Stevenson criticises, 23–4; and Dreiser's works, 23, 185, 187–9, 194, 196–202; Henry James criticises, 24; Lawrence and, 38, 40, 45, 53, 213; interrelationship with *Jude*, 45–9, 125; TH gives to Powys, 66, 80–1; echoed in Powys, 71–2; French translation, 125; hampered sexuality in, 128; Alain-Fournier on, 135–9, 205; and *Le Grand Meaulnes*, 143–4; threshing scene, 163; Fowles and, 167; US stage version, 175, 185; effect on Ellen Glasgow, 178–81; influence and inspiration, 205–6; V. Woolf on, 206; tragic beauty in, 211–12
thrush *see* snail and thrush image
Tolstoy, Count Leo, 36, 45, 135, 185
Toynbee, Arnold J., 183, 193
'Tragedy of Two Ambitions, The' (TH), 25, 112, 116–17
'Transformations' (TH poem), 153
Trumpet-Major, The (TH), 79, 111
Tryphena *see* Sparks, Tryphena
trysts, 161
Turner, J. M. W., 10, 44, 210
Tuttleton, James W., 180
Two on a Tower (TH), 37

Index

Under the Greenwood Tree (TH), 126, 173
United States of America: Hardy's popularity and reputation in, 173–5, 183–4, 187
unities (time and place), 72–3

Virgil, 215–16
vivisection, 93

Weekley, Barbara, 37
Well-Beloved, The (TH): Proust reads and refers to, 30, 112–24, 128, 130–2, 205, 207; Lawrence dismisses, 40; and Powys's works, 63, 85, 89, 92–3, 205; Fowles and, 89, 150–1, 160–2, 164–5, 169, 171–2, 205, 213; and sexuality, 101, 114, 125, 128–9; autobiographical elements in, 113–14, 169–70; and lost mother, 127, 161; Swinburne and, 131–3; accused of immorality, 132; rewriting, 152; and love, 157; multiple ending, 160; writing, 168; reputation, 204
Winter Words (TH), 79
Woodlanders, The (TH): R. L. Stevenson reads, 23; echoed in Powys, 72–3; homecoming theme, 73, 165; cruelty of nature in, 82, 210; hampered sexuality in, 128; satirises platonic Ideal, 133; preface, 151
Woolf, Virginia, 25–9, 111, 147, 205
Wordsworth, William, 66, 88–9, 108, 200
World (journal), 132–3

Zola, Emile: *La Terre*, 147